KU-267-424

...FITH COLLEGE DU...
...CIRCULAR ROAD DU...
...) 4150490 FAX: (01)...
...: library@ge...

NILE
RODGERS
LE FREAK

AN UPSIDE DOWN
STORY OF FAMILY,
DISCO AND DESTINY

sphere

920
ROG

SPHERE

First published in Great Britain in 2011 by Sphere
Reprinted 2011 (twice), 2012
This paperback edition published in 2012 by Sphere
Reprinted 2013 (twice)

Copyright © Nile Rodgers 2011

The moral right of the author has been asserted.

All rights reserved.
No part of this publication may be reproduced, stored in a
retrieval system, or transmitted, in any form, or by any means, without
the prior permission in writing of the publisher, nor be otherwise circulated
in any form of binding or cover other than that in which it is published
and without a similar condition including this condition being
imposed on the subsequent purchaser.

A CIP catalogue record for this book
is available from the British Library.

ISBN 978-0-7515-4277-6

Printed and bound in Great Britain by
Clays Ltd, St Ives plc

Papers used by Sphere are from well-managed forests
and other responsible sources.

MIX
Paper from
responsible sources
FSC
www.fsc.org FSC® C104740

Sphere
An imprint of
Little, Brown Book Group
100 Victoria Embankment
London EC4Y 0DY

An Hachette UK Company
www.hachette.co.uk

www.littlebrown.co.uk

This book is dedicated to my biological, spiritual, and musical family. Without you there'd be no me. I love you very much.

Le Freak

contents

The Theory of Relativity

*Life isn't about surviving the storm;
it's about learning how to dance in the rain.*
—Unknown

"Sweetie, I never see you," my mother said. "If we continue like this, I'll only see you a couple more times before I die."

It was eight days after 9/11, the morning of my forty-ninth birthday, and like so many people in America at that moment, my mother was thinking about the importance of relationships, especially among family. Her take on it was a bit darker than most, but it was harder to see on September 19, 2001: The rest of the country had finally caught up to Mom's gift for morbid melodrama.

The truth is, she was right. I didn't see her enough—though some people might say I had good reason to never see her again.

But after 9/11, as we all know, everything changed, and I resolved to spend more time with my crazy clan. Not just Mom, but my aunt, uncle, cousins, and the rest of my immediate family, which included the other parental figure who made me what I am, my stepfather, Bobby.

We needed an occasion, of course, and there's nothing quite like Thanksgiving to gather our tribe. Though they had long since separated, Bobby was still very much in Mom's life, despite all they'd been through. And in many ways the holiday meal neatly mirrored the mixed makeup of my family. There was the dark meat—me and Aunt Mabel and her offspring, a clue that we were direct descendants of slaves from the South; Mom and my brothers are the same beige as the mushroom stuffing. And Bobby was the white meat— an unrepentant Jewish junkie from the Bronx. Drugs, crime, and love were the gravy that kept us all together.

AND SO WAS BORN our annual raucous all-the-trimmings repast at Mom's place—the home I bought for her on her fifty-seventh birthday—in that most family friendly of cities, Las Vegas.

Vegas was the perfect place to reunite my parents. It was, after all, Bobby's town, where he passed bad checks, counted cards, played the ponies, drank like the town drunk, and did heroin. In fact, he got down there with such gusto that during the mid-sixties he was barred from entering the entire state of Nevada. And Mom wasn't afraid to go all-in in their no-limit game back then either.

By 2001 things were a little different. But Bobby still loved to gamble (except now he slow-played), still loved to get high (and could do so for days at a clip), and still had that same Lenny Bruce beatnik humor. Mom was just as quick on the draw with her scalding quips. They could still go toe-to-toe.

Thanksgiving Vegas-style made us feel like we'd never stopped living together. It was business as usual: fun, laughter, and complete and utter dysfunction—and I don't think we'd have it any other way. In fact, it was so successful that our newly minted tradition continued unabated with a twist—every year there would be one major revelation retrieved from the family vault of secrets and brought to the dinner table to be examined like an old heirloom. We kept it going until 2009, when once again, things changed.

THAT THANKSGIVING, the family diverged from our annual get-together in Vegas and instead convened at a cousin's house in Hemet, California—coincidentally, the town where L. Ron Hubbard died and was cremated within twenty-four hours. We had to accommodate my ailing aunt—and to make things easier for Bobby, who now needed our help getting around. Though we were in a different place, the laughter, feasting, and recycled family stories felt as familiar and welcome as ever. One of the reasons our Turkey Day never gets old is because of the yearly Big Secret. Actually, given how open-minded my family is, the real shock of these secrets is how anyone ever managed to keep them under wraps for so long! After fessing up, we'd mercilessly make fun of the secret sharer (which maybe explains why they kept it secret). And that Thanksgiving was no exception.

The next morning we all met at the Marriott Hotel in Riverside, California, for breakfast. In a matter of minutes, the whole joint was caught up in our out-of-control breakfast, with jokes and secrets flying back and forth throughout the rambunctious meal. We might have stayed there for hours, but this morning was different.

Bobby had a very important appointment. And for once, we needed to be there on time.

We all got into our cars. I took the lead. I'd memorized the directions. We drove about eleven miles to 22495 Van Buren Boulevard. We met up with the chaplain from the Veterans Administration home in Barstow, California, Bobby's most recent residence. It was now 10 a.m. Despite the early hour, we quickly had the chaplain cracking up as loudly as the rest of us. In Mom's haste to get Bobby there, she'd forgotten to stop at the VA home to pick up his flag, as the chaplain had instructed. "Don't worry," he said. "We've got you covered."

The chaplain told us how lucky he was to know Bobby and meet the rest of his family. "He taught me how to have fun again," he said. "I can see why you're such a happy family—he seems to have taught you the same thing, too!" We laughed, hugged, and agreed. Then we all started crying.

A three-gun volley went off and the Honor Detail marched away after the bugler blew taps. The sergeant then presented Mom with the flag they'd folded at the end of the ceremony.

At 10:45 a.m. PST on Friday, November 27, 2009, we interred Bobby's ashes at Riverside National Cemetery. Mom and the family had brought his remains from Las Vegas, where she had protected them since Bobby's death about six months earlier, so he could join us for the annual family dinner.

I'd wanted all of us to spend a happy Thanksgiving together—one more time.

part I

Can They Be That Close?

one

The Ballad of Beverly and Bobby

IT TOOK ME A LONG TIME TO REALIZE THAT THE THINGS MY PARENTS did were not exactly normal. I was about seven years old, and it was the tail end of the 1950s, when it started to dawn on me that they were . . . well, let's just say they were different.

For instance: My friends and I got shots when we went to the doctor, and we hated them. But my parents stabbed themselves with needles almost every day, and seemed to enjoy it. Weird.

Most of my friends' parents sounded like the adults in school or on TV when they talked. People understood them. My parents, on the other hand, had their own language, laced with a flowery slang that I picked up the same way the Puerto Rican kids could speak English at school and Spanish at home with their *abuelas*.

And then there was the matter of how they talked. My parents and their friends spoke this exotic language very slowly. There were other odd things. For instance, they often slept standing up, and this group narcolepsy could strike right in the middle of the most dynamic conversation. Someone would start a sentence: "Those ofay cats bopping out on the stoop are blowin' like Birrr . . ." and suddenly the words would begin to come out slower. And. Slower. Soon they wouldn't be speaking at all. Eventually our living room would be filled with black-and-white hipsters suspended in time and space, while I ran through the petrified forest of their legs. My favorite game was waiting to see if the ashes from the cigarettes they were smoking would ever drop. Somehow they almost never did.

I can still remember the day when I finally realized that there was a name for this unusual lifestyle. My parents were junkies! And their slow-motion thing was called nodding out.

Oh well—it was nice to be able to name the thing. This was my life, and as far as I was concerned, there was nothing uncommon or uncomfortable about it at all. In fact, for a while at least, it was a carefree Shangri-La.

MY MOTHER, BEVERLY, was a beautiful, brilliant black girl whose family was a generation from southern sharecropping. She got pregnant with me when she was thirteen, the very first time she had sex. Bobby, my stepfather, was white, Jewish, and central-casting handsome. They were an unusual progressive pair: They smoked pipes, dressed impeccably, and read *Playboy* for the articles. Even in Beat Generation Greenwich Village, New York City, circa 1959, interracial couples weren't exactly commonplace.

Mom's maiden name was Goodman. Technically, it was Gooden, but her father, Fredrick, appropriated the name from a huge Goodman's Egg Noodles billboard that hung outside of the Lincoln Tunnel on the New Jersey side. The family story is that Fredrick had been forced to flee the cotton fields of Georgia after he used a tree branch to beat a white man he'd caught raping his sister. Grandpa Fredrick (never one to let a good story go to waste) told me that he saw the sign for Goodman's Egg Noodles just after his car exited the tunnel connecting New York to New Jersey, the state where he'd begin a new life. When he emerged from the Hudson River baptism, he was a new man. Better than new: He thought the name would help people up North think of him as a "good man." In the end, I guess it sort of worked. Twenty long years later, after the Woolworth CEO he chauffeured passed away, Grandpa got the Cadillac as thanks for his devotion and service.

By the time Beverly Goodman was twelve, she was already what they used to call a fast girl. She ran with a street gang called the Taejon Debs. They dated members of two different rival male gangs, the Copians and the Slicksters. But she wasn't just beautiful and bright. She was hip. She and her cadre of friends were aware of the fact that they knew things that most civilians didn't. She listened to Nina (Simone), Clifford and Max (Brown and Roach), Julie (London), Monk (Thelonius), TB (Tony Bennett), and Ahmad Jamal on a regular basis, and was so down she called them by a single name (except Jamal, maybe out of respect for the fact that he'd gone through the trouble of changing his name from Freddy Jones). She spoke with confidence, just a peg down from arrogance, which only big-city intellectuals could get away with, even if they were only twelve. She had art, literature, and music all around her.

MY EARLIEST RECOLLECTION of life with my mother is of two young people—one so young he'd barely finished wearing rubber pants— living together as roomies, a strange friendship instead of the standard maternal setup I'd see with other kids and their mothers. I always called her Beverly instead of Mommy. She never asked me to do otherwise. Even as a very young kid, I was utterly convinced that my mother was the most beautiful woman in the world. Mom's looks were a combination of African American, Native American, and Irish. This was no accident. Mom's bloodline goes something like this: My great-great-grandmother Mary Ellen was the child of a partially African mother, whose slave name was Caroline, and an Irish doctor and slave owner, Dr. Gough, who was, um, intimate with his property. Though he was married to a respectable, proper English woman, he apparently fathered at least more than one child with his slave housekeeper.

As the daughter of a white man, my great-great-grandmother Mary Ellen was more privileged than the average ex-slave's child, and she was better educated than the darker-skinned blacks around her. This fact was not lost on her. Later, when her own daughters came of age, she passed along some interesting advice: "Protect your children and the benefits you've gotten from my being half white," she told them. "Marry the fairest man you can so your children will have good hair." My great-great-granny and her husband, Lee Randal, had five children with very good hair. One of them, Mabel Ethel (born October 12, 1891), would marry a man named Percy Stanley Mickens, who was born on December 6, 1888.

Percy's father was Abraham Lincoln Mickens. One day a woman named Wicke dropped off a child at his home. Abe's wife, Alice, couldn't bear children and Wicke had agreed to have Abe's baby (Percy) for them. She was a full-blooded Indian woman (FBI, as they say back on the rez). Percy's birthmother was of the Iroquois Nation, so his hair was also very good. Percy's wife, Mabel, had four children. One was called Alice, after the mom that raised him but couldn't have children of her own. That Alice is my mother's mom. Today those Iroquois and Irish genes are very apparent in my family. Most of us resemble to varying degrees Lena Horne, Halle Berry, Cab Calloway, or Lenny Kravitz.

Except for me.

I inherited my biological father's genes: I'm dark-skinned. "The only spot in the lot" is what some friends and family called me. As screwed up as it is, my great-great-grandmother knew what she was talking about when advising her daughter to "marry light." It's hard to describe how horribly ugly I felt as a dark-skinned kid in the fifties. Thank God for the sixties, when black was suddenly beautiful, no matter the shade.

Which brings me to my stepdad: Bobby Glanzrock. It's not fair to call Bobby a black man in a white man's body, because his style was genuinely his alone. Bobby was a beatnik Ph.D. His observations had angles and perspectives that would make Miles Davis contemplate his own sense of cool. Bobby spoke with a slow, deliberate syncopation that was constantly modulating through the musical scale. This was the preferred style of speaking amongst the hipster class. Think Mitch Hedberg or Jimi Hendrix.

Some of his black friends called him "White Bobby," but my stepdad acted more like the black avant-garde jazz musicians he idolized than the haberdashers in his lineage. He only dated soul sisters, most of whom could have doubled for Cleopatra Jones, all Afro and attitude. That included my mom, who sported the latest Carnaby Street duds and a towering nimbus of kinky hair. Bobby's uncle Lew, who had no sons of his own, groomed his nephew to take over his clothing business. But Lew disowned him for marrying a black woman, even one with a nice Jewish-sounding name. Bobby threw away the glory of the schmate business for Beverly. And in return, he became the love of her life, and she had more than a few lovers. Me, I was their little groupie. I loved them both like crazy.

And "crazy" may be the operative word. Beverly and Bobby may not have been model parents, but they were a really good fit for each other; art, literature and especially their love of music bonded them together. But as they spiraled deeper and deeper into addiction, they were also increasingly self-centered, not infrequently criminal, and less and less interested in the responsibilities of raising a kid. On some level it was great to be treated like a peer, to be on a first-name basis with my parents, but it wasn't exactly a substitute for the usual parental cocktail of nurturing and discipline. Respect? Yes, there was plenty of that. If I had a problem, we'd "rap on it." Then they'd ask me something like: "Are we copacetic?" If I answered, "Yeah, I guess so," the matter would be settled with a "Solid!" and a five slap or some other affirming gesture.

Bobby always affectionately called me by my nickname, "Pud," short for "pudding pie." Once, after I'd accidentally set fire to the apartment while playing with matches, he sat me down. More disappointed than angry, he stared woefully into my eyes for about five minutes or so, then finally broke the uncomfortable silence.

"Pud, dig yourself," he said.

This was the harshest discipline Bobby ever doled out. My mother then asked me if I wouldn't mind walking over to her and lying down on her lap. She gave me a few whacks on the behind and asked me if I understood why.

"Yes."

She looked me in the eyes and said, "Pud, you really have to start digging yourself."

"OK, Beverly." I cried more from shock than pain, because she'd never hit me before. Then again, I *had* set the house on fire.

BUT THAT INCIDENT was an accident, not pyromania. In fact, I was rarely a burden to adults. Our cigarette-fogged living room was regularly dotted with junkies in full nod, like a twisted beatnik version of Ingmar Bergman's chess game with death: adults of every hue in suspended animation, waiting to move to the next square. Shooting, drinking, snorting, and smoking any and everything right in front of me was all part of the daily script. But I knew better than to mess with anyone's high.

"Shit, man, little Pud is cool as a muthafucka." An old family friend and a truly gifted artist, Harold, used to say at an excruciatingly slow tempo. "You don't have to worry about Pud, man, he's all right." Harold was one of the finest gentleman-junkies I've ever known.

By the time I was seven, I'd become fairly independent. The Zenith black-and-white screen in our apartment had been unofficially designated as my primary guardian. I had a bottomless appetite for grown-up TV. Insomnia kept me up until the wee hours and I'd watch *The Late Show* and *The Late Late Show* every night. Since I was always alert and functional during the day, no one was much concerned with the fact that I hadn't quite figured out how to sleep.

Most of the people in my life back then may have been constantly high, but they were pretty stylish. Coming home from school, it wasn't unusual for me to see berets or tams, jackets with elbow patches, ascots, dickeys, turtlenecks, groovy "slacks," highly designed cigarette holders and cases, hashish and rolling papers from all over the world, sketch pads, record albums, shoebox lids to clean the seeds from marijuana, magazines of all types, books, music manuscript paper, various sets of works and different ligatures to wrap around your arms to make the veins pop up and easier to hit with the needles. This was the paraphernalia of a junkie pad at the twilight of the fifties. Some visitors were famous artists, all were friends, and all were welcome. Once, Thelonius Monk himself came over to buy my mom's fur coat for his girlfriend. Heroin often turns addicts into gifted salespeople. Some families go to Disneyland for fun; we went to the pawnshop. In most junkies' wallets, the pockets where you'd expect to find family photos or business cards are instead crammed with pawn tickets.

WE MOVED AROUND A LOT—Chinatown, the Lower East Side, the Bronx, and Alphabet City—but our lives first started to change when we lived in a two-bedroom apartment on the corner of Greenwich and Bethune streets, sometime in the summer of 1959. This was the last moment in my parents' lives before junk began dictating everything about how and where they lived. Ironically, this part of New York is now the high-rent West Village, but I still associate it with the sewage-perfumed brine of the Hudson River that used to fill those cobblestoned streets. This was before America learned how to monetize geographical assets by simply renaming them, as my Grandfather Goodman and the soon-to-be-ordained-beautiful blacks in the sixties would surely applaud.

Bobby had a round-the-clock sarcastic wit. When he was about to move us to Greenwich Street, he told Beverly that he ran a great line on the doorman. "Excuse me. Do any black people live in this building?" he inquired in a highly concerned voice.

"Absolutely not," proudly replied the doorman to the new tenant.

"Well, guess what? There's some livin' here now." Bobby snickered.

I CAN STILL PICTURE life on Greenwich Street. Our brand-new French Petrol Blue Simca was parked curbside, right out front. It looked like a frowning flat-faced barracuda with its dorsal fins chopped off. It was the most unusual car in town. Our pad was in the first wave of newer buildings in the Village, most named after famous artists like Van Gogh, Cézanne, or Rembrandt. Though my folks weren't artists, they had the Bohemian style down. Many people in the building often smelled of linseed oil and turpentine; the girls wore their hair up in buns and walked with their toes turned out, radiating grace even when they were dumping the garbage. You could look into the windows of your neighbors and see and hear composers writing show and jazz tunes at their pianos, like something out of Hitchcock's *Rear Window.*

From the south corner of our block looking right was the Bell Telephone Laboratory, with an elevated railroad track that ran right through the middle of the building. Today it's part of the High Line Park, but back then, to my eyes, it was a world within a world, complete with a private transportation system. Standing in the lobby of my building and looking across narrow, Victorian-sized Greenwich Street, I'd see slaughtered livestock being moved onto loading docks, the meat swinging from large hooks. Anyone who's seen *Rocky* knows what these huge dangling headless bodies look like, but on celluloid they have no scent. In the winter it wasn't so bad, but during the summer months, the stench was unbelievable—tons of flesh in a race against rot that the meat workers almost always lost. Today it's still called the Meatpacking District, but back then it wasn't an ironic name for a shiny upscale neighborhood, it was a literal description of the foul and bloody business going on. I was seven years old and almost always alone. I would sing as I explored the streets, adding an appropriate underscore to my solitary wandering. I was a boy composer and my strange and exhilarating new hood provided endless melodic and lyrical inspiration.

I was exceptionally weird-looking back then. Super skinny. Thick glasses. And my mother dressed me like my dapper stepfather, which meant I dressed like a blue-blooded, old-money, prep-school WASP.

I desperately tried to find friends and companions, but there were no other kids my age in our building. Other than the doorman, who was actually a cool guy, my only friend was a schoolmate named David. David's mom was white and his father was black, an interracial combination that was a little more common than my parental situation, but still stopped traffic in 1959. David lived on the border of Little Italy, which was less than a mile from my house but seemed as far away as Big Italy. Maybe because I looked so silly, with my Jerry Lewis glasses and Tom Wolfe getups, the Italian kids near David's place always wanted to beat the shit out of me. "Get da fuck outta ere, you fuckin' black booger," they'd shout. Asthma or not, I was a fast runner, and after I got over the fear of getting killed, it became a game for me. Picture me like a playful puppy running from everybody, singing songs like "Old Joe Clark" and "Run Red Run," with oversized glasses bouncing around on my face. I was impossible to catch. Adults in Little Italy would shout things that were far worse than what the kids said. But visiting David and his family was worth it, so I ran that gauntlet every day.

THE INTRODUCTION OF A MONKEY into our lives was the first ominous sign that my Village idyll—running from murderous Italian kids, dodging racks of rotting meat, crawling through the legs of nodding junkies—wasn't going to last. At some point, Bobby met a woman named Daisy. In the scheme of things, Daisy isn't all that important to this story. I don't even remember her last name, or what she looked like. What I remember most about her was her primate companion, which was kind of out there, but I'd come to expect strange things.

Bobby made the mistake of bringing Daisy and her pet monkey to our apartment. While the monkey explored our place, the two humans were up to a little monkey business themselves when Beverly and I unexpectedly walked in. Mom acted as if everything was perfectly normal. "Would you like me to make some dinner?" she said in an almost festive tone. Bobby was visibly unnerved by our sudden entrance, and even more by her nonchalant reaction. I was stunned to hear the normally super smooth Bobby lose his poise.

"Uh, no thanks, babe," he mumbled. "We were just talking, and I was about to take Daisy and her monkey downstairs and get her a taxicab. She's got to make a few runs and then she's gonna go uptown and do her thing." The two of them—and the monkey— scrambled out, and when Bobby returned a few minutes later, Beverly was still completely cool, as if nothing strange had happened. "Hey, Bobby, are you ready for dinner now, baby?"

As you might suspect, this story has a second act: Two days later Bobby came home and found Beverly in a romantic embrace with Ralph, her boss (at the time, my mom was working as an IBM keypunch operator, making a pretty good living). "Dig this shit," he said in a low voice, pissed off but still keeping his beatnik cool and contemplatively tugging at an imaginary goatee on his clean-shaven face. "Beverly, what the fuck's going on here?"

"Oh, Bobby, we were just talking."

"Talking?" he said, his voice still a whisper. "My ass."

"Yes, talking, 'bout some of the same subjects you and Daisy were discussing the other day!"

THUS BEGAN THE FIRST of many breakups that followed the monkey incident. Mom loved Bobby, but the Daisy incident really kicked her ass. So Beverly and I split Greenwich Village and moved up to the Bronx with one of her exes, a guy named Graham.

Two years before marrying Bobby, Mom had been with Graham, who was the father of my then one-and-a-half-year-old half brother Graham Jr., a.k.a. Bunchy, who was living with Graham's mother, at

1313 Needham Avenue in the Bronx. Graham was one of many men who were as hooked on my mother as they were on drugs. And like the rest of them, he would do just about anything for Beverly, even after she'd dumped him for Bobby. So when she called him desperate for a place to stay after the monkey incident, he was happy to have her, even if that also meant taking in her skinny, asthmatic, near-sighted, insomniac son.

Life at Graham's place, a house in a desolate industrial area of the Bronx, was even lonelier than my life in the Village. Fortunately, after a few awkward weeks, my mom's brother Freddy Boy phoned us at Graham's with a better offer. He was the superintendent in a building on East Eighth Street and told her there was a vacancy "and it's really cheap."

Since we'd been living rent-free with Graham, my mother had saved enough to make it work. Not only did Graham let her go, he helped us move in. Meanwhile, Bobby was heartsick without her; he'd been calling her constantly, begging for forgiveness. Bobby and Beverly loved each other madly, so everybody, even Graham, knew they'd eventually get back together, which is exactly what happened. And that's how my mother, Bobby, and I wound up in Alphabet City, in a railroad flat on East Eighth Street, between Avenues B and C, in Freddy Boy's tenement building. We were less than two miles east of our groovy pad on the West Side, but we might as well have been light-years away.

Most of the residents of Alphabet City were Puerto Rican, including Uncle Freddy Boy's new wife, Bienvenida, whom we called Bambi. Suddenly I had a whole new Puerto Rican family. My new kinfolk spoke Spanglish, especially on the phone. "*Hola*, Margie, when you go to the store *tráigame un paquete de* Kools, *y un* container *de leche. Sí, para mi*. For real, no foolin'. I changed to Kools last week. OK, bye. *Muchas gracias*." I only understood half of what they were saying, but I was used to figuring out what adults were talking about. Bambi and her Puerto Rican friends and relatives were sexier than any people I'd ever met. I was eight and obviously didn't know the full meaning of the word "sexy" yet, but in retrospect, I'm sure that's what it was. They were exciting and they made me feel funny in a strange way, but it was good funny. I was always happy to be around them. Much later on in life, I'd learn that the sexual atmosphere I'd detected as a kid came from all the actual sex that was going on.

IT WAS DURING THAT PERIOD when I joined the Cub Scouts, which back then had a strong presence in the hood. I remained a scout until my early teens. After-school programs were the most solid part of my unsteady life. My uniform told the world I belonged to a collective where helping little old ladies and blind people cross the street was a daily duty, a movement that stood for certain values. They used to say, "Scouting is all about the boy you are and the man you will become." Looking back, it's hard to say they weren't right. Almost everything I've ever done passionately is a variation on the platoon consciousness of scouting. I liked helping people and my folks were proud of me.

I was also proud of both my parents. Being in such close proximity to these cool people made me feel cool too, or as close as an eight-year-old Boy Scout can get to it. They exposed me to such disparate things as Shel Silverstein, Gahan Wilson, Lenny Bruce, sexology, Mikhail Botvinnik, Go (a Japanese board game), and

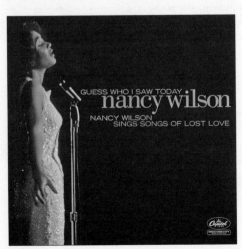

the Village Vanguard, which featured the top jazz artists in the world. I knew about all these things and more, and I could discuss them in depth. It was an exciting education in progressive thinking. But it was music I loved in an all-encompassing, obsessive way. One day for elementary school show-and-tell, when other kids brought dolls, model cars, and toys, I brought Nancy Wilson and Billie Holiday records to the class.

I would have been happy to just learn from my parents and their friends. But the law said I had to go to real school too and I vividly remember the day my folks enrolled me in the local public school in Alphabet City. People were pointing at us, and some were even gasping. There was a lot of chatter among the students, but all I could decipher through the din was, "Oh shit, his father is white!" I'd already experienced my share of racial tension, but until then the difference between Bobby and me hadn't had any negative effect. I'd never for a minute thought there was anything weird, and certainly nothing wrong, with Bobby being white. But that day I realized that other people actually found something shocking about our situation.

They didn't know the half of it—and neither did I. Bobby was falling apart. For years he'd managed to stay highly functional, on the surface, at least. He had worked at a preppy clothing store on the northwest corner of Greenwich Avenue and Christopher Street, called Casual Aire. It was directly opposite the infamous Women's House of Detention, New York City's notorious all-female prison. On any given day outside the House of D, passersby were treated to the taunts and screams of the inmates, but Bobby got nothing but compliments and whistles. The things they promised to do to him when they got out were so graphic my ears still burn when I think about them. To their credit, they were equal-opportunity harassers, and offered the same services to Beverly.

Bobby's natural sense of cool gave him a leg up on everybody else, and that extended to the clothing business. He really knew his stuff, and he was so with it that no customer dared disagree with his grooming or fashion recommendations. He scored hefty commissions that kept us in our righteous West Village pad and kept him well supplied with drugs. But it didn't last. By the time I was enrolled in public school, Bobby had more or less stopped working and was basically just living to get high.

On Thanksgiving Day 1959, I came home to our place in Alphabet City after a fierce game of tag in Tompkins Square Park, exhausted and ready to feast. As I rounded the corner, I saw a handful of police-men wheeling my stepfather out of our building on a gurney. He looked dead. He was blue. He wasn't breathing, even though they had an oxygen mask on his face. My mother was crying hysterically; all the people in the neighborhood were on the street or watching from win-dows. In those days the police did the emergency ambulance work for the city hospitals. So even though the police weren't there because of a crime, it still looked like a major tactical law enforcement operation.

And in a way it was. I had been around junkies since I was born, and I'd seen their rituals for some time now that my eighth birthday was a couple months behind me. Heroin was always sold in elabo-rately decorated packets, making them traceable to a source. If Bobby died from a bag of a Puerto Rican or black dealer's scag, there would be a serious investigation, because he was white, and being white seemed to make a difference. I could hear everybody talking about it openly, because nobody knew I was the white guy's stepson. How weird was that? In my eight years of life, a few of the junkies around me had died, but they were all black. *"Oh shit, his father's white."* I finally got it, what the other little kids already knew: So many things in our lives had to do with race. I suddenly realized that when you were talking about anything, if you switched the race of the person, everything looked completely different.

Over the next few days, I stealthily eavesdropped on my neigh-bors. Even though Bobby, Beverly, and I knew what our relationship meant to us, it apparently meant something completely different to others, family and friends included. Who was right and who was wrong? I concluded everyone was both—from a certain point of view. I was only eight, but that day marked the birth of my racial consciousness.

Fortunately, Bobby lived. He came home from the hospital a few days later, and I thought life would get back to normal. Looking back on it, though, the day Bobby came home was the day our lives changed forever.

* * *

SHORTLY AFTER BOBBY'S RETURN, my mother developed an interest in heroin. Up to that point, she'd never done hard drugs, despite being surrounded by addicts, first and foremost Bobby. But these addicts were her lovers and friends, all of whom, like Bobby, were wildly interesting and original people, the kind of people Beverly needed to surround herself with. And somehow, some way, Beverly, even though she was just a kid herself, had protected us from all these addicts running in and out of our lives.

But this new interest in heroin was just a ruse on my mother's part. She thought if she got high with Bobby, she could wean him from the habit. When Bobby overdosed, he was very thin, and Mom thought the problem might be that he was shooting too much for his body weight. So she'd say, "Can I share half of that bag, baby?" whenever Bobby got started on his complex preparatory ritual for shooting up, which culminated in him tying up his arm and shooting up with a syringe. Beverly, on the other hand, would pretend to snort her half in the bathroom, but instead flush the scag down the toilet. This deception worked for quite a while. She'd been around junkies for a long time and could imitate their mannerisms to a tee. So she kept up this charade, vanishing into the bathroom, flushing away half of Bobby's fix, and then faking a junkie nod for the rest of the day. She was afraid if she didn't, Bobby would OD again, and this time die for real.

One day, while preparing his ritual, Bobby barged into the bathroom to ask my mother for a cigarette lighter. When he opened the door, he caught her in the middle of her ritual, flushing his precious junk down the toilet.

"This is the first time I've flushed!" she said when she was busted. Bobby didn't buy it. But shrewdly testing her story, he said, "Well, don't worry, you can still get high if you need it. We'll do it together and I'll show you how to get higher with less junk. Don't snort it, shoot it, babe."

Bobby assembled the homemade syringe. And this time the nod and slowed speech she'd been affecting were no longer an act. It wasn't long before they were both getting straight every day.

And me? I was the oldest eight-year-old on earth.

two

Nothing to Fear but the Fear of Fear Itself

CHRISTMAS WAS COMING AND IT WAS EXCEPTIONALLY COLD. I WAS depressed because our family was completely disintegrating: Bobby and Beverly were using almost all the time. That was plenty for any kid to contend with, but to fully understand the depths of my depression, and my constant sense of loneliness, we need to briefly turn the clock back a few more years.

I was born with a number of congenital medical conditions, the worst of which was asthma. Asthma dominates my earliest and worst childhood memories: Every high-pitched breath I took used to sound like I was blowing through the top of a torn balloon; simply breathing made me feel like a carnival strongman was bear-hugging my ribs. My respiratory pathways burned from extreme swelling; the pain was beyond excruciating. Inhaling the smallest amount of dust or car exhaust would send me into a panic: *Will this be my last breath?* My body would heave and writhe like a tortured house cat trying to cough up a fur ball. When I finally dislodged the blockage by coughing up phlegm, the whole ordeal would start all over again.

When I was about five and a half, my asthma got so bad that Beverly had no choice but to put me in a hospital oxygen tent, which meant a stay at Lincoln Hospital in the Bronx, where we lived with her mother.

The hospital ward bustled, but in my tent there was nothing but silence. The enclosure was about three feet high by three feet wide, and not much longer than my normal bed. I'll never forget the confining chrome retaining bars, which were always pulled up, even though I was no longer a baby in danger of rolling off. I got fevers all the time, and my caretakers regularly felt my forehead to track whether I was hot or cold, even though the temperature in the tent was kept at subtropical levels.

Living in the confines of that vinyl keep, I felt contaminated and worthless, an isolated island in an overcrowded sea of staffers, patients, and their visitors. The smell inside was strange, almost like what you'd imagine the inside of an alien spacecraft to smell like. I felt as though I was a human specimen in an experiment sanctioned by my family. I guess the tent was supposed to feel less restrictive than wearing an oxygen mask. That didn't mean much to me at the time: Sure, I could move, but I was still imprisoned within the perimeter of a clunky Saran-Wrapped bed. I'd sing to myself to survive the loneliness.

WHEN I FINALLY returned home after a few weeks, I'd developed an unintended side effect: I now sang to comfort myself when I was lonely, and I started to depend less on my family for security. As much as I wanted to be around them, especially my mother, I believed it would never last. For some reason, Mom always seemed to be giving me away. I felt like I wasn't good enough to keep. I remember improvising tunes and holding on to her leg, riding on it while she walked around. Sometimes it was just a game; other times

I was holding on for dear life. I never wanted her to leave me alone—ever.

Meanwhile, my asthma continued to get worse. I needed medical care often, and much of the time I was tended to by a great man called Dr. Green. Dr. Green's brother just happened to be the famed composer Adolph Green, who wrote "I Won't Grow Up," "Singin' in the Rain," "Just in Time," and scores of other songs in my personal repertory. Dr. Green was a kind and caring physician whose practice was dedicated to mostly black and poor Jewish patients in the Bronx. There was a link between black and Jewish culture in the city back then; we knew the details of each other's rituals and idiosyncrasies. Dr. Green felt like part of our family. He tended to the Glanzrocks as well as the Goodmans.

But even the great Dr. Green couldn't cure my asthma, and one day, after yet another attack that resulted in convulsions, things descended to a new low.

"How you doin' today, Nile?" the doc asked in his comfortingly familiar Bronx Yiddish accent. "We're gonna fix you up real nice," he said. "Say 'Aaaah.' " Dr. Green stuck a huge piece of wood in my mouth, the bone-dry tongue depressor depriving me of my already limited air supply. This time, though, his tone had an edge I'd never heard before. He shook his head again and turned to my mother. "His asthma attacks are coming more frequently now," he said to her, "I'm afraid we're going to have to send your boy to a convalescent home."

As UNCOMFORTABLE AND FRIGHTENING as this news was, I didn't freak out. I'd become quite the little stoic. At that point in my life, the injections that made most kids cry didn't bother me. I was developing a very high threshold for pain.

And so it was that my bags were packed and I was off yet again. Only this time my destination was a home for convalescent boys.

The home had a turn-of-the-century feel with a little *Dick Van Dyke Show* thrown in. You could picture people picnicking on its pastoral grounds, playing croquet. Boys rolling hoops with sticks and men on high-wheeled bicycles would have been right at home, too. Only the gazebo for the barbershop quartet was missing.

But looks can be deceiving. Once you climbed the series of steep steps and passed through the waiting room doors, it became clear that this was a first-class facility, with cutting-edge technology. To a loving parent, the atmosphere was reassuring. Your child was in the very best of hands.

When I was dropped off, my stoic's mask dropped. I didn't realize my mother wasn't staying. I was, of course, wildly uneasy about being left alone again. I threw a tantrum. I was hysterical. I cried so violently, it took almost the entire staff to get me under control.

But once I settled down, I wound up bonding with the kids there more than anyone I'd befriended in my short life. We were almost always laughing when we weren't coughing from our chronic illnesses. We enjoyed a kind of foxhole camaraderie, far from home, thrown in with strangers, battling for our lives. Playing and fun were our weapons. We had a lot of freedom to roam the expansive grounds, which extended over many acres. Compared to the crowded streets of the Lower East Side or the South Bronx, it was like having our own planet.

For meals we marched to the mess hall, which looked exactly like the dining room at Hogwarts in Harry Potter films, minus the floating candles. Most of the kids at the home were older than me, but we traveled as one large group. To a five-year-old skinny asthmatic kid, the thirteen-year-olds and the caretakers were like giants with loud, frightening basso voices. The caretakers made us sing while we marched:

"God is great
God is good
And we thank Him for our food
By His hands
We all are fed
Give us this day our daily bread
Ahhh-men"

My intellectual development blossomed at the home. I quickly learned how to read like a much older kid, almost at an eighth-grade level, something that would greatly improve my odds for survival when I went back to my nineteen-year-old mother in the South Bronx.

And beyond reading, the institute's old rabbit-eared black-and-white television played a huge role in my development. Just like when I was back home with Beverly, the tube molded my concept of the world. There was no such thing as age-appropriate viewing. If you wanted to watch it—*Howdy Doody, You Asked for It, Popeye, Burns and Allen, Frankenstein, Dragnet, Charlie Chan*—you could watch it. If we didn't understand something at first, it wasn't long before we'd figure it out. Soon we were conversant in current events, geog-

raphy, drama, horror, comedy—even in its subtle forms, like sat-ire. We got almost all the jokes between George and Gracie, as well as the ones Popeye said under his breath. In one episode Olive Oyl was being romanced by a suave dancer  who taught her a new Brazilian dance called the samba. When Olive summoned Popeye to the dance floor, he said under his breath, "Uh, I don't do no Sambo dancing." It was racial, it was funny, and we got it.

We knew where Brazil was, and that LSMFT stood for "Lucky Strike means fine tobacco!" We knew that what we were seeing was entertainment and information. It was making us smarter, and it made us want more. We were like early cyberpunks, and even if our process of absorption was considerably slower, the knowledge in the TV box eventually became the knowledge in our heads.

* * *

ON VISITING DAYS they'd bring us kids out to a common meeting area that was decorated like *Terrytoon Circus* meets *Pee-wee's Playhouse.* My mother never missed a visit, but she only saw some of the home. For instance, she never saw the room where I slept. I'm not even sure she ever met our caretaker, a freckled, rotund, and somewhat odd-smelling man whose name I can't remember. Even if she had met him, I doubt she would have had the slightest idea that this man, so deeply entrusted with our care, was the snake in our Eden.

At bedtime the caretaker would scream, *"Lights out!"* in his scratchy voice. All the rooms on our floor would go pitch black. Within a few minutes, the silence would be broken by the sound of a kid coughing, choking, or gagging. First one kid, then another. I couldn't see anything because they removed my glasses at bedtime, but under the coughing I'd hear the caretaker traveling from one of the small dormitory-like rooms to the next. His hoarse voice would whisper, "This is what you're supposed to do." The terrifying darkness hid his whereabouts and kept me from seeing what he was actually doing, but the sounds revealed what my eyes couldn't perceive: He was putting his penis in a kid's mouth. The coughing and whispering went on for what felt like an eternity. And then, in an instant, it would stop, and like magic the caretaker would be asleep. We'd know he was asleep because we'd hear him snoring.

Sometimes he'd wake up and start bothering another kid. As long as the lights were out, I could never relax or fall asleep. I'd stay awake every single night until the dawn light illuminated the room enough for me to see there was no one lurking. Only then would I sleep until "wake-up," which was about two hours later. During the day, we'd all talk about the bedtime incidents. We were terrified of him. His loud voice could make us cry in the day, but his nocturnal whispering frightened us even more. I don't remember him ever touching me. I've often asked myself, How can I remember the details of these incidents so vividly if it didn't happen to me, too? I only remember trying to get my mother to understand what was going on. I'd try to paint her a picture. The problem was that at five and a half years old I lacked the vocabulary required to make her understand.

"I want to leave this place please, Beverly," I'd say.

"No, Pud, you have to stay here."

"But why?"

The doctors had told her it was the best thing for me. So life at the home went on.

Eventually I got as well as I could, and they sent me back to the South Bronx. When I finally returned home, my mother noticed I had developed an unnaturally heightened fear of the dark. Actually, I was terrified. I haven't slept through the night since.

BACK IN THE CITY, I found myself again in the daily care of my nineteen-year-old mother. To somewhat understand what Mom was like, it's instructive to hear a story I've heard since my earliest memories, of the albino woman who nearly adopted me. I might well have grown up as "Gregory," if not for the determination of Beverly Goodman.

Mom was a junior high school student when she got pregnant with me. Though it wasn't clear what law she'd broken, the New York City school system shipped her off to a prison ward/reform school on Welfare Island. After she'd delivered the baby, it was understood that she would give it away, which is how I ended up in the care of the albino woman, who for some reason couldn't have children of her own.

What no one had counted on was Beverly's strong maternal instinct. She decided to get a job instead of returning to school. Since she no longer went to school, she didn't have to abide by their rules. She had to convince her own mother to get me back. Beverly's mother's name was Alice Clarice Goodman, but everybody called her Goodie. Her kind and loving nature fit her nickname, but no matter how nice she was, I always felt like I was taking care of her when I was in her company. Mentally, Goodie was not much more than a child herself.

She was born blind as the result of a serious venereal disease her father had transmitted to her mother. It took some time to gain her eyesight, impairing her early ability to learn. As a young girl, she also contracted rheumatic fever, which resulted in the worst form of Sydenham's chorea, or St. Vitus's dance, a neurological disorder characterized by aimless involuntary movements of the arms, legs, trunk, and facial muscles. In Goodie's case this meant muscular weakness, frequent stumbling and falling, slurred speech, difficulty concentrating, and emotional instability.

One day she found herself alone with her cousin's boyfriend, Fredrick Goodman. He raped her and she got pregnant. His family made him do the right thing and insisted he marry her. It was around that time she started to gain control of her muscles and started to learn at a quicker pace. In those days they believed hormonal changes due to pregnancy could positively affect people with SD. We now know it more often reverses itself with aging.

She was getting brighter and becoming a much better mother, both at a quicker pace. Goodie had a strong sense of right and wrong, and she always leaned toward right. She and Beverly thought it was wrong to give away the baby. It was only a matter of time before Goodie, Beverly, and the authorities were knocking on the albino woman's door. Back then mothers had very powerful custodial rights. Sadly, the albino woman had already completely accepted me as her son and even named me Gregory. The retrieval was not going to be easy.

When my mother finally got her hands on me, and was leaving the woman's house with me firmly in her arms, the woman fell to her hands and knees and started kissing my mother's feet. "You're so young and so beautiful . . . you could have children anytime you wanted," she reasoned. When that didn't work, she wrapped her arms around my mother's legs so she couldn't walk away. She was crying hysterically, pleading, "Take all of my money. I'll give you anything you want, but don't take Gregory. Please, don't take my son." Of course, my mother kept moving and never looked back.

But from that point on, I was forever to be known as Nile Gregory Rodgers.

My mom continued to call me Gregory because I seemed to respond to the name. But my paternal grandma, Lenora, never did. She called me Junior. Though Beverly never married her son (and my biological father) Nile, Lenora—or Nora, as she was called by almost everyone—treated her like a daughter. And Nora came into Beverly's life at a propitious moment. Goodie's husband suddenly divorced her when she supported Beverly getting her baby back. Nora more than any force on earth is responsible for the turbo-charged development of Bev's personality and values. She was very different from Goodie.

Lenora had a classical education, was well versed in Latin and extremely bright. She was like Josephine Baker meets Clarence Darrow, with Pearl Bailey and a little Rosa Parks sprinkled on top. She was a tough cookie and had an unmatched instinct for survival. She took Beverly under her wing as her apprentice. And Beverly was starstruck around Nora—this was no ordinary mother-in-law.

Nora taught my mother how to use men. She did not censor her feelings or her philosophy. She hated men, and felt they'd earned it. Her father had raped her older sister for years, which resulted in a pregnancy. After Nora's sister delivered her baby girl, whom she named Naomi, a Hebrew name meaning gratitude, she committed suicide. Baby Naomi lived in foster care until she came of legal age, at which point she went to live with her aunt Lenora, who treated her more like a daughter than the half sister she was. Lenora's love for her couldn't save Naomi from whatever god-awful nightmares must have plagued her. She spent most of her life in and out of state hospitals, suffering from extreme depression that required shock treatments. She finally died at a relatively young age in Hartford, Connecticut.

Lenora couldn't save Naomi, but she did everything she could to try and save her own sons. As much as she hated men, she loved her boys. More than she loved her sons, she loved me, her one and only grandson, Nile Rodgers Jr. (She overlooked the Gregory part of my name.) She adored me. She gave me everything she possibly could. I knew Lenora would lay down her life for me, and do it with a smile on her face.

Meanwhile, Lenora's own two sons were already disappointments. Her eldest son, Demetrius, was a musician and wasn't motivated to do much more than sing, get high, wear cool clothes, and get laid. Her youngest, Nile, also a musician, was also mainly interested in playing drums, getting high (he was a heroin addict with a daily habit), putting on his glad rags, and pursuing females—including Beverly, the mother of his child.

Now Lenora had one more shot at getting it right: She had me. Maybe I would turn out to be a better man.

LENORA'S DEVOTION TO ME was trumped only by her devotion to Catholicism. But she was no stiff either. She could drink any man under the table. Her favorite libation was Chivas Regal. She had a rum keg hanging on the wall that was split down the middle. It opened into a bar, complete with Art Deco glasses and a chrome martini-mixing bottle. She would frequently ask me to pour her "a taste," and I loved playing bartender. She was a missionary who also happened to be a Lindy Hopper. I guess the two aren't mutually exclusive, and she was equally comfortable wearing either hat. And, brother, let me tell you, be it pillbox or full-on Ascot Races bonnet, she always sported a stylish chapeau. My earliest memory of her was the day she gave me Elvis Presley's recording of the Otis Blackwell song "Blue Suede Shoes." She also gave me the shoes to go with it, along with a navy blue suit, both of which I later wore for my First Holy Communion, bringing her passions for music, God, and grandson into a harmonious circle.

LENORA WAS A HARD-CORE Roman Catholic, but with an Afro-Caribbean slant. She had a closet full of images of black saints, and her apartment had the feeling of a voodoo shrine. We went to church in the Bronx, but she filled in what they had left out when we came back home for our own religious services—and her addenda tended to be a little bit more disturbing than the official version. Until I saw her black saints, I was under the impression that Christian personalities were always white, the way they were in the movies and church. Seeing those black saints—before black got beautiful—was unsettling.

As religious as Lenora was, Mom was just as devoted to a science-based belief system. She had dropped out of school in junior high school but compensated by using whatever she had learned to the fullest. Though she idolized Lenora and listened and learned about men and survival, she had no use for Lenora's belief in the supernatural. It made for a fairly entertaining mix for a little kid.

Things weren't so bad at first, but over time, Lenora's nonstop religious lessons grew more frightening the more she tried to compete with my mother's cold atheism for dominion over my heart and soul. Like the nuns I'd soon meet in my new school, she tried to connect spirituality to everything. She always told me God was everywhere and always watching me. So many things that I had heretofore thought were fun now had dire consequences.

I can still remember what went down as one of the most confusing days in my life: my First Holy Communion. After confession, a ritual I thought I'd aced, Lenora asked, "Did you tell the priest that you had been playing cards?"

"What?" I said.

Could this be a real question? It felt like this was the West Indian Inquisition. I had no idea what to say. So I decided, for the first time in my life, to lie. "Yes," I said sheepishly. She put a little spit on her hankie and wiped some sort of smudge off my face.

"Good boy, Junior," she said.

THE AUTUMN AFTER I returned from Milbank, Lenora saw to it that I was enrolled in St. Pius V, the best parochial school in our very poor district of the South Bronx. To get into St. Pius, I had to take a reading test to prove I could keep up with the class. They gave me what was called back then a "first-grade reader." "See Dick run. See Jane run. Run, Jane, run. Run, Dick, run . . ."—that sort of stuff.

Since I'd already learned to read that same book at Milbank, I recited it effortlessly, the words rolling out of my mouth as easily as I could make a Duncan yo-yo "sleep" or "rock the cradle." (Not only could I read, I also happened to be the block's yo-yo and spinning-top champ, another one of many benefits from my extended stay in Milbank.)

Sister Ann-Marie seemed startled. She gave me a second-grade reader. It was basically the same stuff with a few "bigger" words, like "funny" and "jump." I aced this test, too. It wasn't until I got to the eighth-grade reader that I started to stumble on unfamiliar polysyllabic words. But by then I'd made an impression.

"This child is a miracle," one of the sisters cried. "He's been touched by the hand of God!"

I'd never felt so loved and accepted in my whole short life.

There was only one problem: My atheist mother quickly dismissed anything of the sort. All she wanted was to get me into school and get out of there as quickly as possible. She seemed disinterested in hearing any praise.

I started thinking that the albino woman was my real mother, and that Beverly had stolen me.

ON SEPTEMBER 28, 1958, my mother gave birth to my first little brother. He was named Graham, after his father, but we called him Bunchy. I told the nuns how happy I was about having a little brother. Sister Ann-Marie was less pleased, since my mother had no plans to baptize him.

"When he dies, he is going to hell for eternity," she told me.

The concept of eternity was completely overwhelming. I cried for weeks in bed at night, but dared not mention it to my atheist mother.

As I tried to comprehend my brother's inevitable fate, I'd sing myself awake, reassuring myself that no one could kill me because I never let my guard down by falling asleep—except when I was on the subway, where I slept peacefully. Poor inner-city kids took public transportation to school. The first time I took the train by myself, I fell asleep so quickly that I missed my stop. The same thing happened on the trip back. Now I could sleep anytime at all—as long as I was on a train. But I was very young and couldn't come up with many plausible reasons to ride the train at night.

Meanwhile, I began daydreaming during my waking hours. I loved fantasizing about wild adventures complete with the musical underscore during class. My first report card read "Nile is a bright student, but doesn't pay attention in class and doesn't play well with others."

Were they crazy? I played well with others—lots of others! They were just mostly in my head—but play we did.

MEANWHILE, BEVERLY HAD DEVELOPED an extremely acute case of postpartum depression and was literally contemplating killing my little brother Bunchy every morning. For a few months she adopted a bizarre daily ritual: She'd prepare two sack lunches, slam a large butcher knife down in the center of the table, make a phone call, hang up, and say, "Take care of your brother, because if he doesn't stop crying I'm going to bash his head in."

She'd literally lock us in the apartment and leave. By the time she returned, I'd have eaten my sandwiches, given my brother his bottles, and changed his diapers. We stayed out of sight in the bedroom, watching TV. Our electronic babysitter did an exceptional job. My little brother and I were as well behaved as two kids ever were—well, that is except for his constant crying. It was as if he knew his short life was in jeopardy, and he wanted to make sure he didn't leave this world without making some noise first.

In fairness to Mom, by now she'd had three coat-hanger abortions that had resulted in two very-near-death experiences. She'd had another child snatched away from her as soon as he was born—me. It's easy to understand why she'd developed such a complicated psychological relationship to pregnancy and childbirth, aside from whatever hormonal swings she was suffering. Bunchy's father never wanted children and he was not very involved in his young son's life. Most of Beverly's support came from Goodie and me. She could have snapped any day. This went on for a few months until a psychiatrist convinced my mother that she was not emotionally fit to take care of children.

Which meant Bunchy was sent to Graham's mother in the Bronx, and I went by Greyhound bus with Goodie, to live some three thousand miles away, in sunny Los Angeles, California.

three

Go West, Young Boy

WHEN THE GREYHOUND FIRST PULLED INTO THE EAST SEVENTH Street Terminal in Los Angeles, I did a double take. Had we come full circle? Downtown L.A. felt just like midtown New York, where our journey had originated days before. It was as if I'd just awakened from a cross-country dream and found myself in the same place I'd started. Even the summertime temperature was the same.

I'd soon learn that the bus station that welcomed us to L.A. was in a section of town called Skid Row. No wonder it felt so much like home: It was cramped, smoggy, and teeming with the same urban detritus—bums, hookers, runaways, cabs, newspaper boys, policemen, buses, and screaming fire engines—I knew so well from New York. There was the same ratio of derelicts to working people as in the Port Authority bus terminal we'd just left behind.

But that was where the similarity to New York ended. Instead of subways, my new town had trolleys, which they called streetcars. The Puerto Rican culture I knew so well back home had been swapped out for Mexican. The streets had south-of-the-border names like "Alameda," "Santa Fe," "Olvera," and "Figueroa." Taco stands were on every other corner.

En route to the house we'd be staying in until we got our own place, I saw highway signs directing motorists to destinations like San Pedro, Santa Monica, and Santa Ana. I'd read about Santa Anna fighting against Davy Crockett. He'd been portrayed as an enemy of the United States in school when I was back in New York. Out here they'd named a city after him. Now, that's impressive, I remember thinking. Out here they name streets and cities after bad guys too!

Goodie and I would have a helping hand in our strange new environment. My grandma Lenora had also come west, a few months before us. Back home, her husband, Leroy Rodgers, my biological father's dad, was terminally ill, and the Jack Frost Sugar Company, where they both worked, expected her to pay back the money they were spending on his hospital bills. Instead of paying, Lenora skipped town with her new boyfriend, Walter James Adams, aka Bill, aka Pretty Bill, who happened to be a master tailor—and convicted murderer. Lenora changed her surname back to her maiden name, Clare, and dropped off Jack Frost's radar with her life savings intact. She sent Leroy extra money under the table until he died. Had she paid his employers back, it would have bankrupted her.

Lenora was thrilled that Goodie and I were joining her on the West Coast. Bill was less than pleased, but he knew it made Lenora happy. And happy is the only way you'd want Lenora to be if you had to deal with her. Trust me.

Lenora wasted no time laying down her rules to me. Without the intervention of my mother, her missionary work on me was going to be a lot easier. She made it clear I was going to continue attending Catholic school, just as soon as Goodie got settled.

* * *

WE FOUND AN APARTMENT in a housing court. All the units faced a common yard filled with lush foliage like apricot and avocado trees, tropical cacti, and bushes filled with wildflowers and berries. Everybody could see the comings and goings of everybody else.

St. Cecilia (named after the patron saint of musicians) was the local Catholic primary school in our district. When I checked into school, I'd be going into the second grade, and yet again, I'd be checking in late. They didn't roll out the welcome mat for me the way they had on my first day of school in the Bronx. No, these were not the same loving nuns who were so impressed with my precocious reading skills. Actually, they were pretty cross with my grandmother and me for checking in at such a late date. The head of admissions pounced on Goodie when she sensed her docile nature.

"I don't think we can accept this child here," the headmistress said. "You don't have his records and he's not even your son!"

I'll never forget that. Nobody was more aware of the fact that Goodie wasn't my mother than I. In the end it was Lenora who got me admitted. Beyond being a raging bull, Lenora was in very good stead with the Roman Catholic community. So she worked her black magic and got me in. Still, they didn't want me there, and I didn't want to be there.

Our housing court was on the corner of Budlong and Vernon avenues, in the Exposition Park area of Los Angeles. It bordered a nicer area called the Historic West Adams District. Compared to the West Adams District's houses, where most of my new fellow students came from, our place was bleak. It was one story high and made of adobe-colored stucco. There wasn't a designated play area, and no other kids lived there. The West Adams District's houses were grand and palatial in comparison. Their gardens were all beautifully manicured; during Christmas season, cars would drive through the neighborhood to see the magnificently displayed lights.

I don't have a single fond memory of my L.A. Catholic school classmates. I only remember feeling unhappy and receiving more punishment than the other kids, most of which came from the standard parochial school playbook: ruler slaps on the palms or knuckles, standing with your arms outstretched mimicking Jesus on the cross with books in your upturned hands, or worst of all, swats. These were administered with a handball paddle or a cricket bat, and delivered by a teacher with a full-on Babe Ruth swing.

I acted out and was sent to a classroom for older kids as a punishment. Instead of learning with kids my own age, I was sitting in a corner, or standing in front of the class holding books, and occasionally wearing a conic dunce hat. I hated it. One night I saw a film called *I Accuse,* the story of Jewish military captain Alfred Dreyfus, who was wrongly convicted of treason. I projected his story onto mine as the explanation for my misery.

I started to role-play even more, daydreaming, fantasizing, and scoring it in my head almost all day long. I pretended the nuns had convicted me of something that I didn't do. I imagined that St. Cecilia was Devil's Island and I had to escape. The school continued to dole out cruel and unusual punishment, but I kept thinking about how I was going to break out, which certainly made things at lot more fun.

One day I decided to stop plotting and act. My action plan was as complicated as D-day, but I had every detail worked out: Every morning, Goodie and I left home together and walked to the bus stop. Goodie worked for Lenora, who had a small business cleaning homes and offices. Normally, she'd wait there and I'd go west toward Normandie Avenue to school. Today, however, I sat with her until her bus came and then sent her off. "Junior, why aren't you going to school?" she asked in her trusting voice.

"I am going," I lied, "but they changed the time our classes start, and I don't have to be there until nine-thirty."

Goodie, of course, believed me. She didn't think I was capable of lying. She was happy just to sit with me at the bus stop.

I waited until she boarded the bus and watched it rumble out of sight. Then I fished out my key, turned around, and headed back inside our apartment. It was that easy. I skipped to the kitchen, filled a pot with milk, and brought it to a simmer. I measured two heaping tablespoons of Nestlé's Quik chocolate powder into a giant glass and poured in the warm milk. Then I turned on the TV, adjusted the rabbit ears antennas to get the picture sharp, and kicked back like Dean Martin with a cocoa martini. I watched in a trance until there was nothing good on. Around 10 a.m. I went outside to play by myself.

I was running through the bushes with my tree-branch spear and reciting dialogue from *Tarzan* when a man emerged from the apartment across from ours. He really caught me off guard—I hadn't planned on running into anyone. I thought every adult started work around the same time as Goodie did.

"Hey, kid," he said. "Whatcha doin? You live around here?"

"Yes, sir, right over there," I said, cautiously pointing to the rear apartment. "My name is Gregory." (I always used my middle name to try and fit in with the other kids; at the time the name Nile only generated dirty African river jokes.)

"How come you not in school?" the man asked.

"I go to Catholic school, and we don't have regular hours," I said in my polished "New York" accent. Then I confidently asked: "Where do you live, and what do you do, sir?"

"I live here and I'm on the county." I had no idea what that meant. "On the county?" It sounded official, like he was an FBI agent or a cop. Thinking I was busted, I tried to flatter him, and said, "You're probably important doing that, sir?" He burst out laughing. "Yeah, I'm important," he said with a laugh. "I sit around here all day, and don't go nowhere. I'm just headed over there to get me a little taste." Finally! Here was something I recognized and understood. I knew what "a little taste" was. In the end I'd find out he was a wino named Ernest, living on welfare ("the county"). After our little chat, he waved bye and sauntered across the street to the liquor store. I wasn't in trouble but decided our house was safer.

Back in the apartment, I watched Lucille Ball, Loretta Young, *Father Knows Best,* and other reruns the rest of that day. This was amazing. It was much better than school. And if you asked me, I'd say I learned a hell of a lot more from the TV.

When Goodie came home after work, she was none the wiser. I'd played hooky and gotten away with it. I was jumping up and down inside. I didn't think they wanted me at that school anyway. It was win-win.

The next day Goodie went to work and I followed the same plan, but this time while I was outside playing, a woman who said she was a substitute teacher questioned me. I ran the same rap I'd used on Goodie, but the teacher often worked at St. Cecilia and she wasn't buying it. She wound up calling my school, and for a short time I was in the doghouse with Lenora and Goodie.

As LUCK WOULD HAVE IT, I had another asthma attack and needed to stay home for a few days. When I returned to school with a doctor's note from my grandmother, the nuns all seemed much nicer, and this didn't go unnoticed by the dreamer and schemer inside me. It wasn't long before I was playing hooky again. But now I got Ernest, the wino next door, to forge a note that I would keep in my pocket, just in case I got caught. I thought it would allow me to do anything and go anywhere, like the "letters of transit" in *Casablanca*.

I dictated the contents and can still remember what the note said as if it were yesterday:

To whom it may concern,

Please excuse my grandson Nile's absence from school. He was suffering from an asthma attack, and had to stay home.

Thank you kindly,
Alice Clarice Goodman

Thus began the most exciting seventy-five days of my life.

I was on my way to setting the national truancy record for the entire parochial system in the United States of America. I hope you can understand why I'm still sort of proud of this accomplishment.

To make a little extra money, on school holidays I sometimes worked with Goodie or Lenora. At the time, Lenora's business had a cleaning contract with the Franklin Life Insurance Company, located on the corner of Wilshire and Western boulevards. I knew how to get there by surface transit.

One day, however, I took the bus on Wilshire in the opposite direction, and when it got to Pershing Square, I got off. Wow. I was back in Skid Row near the Greyhound Bus terminal. When I arrived, I was blown away at the sight of all the movie theaters, which reminded me of Forty-second Street and the grind-house theaters of the South Bronx—only this was that to the tenth power. I'd been dreaming about this day since our bus pulled into downtown L.A. Downtown L.A. was better than Disneyland and Coney Island's Steeplechase combined.

After exploring awhile, I'd go to a movie theater box-office window and say, "One children's ticket, please." They rarely asked me, "Why aren't you in school?" But if they did, and I had to resort to the asthma note, I would tell them, "When I woke up this morning, I was very sick. When the attack went away, it was too late to go to school."

It always worked.

I could tell this story to cops, and it seemed to work even better. Sometimes they would escort me to a Skid Row movie theater. At least once, they even drove me in a cop car! There were no ratings, and anybody could see any film they wanted. For the next two and a half months, I saw almost every movie that was released, many times over.

The trick was, never go to the same theater too soon. This was easy, because there were a seemingly endless number of grind houses on Skid Row. In those days they didn't turn the theaters over, so you could stay in one all day. It was a common practice to arrive at the theater anytime you wanted. If it was in the middle of a film, you'd simply wait until it came around again to see what you'd missed. With the multi-feature grind-house format, you could sit for six to eight hours before the part you missed cycled back. It was fantastic!

I always went home at the same time I would have had I actually gone to school. This had many advantages. If the truant officer visited and left a letter, good old Ernest or another wino in need of a taste would write and mail back the letter explaining my absence for as little as ten or fifteen cents. In those days you could purchase a small bottle of Thunderbird wine for not much more than that.

ONE DAY GOODIE GOT SICK with the flu, and it was horrible. She had a high fever and was bedridden. I asked her if she wanted me to stay with her to help out, but she said, "I don't want you to miss school. I'll be all right."

I left the house and headed downtown to see *The Sword and the Dragon*. A character, the Wind Demon, reminded me of my asthma and made me worry about Goodie. I wanted to go home and take care of her, but I couldn't show up before three-thirty. When I finally got home, I found not only Goodie but Lenora, and judging by the way she glared at me I could tell she wasn't happy. Also in our living room were a truant officer, a policeman or two, and someone from St. Cecilia. "Excessive truancy," they called it. Who had written the excuse letters in response to the truant officer's summonses? They accused Goodie of turning a blind eye. I insisted that I had acted alone. I knew that if I told on Ernest or any of my wino friends, they'd be in deep trouble; they'd be contributing to the delinquency of a minor. And I'd seen enough Cagney films to know you didn't rat.

Everyone knew I was lying. They agreed that I should be sent back to my mother, a punishment in their eyes. But earlier Lenora had given me a serious whipping with an ironing cord that had left painful welts on my body. My mother would've never done that, no matter how mad she got. I couldn't wait to get back to her.

And I was right. The postpartum depression that turned Beverly into a potential murderer had at long last disappeared. In fact, she felt so well, I would soon find out, that she'd had a third child, Tony—my second half-brother—with yet another man.

So at age seven, I was put on a TWA Super G Constellation to fly, by myself, from L.A. to New York City. We hit a bad storm over St. Louis, and I urinated in my pants. I was cold, frightened, and miserable. I peed on myself again during another encounter with air pockets, and discovered that I momentarily got warm and slightly more comfortable. I realized that I was looking forward to the next time my bladder filled, and to the peace and warmth that accompanied the release. But soon again I was freezing in the air-conditioned pressurized cabin, lonely and ashamed.

When I finally arrived the next morning at La Guardia Airport, my mother was waiting for me. She freaked out when she got her first glimpse of me as the crew walked me off the plane. I was scared stiff, cold, in soaking wet pants, my face tear-stained.

"Oh God, Pud, what happened?" my mother said.

"I don't know," I replied in a timid monotone.

That response was becoming my standard explanation for all the idiosyncratic habits I was developing. And it was true.

four

Like Fathers, Like Sons—Variations on a Mormon Theme

THE MINUTE THE BELL RANG AT P.S. 41 IN GREENWICH VILLAGE, I'D HIT the push-release door without breaking stride and leave school behind like a thoroughbred erupting from the starting gate. It was a warm late spring day in 1960. Summer was almost here. I was seven and a half years old and back in my hometown.

I never slowed down as I stripped off my jacket and rounded the corner from Eleventh Street onto Sixth Avenue, crossing it diagonally. From this vantage point, the Women's House of Detention was the largest freestanding structure among the countless eateries and novelty shops. As I closed in on Ninth Street, I could hear the constant catcalls and insults flying from the Art Deco prison's tower. Even at this pace, I would greet the street's familiar faces. "Hey, Antonio," I said to my blue-eyed Italian friend who sold me pizza at lunchtime.

Quickening my pace, I waved to my bearded beatnik poet buddy on the corner of Eighth Street and smiled at girls who were in between fashion trends, some still in poodle skirts, the new breed wearing Empire-waist dresses. When I got to Waverly Place, I took a hard left. The pizza and fast-food joints gave way to stately residential brownstones. Once I hit MacDougal Street and the chess tables scattered just inside Washington Square Park, I slowed my pace and scanned the faces for my favorite chess opponent. I can't remember the guy's name, but his game is still clear as a bell: He started nearly every match with the Petrov opening, bringing his knights into play before my breath and heart rate slowed down. After an exciting thrashing at the hands of my ever-willing rival, I took the long way home.

I'd kept to this routine every day—but today would be different.

As I walked west down Bleecker Street from La Guardia Place, I noticed a large crowd of people gathered around the Hotel Greenwich, right by the famous Village Gate nightclub. The hotel had recently been converted into an SRO (single-room occupancy) flophouse and was filled with mental patients who had nowhere else to go once New York City's state hospitals started closing.

The SRO residences gave the Village an edge. I remember feeling comfortable around their eccentric tenants. I was used to irrational behavior. As I drew closer to the crowd, I realized everyone was looking up and pointing. "Is he going to jump?" cried one man. "Think so," answered another. I craned my head and immediately recognized the naked man raving incoherently and flailing his arms on the fire escape: Nile Rodgers Sr.

IF BIOLOGY IS DESTINY, then I was born to be a musician. Nile Rodgers Sr. was a brilliant percussionist who came of age during the Latin music boom of the late forties. Dances like the mambo, cha-cha-cha, merengue, and rumba had a huge influence on the big bands. My father specialized in Afro-Cuban beats and was considered a virtuoso by the time he was a young man.

NEW YORK

703   Furnished   West   Side   703   Furnished   West   Side

BLEECKER ST., 160   THE NEW   777-0347

GREENWICH HOTEL

FOR MEN

$2.75 Per Night $18.50 Weekly

FIREPROOF BLDG, PRIVATE ROOMS, SEPARATE SHOWERS
EXCELL CAFETERIA & LOUNGE INSIDE HOTEL
OPEN DAILY—THRIFTY PRICES

SUBWAYS: IND W. 4th ST.   IRT BLEECKER ST.

Paul Whiteman, "the King of Jazz" and popular big-band leader, was the music director for an ABC show that premiered in 1949 called *TV Teen Club,* and he occasionally hired my dad. The show featured a young announcer named Dick Clark and would later be renamed *American Bandstand.* The Whiteman gig was a huge break because Paul's orchestra was, true to his name, all-white. It's a well-known fact that Paul wanted to hire more black musicians but his management pressured him not to. My dad was actually working with Paul on the day I was born, September 19, 1952. Unfortunately, Paul couldn't hire him full-time, and Dad had to supplement his income with a day job in the Garment District, where most of my mother's family also worked (as well as Bobby, my stepfather-to-be).

Nile charmed everyone who crossed his path. If he didn't have an instrument with him, he could turn any object into one. He loved music: He lived it, walked it, talked it, and played it all the time. He loved music more than anything—except maybe getting high.

By the time he was sixteen, my father was more or less a daily drinker and a recreational pot smoker. Because of his relatively well-paying job running racks in the Garment District—"flying Jewish airplanes," they called it—he had extra spending money, just enough cash to develop a taste for a new drug that had recently turned up in the neighborhood: heroin.

Nile worked with a guy named Freddy Boy, who had a brainy and very beautiful kid sister named Beverly, whom Nile took a liking to. He was sixteen and she was thirteen—and very soon she was pregnant.

For a while Nile loved Beverly even more than music and drugs, so much so that he was nearly killed defending her honor, after a jealous Copian gang member called her a whore. Nile spoke up, and without warning, the Copian plunged a huge knife into his chest. He collapsed in the street, but was rushed to the hospital and somehow recovered. Beverly, on the other hand, liked Nile, a lot, but was absolutely not in love with him. But once she was pregnant with me, Beverly's father, whom she deathly feared, convinced her she had to get married. And so the wedding was set for June, just three months before I was born. Nile was ecstatic.

In preparation for the big day, they got blood tests and secured a marriage license. But when they reached City Hall, my mother decided she just couldn't do it—she'd just turned fourteen, after all—and caused a big scene. Crushed, Nile slapped my mother across the face. According to her, that was the only time in his life that he'd ever struck another person.

But once was all it took. Besides, it was a perfect excuse to cancel a wedding she didn't want. And so it was that Nile Sr.'s fourteen-year-old fiancée humiliated and disappointed him on what was supposed to be the happiest day of his life. That night he did so much dope and booze he almost died. I would hear about the wedding day binge that he blamed on Beverly every time I saw him for the rest of his life.

Now on this hot late spring day, at the age of twenty-four, eight years since he'd last played with Paul Whiteman, my father was spotlighted in sunlight, and the ledge of a flophouse was his stage.

The gawking crowd would have to do as an audience. That was Dad, all right, but it was hardly the image I'd kept in mind. His handsome features and optimistic smile had been replaced with a maniacal grin beneath a pair of unfocused eyes. He'd already jumped out of the fourth-story window and fallen onto this landing over-looking Bleecker Street. A small brigade of cops and firemen were trying to bring him in. I frantically ran into the hotel and told the desk clerk, "The man on the fire escape is my father. I don't think he'll jump if he sees me." Which is exactly what I believed.

"He is a very nice man," I added. The clerk brought me over to the policeman in charge, and after a quick chat with the fire chief, they escorted me up to the fourth floor and the window closest to my father.

"Hey, Nile, hey, Nile, it's Little Splash," I said to him in a gentle voice.

Splash was my dad's nickname on the street, because he drank a lot of cheap bathtub gin. He needed to. He was always high and it was a simple matter of economics. Over the past few years, he'd become a full-fledged alcoholic and drug addict, lost his job in the Garment District, and ended up on welfare in an SRO. He was on the city's methadone program and made extra money by selling "spitback" to addicts. Spitback is resold methadone that junkies lit-erally spit into a hidden receptacle after they swallow just enough to get straight. He liked it when his friends called me Little Splash, and I thought this would get through to him. It did. He recognized me instantly.

I hadn't realized that he lived so close to us. I hadn't seen him for about six months. Beverly didn't allow it because she felt embar-rassed for him. But she didn't understand how much I loved him, and that he and I got along great. On our last get-together, we'd gone shopping and seen the Steve McQueen sci-fi film *The Blob* in the Bronx. He'd always give me a present, a record or a cool ethnic percussion instrument, or a bag of green plastic army men from Woolworth's. But now he looked at me with a sorrowful, nearly empty stare: "Pud, Beverly fucked me up. She left me standing on the steps of the chapel. Why did she do that to me? I loved her so much."

"I know, Pops, come inside now."

"Hey, son, are you all right? You all right, Pud?"

"Yeah, Pops, I'm fine, but I think you should come inside now."

"But Bev keeps fucking with me. I saw her standing out here, so I just came over to rap with her for a tick, to tell to her how much I still love her, then she split on me again."

At that moment I realized he wasn't trying to commit suicide at all. He was hallucinating, maybe a wee bit schizophrenic and suffering from delirium tremens (the DTs). I'd seen this kind of behavior before and I wasn't afraid of it. Many of the winos and SRO people had these colorful symptoms regularly. After a little coaxing, my dad was back inside the hotel and we were making our way down the hall to his room. Other than the fact that he was totally naked, everything was solid, maybe even copacetic. And with that, the cops just left. No indecent-exposure booking, no psych ward at Bellevue. The hotel returned to its normal state—i.e., insane, but not on ghoulish suicide alert. The streets cleared.

Just another day in paradise.

As soon as we reached his flat, my dad snapped out of his psychosis, almost as if seeing me had jump-started him back into the regular old Nile. We acted like the fire-escape incident hadn't happened. My dad's tiny room reeked of piss and other putrid odors I couldn't identify, so I waited in the hall, which also stunk, but not as bad. While he washed and dressed, a female SRO resident tried to make a quick buck for a fix.

Although the place was seedy, the Hotel Greenwich still had a certain grandeur. The woman who approached me was backlit by the stairwell lighting and she looked very alluring, although I didn't know that word yet.

She leaned down and spoke to me: "You got any money, youngblood? You wanna blow job?" That was the first time I ever heard the expression. She looked like a French beatnik in a tight black-and-white-striped blouse and peasant skirt, which she lifted while repeating "Wanna blow job, wanna blow job?" endlessly, almost like a Buddhist chant, pantomiming a blow job. But all I could hear was "Bluto done it, Bluto done it!" It sounded like the refrain from a *Popeye* cartoon where a bullfrog was fingering Popeye's nemesis, Bluto.

I'm sure if I'd been just a few years older, her voice would've reverberated in that stairwell as sexily as Donna Summer's "Love to Love You Baby." But to Little Splash it just sounded funny. All I could do was laugh as she drifted away.

Suddenly my father appeared, in slightly tattered, hip beatnik clothes bathed in Zizanie cologne, and we left the building—through the front door. We walked to the fast-food joints on Eighth Street. He took his spitback money and bought me a slice of pizza and a large Orange Julius. I was happy. The normal, kind, giving Nile was back. We spent the rest of the day browsing through every record store and music shop in the Village.

HE MAY HAVE BEEN crazy as hell, but my father's gift to me was his kindness, open-mindedness, and music. Every chance he got, he'd patiently teach me to read rhythm patterns. Because of robust music programs in the public school system, by the time I was fourteen, I could play at least a "tune" on almost any instrument in the symphony orchestra. When I was nineteen, I got my first important professional musical job, but he never saw me turn pro. My father died a few days before that. His life was relatively short. After I die, his bloodline will end with me, as if he never existed. He had no other children and is buried anonymously in Potter's Field on Hart Island, New York's cemetery of the unclaimed dead.*

---

*The family had lost contact with him by the time he died, and I only found that information during the writing of this book.

My dad left no manuscripts, compositions, motifs, or unfinished works. I used to think that was tragic, but not anymore. When I got much older, I traced his DNA back to the Benin tribe of what is now the Edo State in Nigeria. This process started with the National Geographic "Journey of Man" DNA analysis project and ended with the finely focused African Ancestry DNA database. The Benins have a rich artistic heritage that appears to be woven into their bloodline. When I was with my father, I noticed that the musical moments were the happiest of his life. I like to believe that the success I've had is a result of his contributions—or maybe it's just those Benin genes?

five

Hippie Happenstance

BEVERLY HAD A PLAN. BY MID-1962, BOBBY WAS OVERDOSING REGU-larly and she had become a daily user herself. My mother had no intention of watching Bobby die and wanted badly to shake her own addiction. Thus the plan to head back to California. Since Beverly couldn't shoot up around my grandparents, if we moved back in with them, she'd have no choice but to clean up. She could even use the long bus trip out West to kick. And so it was that at the age of ten I found myself back on a cross-country bus, returning to Los Angeles.

Like my first trip out to the coast, we went Greyhound. Once again we left from the Port Authority Bus Terminal, still one of the seediest bum-and-junkie-infested corners of a bum-and-junkie-infested city. As we were getting ready to board, my mother was flabbergasted to see that one of the bums lingering on the street was my dad, good old Nile Sr. In a city of ten million, somehow our paths kept crossing, like some kind of genetic magnetism at work. Beverly hadn't seen Nile in years and was shocked by how badly he'd disintegrated. She didn't even tell me she'd seen him. She waited till I was thoroughly engrossed in a comic book and went over to him.

"Nile, is that you?"

"Hey, Beverly! How are you?" Nile responded brightly, even though he looked like a street urchin.

"I'm fine. What are you doing over here?"

"Oh, I live around here. What are you doing around here?"

"I'm going to L.A.," answered Mom.

"How's Pud?"

"Oh, he's all right. I'm taking him with me."

"Bev, can I see him? I'd really love to see him."

"Nile, I don't think it's a good idea for him to see you like this."

He was clearly strung out on dope and using every ounce of his energy not to fall off into a nod. He pleaded with Beverly to let him see me. He said it was really important to him because he was all alone. The woman he was living with had just died from acute alcohol poisoning—he'd awakened a few days before to find her lying next to him, cold and dead. This story and his disheveled condition broke Mom's heart, so she agreed to bring me around to his flophouse room before we left. But as soon as he shuffled off, she changed her mind. Nile went back to his hotel room, and we boarded the bus.

TO KICK HER HEROIN HABIT, Beverly had packed a bottle of methadone pills, which, as you can imagine, made for a more eventful trip than my first three-thousand-mile journey with my grandma Goodie, two and a half years earlier. We strategically sat directly across from the bathroom. If Mom got sick because the methadone was ineffective, the bathroom assured her privacy. One time she got so unruly (hoarding bathroom time and arguing with the driver) that they threatened to throw us off the bus somewhere in the Midwest. After that she played it a little cooler.

A few thousand miles into the journey, I got it in my head that it would be interesting to meet the driver, even though the sign above him said "Speaking with the Driver Is Forbidden." He made occasional announcements with a thick country accent, using as few words as possible. And those words left out letters and syllables that were apparently unimportant to him. I sidled up to the front of the bus and started chatting.

"Hey, Mr. Driver. What's that?"

"Joshwa trees, son."

"Why do they look so weird?"

"First time I saw 'em, thought the same too."

"I have never seen trees like that. Does Joshua own them all?"

The driver laughed at that. He said, "No, son, Joshwa don't own 'em, just named after 'em. You heard the song 'Joshwa Fit the Battle a Jericho'?"

"Think so." I was trying to imitate his speech pattern.

"Mormons named 'em."

"Those singers on TV named Joshua's trees? Wow, you're really smart. What are their names, do you know 'em all?"

"When them Mormons come here, thought those trees looked like Joshwa's arms raised up."

"Joshua must look pretty funny."

"When I see them trees, I sing the song to myself. Tells me we gettin' near L.A."

He got quiet. Then started to hum, very gently. I knew the tune right away.

"Joshua fought the battle of Jericho,
Jericho, Jericho-o-o-o.
Joshua fought the battle of Jericho,
And the walls come a tumblin' down."

I never really understood what the hell he was talking about, but we chatted all the way till we pulled into the bus depot of my beloved Skid Row. Seeing those familiar landmarks brought to mind all the trouble I had gotten into, cutting school and going to grind houses. Like General Douglas McArthur coming back to the Philippines, I had returned to finish the job. Only this time I was going to get it right. This time I was with my mother, a cool beatnik chick who loved movies herself. I looked south down Broadway when we stopped at the traffic light.

Downtown L.A. hadn't changed much in two and a half years. Everything was still there, just more of it. The cable cars, which were called Angels Flight, were still ferrying crowds of people up and down a steep hill. Funky Broadway was more clouded with car exhaust and smog. The hookers, pimps, and the bums on Skid Row had grown in numbers. Movie posters and billboards were everywhere. Multicolored lights on dozens of theater marquees reflected off my glasses like disco balls.

Grandma Goodie had recently gotten remarried and there wasn't enough room for us at her place, so I moved in with Grandma Lenora on St. Andrews Place, and my mother moved in with my depressed aunt Naomi in a different part of town. Mom's moving in with Naomi brought her out of a funk. This young woman had just barely survived an abusive relationship herself. She was thrilled to be rid of her husband, and to have free-spirited Beverly as a roommate. It was a moment of genuine happiness in her short life. The two of them soon became the dynamic duo of nightclubbing at the black hip L.A. hot spots.

Meanwhile, my life with Lenora wasn't quite so glamorous. Our place was a back house that bordered an alley. Across the alley was a junkyard that mainly housed discarded large appliances. We kids called it Stove Land, and I loved playing there. We ran and jumped over, under, on, or through any and everything, like prehistoric parkour.

The neighborhood may have had a zoning identity crisis, but I wasn't totally unhappy living there. I had a new dog named Tiger and we were devoted to each other. He was a German shepherd crossed with a wolf. "He's been waiting for you," said Lenora's boyfriend Bill, when I first arrived. "He's your dog." Bill was right. Tiger was my dog and he had been waiting for me and vice versa. Tiger and I had many incredible adventures, real Lassie and Timmy material, but the one that pops to mind is the day he rescued me from certain death at the hands of a street gang.

One day a group of Mexican kids happened upon me on my way home. "What set you from, punk?" they asked me.

"Slauson," I said. (Insert buzzer beep sound here.)

"Wrong, punk."

Before they could kick my ass, I took off running, doing my best Jesse Owens impersonation. I ran down the alley. It was deserted and the worst place to be if they caught me, but it was the most direct route to my house. I was almost home, but my frail lungs were succumbing to the L.A. smog and heat. I was starting to slow down, and the gang was closing in for the kill.

With all the air I had left, I yelled, *"Tiger!"* as loud as I could. Somehow he heard me and must've sensed my desperation. Our fence was three times higher than Tiger, but he got a running start and jumped from the steps of our back door and cleared the fence with one leap. He shook off the hard landing and bore down on the gang in full attack mode, like a lion targeting a wildebeest in the Serengeti. The kids scattered in every direction as soon as they spotted the charging canine. They climbed telephone poles, jumped onto cars, and scaled the fence into Stove Land, hoping not to get caught. Tiger heeled on command when he reached me, but remained vigilant. He jumped over my head, his best trick, and then we casually walked home. I was happy for them to know exactly where Tiger and I lived.

BEVERLY HAD MOVED in with Naomi because there wasn't enough space at her mother's, but I thought she just wanted to get away from me again—which made me feel like an abandoned piece of shit again. A feeling further compounded by the unexpected news that she was moving back to New York to be with Bobby—and that she wasn't taking me with her.

I soon found relief for my latest bouts of self-loathing and abandonment: glue. "I'm gonna show you a cool way to get high," a kid my age named Ralph told me. We walked down the palm-tree-lined street to the Laundromat to get the perfect-sized paper bags for glue sniffing from the popcorn vending machine. After we stole a few—they looked like regular beer-can-sized bags but were thinner than lunch bags—and ran back to my house, Ralph trickled the glue evenly around the bottom of one, then closed his fist around it. He blew into the bag, filling it with air. Then he took his left hand and rubbed the bottom of the bulbous bag against the bottom of his clenched right hand. This would ensure the glue spread evenly inside. This was my first up-close experience with the full, mesmerizing performance of a pre-drug ritual.

Ralph started to inhale and exhale into the bag. After a few huffs, he gave me the bag and watched me imitate his every move. After the lesson was over, he said, "OK, here's the only thing you have to remember. When you can't feel the bag on your face, you gotta stop."

My last thought before I passed out was, I haven't been able to feel the bag on my face for about five minutes. Bam. My face slammed onto the kitchen table, like the spaghetti-eating scene in *A Clockwork Orange*.

When I came to, I had a bloody nose, a headache, and glue stuck all over me. I slurred, "Wow. What happened?"

"You should've stopped when you couldn't feel the bag no more," Ralph said.

"I thought that was the high-gettin' part."

When the cobwebs cleared, I felt the way I did after surviving my first roller-coaster ride: "Let's go again." It was fun. And fun, even reckless fun, is the birthright of youth. I was hooked.

Hailing as I did from the Bobby and Beverly school of upscale addiction, I quickly became a connoisseur of glue. I knew the potency of all the different brands, and that Testors was the cream of the crop. By the time I was eleven years old, I was doing glue every chance I got.

By age thirteen Ralph and I had moved on to sniffing other stuff too, like amyl nitrate that we stole from school. We'd break in after hours. I was super skinny, so I could crawl through the Automat-sized windows of the cafeteria, open the door, and let Ralph in. We made our way to the gym and stole the amyl nitrate—they kept a supply on hand just in case a kid passed out during a workout. It was hotter in L.A. than New York, so I guess that made sense. A few sniffs later, we learned that glue was a sedative, and that amyl nitrate was a stimulant. Speedballing 101: At my school it was a self-taught elective.

I'd spend the next five years becoming a full-blown alternative drug addict. I wanted to rebel against my parents, but since they were already pretty cool, I had to find drugs even they wouldn't.

ONE SATURDAY, RALPH and I were hitching to the Sunset Skating Rink in Hollywood from Grandma's place in South Central, Los Angeles. We showed up about an hour late for our intended session, so we needed to kill some time until the next one. We noticed a crowd of white people with hair that covered their eyes, like shaggy dogs, across the street from the rink. They looked . . . interesting, totally different than the few white kids in our school, so we decided to investigate. We were pretty high on glue, and we had an exaggerated sense of how close we were in age to this odd-looking crew coming out of "the Teenage Fair" at the Hollywood Palladium.

We introduced ourselves, and in retrospect, we must've appeared just as strange to them as they did to us. At thirteen, we dressed like miniature pimps: sharkskin suits, ruffled shirts, wrap-around cufflinks over our French cuffs, and of course the obligatory white Italians (pronounced "I-tal-yuns") on our feet. We idolized the Temptations and imitated them in our dress.

We asked the longhairs who they were, and they cheerfully replied that they were "freaks."

"Hey, I know that movie," I said, thinking of the crazy old hor-

ror movie about carnival freaks. I'd seen it many times in my grind-house tour. "We accept them, we accept them, one of us, one of us. Gooble gobble, gooble gobble, one of us, one of us."

They all laughed, and asked us if we wanted to take a trip.

"Sure," we said.

We had time to kill, and we thought that we'd just go joyriding. They invited us to their pad, and as I explained what a pad was to Ralph, we hopped into one of their cars and drove up into the Hollywood Hills. We arrived at a fantastic glass mansion, where we came upon beautiful people in every whacked-out situation you could think of. Coolest of all was that a lot of people were "balling," one of our hosts informed us—a new word to both of us, which meant having sex.

A guy rose out of a pile of women and looked us over.

"Wow, spade cats." He asked us if we wanted to take a trip again. Even though we thought we'd just taken a trip, we said sure, thinking if the next trip was as good as the first, it was going to be amazing. I don't remember how we actually ingested the LSD, because we fearlessly smoked, drank, and dropped everything they offered us.

The next thing I remember, I was sitting in a room in the glass mansion, staring into the shell of an old cathode-ray TV set filled with branches strung with common Christmas ornaments: blinking lights, decorated balls, and glass hair (or "angel hair" as we called it in New York). Somewhere a stereo was playing "The End" by the Doors and other psychedelic songs over and over again. This went on for about a day and a half. During that thirty-six-hour experience, Dr. Timothy Leary and a bunch of other Hollywood heavies came in and out. The crib must surely have belonged to a famous personality, but the name would have meant nothing to us young soul brothers from South Central L.A. at that time.

Twenty years later, Dr. Leary and I met at another house party, in the Beverly Hills home of Hollywood mover and shaker Wendy Stark. It was in the early eighties, and Leary proceeded to tell the entire room—with crystal clarity—the story of two young spade cats dressed in suits who'd taken their first acid trip with him.

I was floored. Here was an example of what I've called "hippie happenstance" to explain the unexplainable in my life. I've been pushing this term on myself since the sixties and my first encounter with the Freaks. For instance: How did I wind up at a party with this guy after all these years? It felt as if I was meant to go to the Teenage Fair, though I'd never heard of it. That I was meant to drop acid, though I had no idea what it was. And that I was meant to do it with Timothy Leary, though I hadn't a clue who the hell he was. I believe I was meant to travel an exact road to get to where I came to be. But I chose the road. This is why I've added the word "hippie" to "happenstance." It reminds me that I walked across the street to meet the Freaks, and that choice affected the seemingly random events that followed.

I RETURNED HOME to find my poor grandmother Lenora sobbing in her living room with a handful of cops who'd spent the past twenty-four hours looking for a missing child.

"Hey, Lenora what's going on?" I asked as I strolled in.

"Where have you been? I've been worried sick."

"I don't know," I said. The old monotonic response still seemed to work as an explanation for my irrational behavior. I'd left the day before a glue-sniffing pimp-in-training and had returned an unwashed, exhausted freak, speaking a new tongue—*balling, dropping, mamas, bikers, heads, Diggers, the clap, tripping, crabs, hassle, speed, peyote, acid, yage, surfers, LSD, Woodrose seeds, belladonna, pigs,* and *MDMA*.

The Temps were replaced by Them, the Troggs, the Doors, Love, the Beatles, and, oh yes, even the Monkees.

SINCE BOTH MY GRANDMOTHERS were now living in Los Angeles, I sometimes moved back and forth. During the summer of '64, I lived with Goodie in Watts. It was two blocks away from the Compton border, which began on a street called Imperial Highway. This may have been one of the hardest-core blocks in the toughest ghetto of Los Angeles, but it was clean and appealing compared to its New York equivalent. Even in Watts, the hedges were trimmed and the lawns were cut, edged, and well kept.

But that didn't mean it was fun. By the midsixties, life with Goodie and her new husband, Dan, was up and down, but the ride was fairly predictable. Dan was from Georgia, a black good ole boy and a heavy drinker. When he got drunk, he became abusive, but luckily he only got drunk on the weekends. His abuse was mostly verbal. And while Goodie wasn't fond of Dan's weekend rants, she'd learned to put up with them. Sometimes, however, he'd take out his shotgun and threaten to shoot her. It wouldn't have been a stretch for him. He had done hard time for shooting and killing a man in Chicago. They say the second time is easier. We hoped we'd never find out.

Life at Goodie and Dan's wasn't always bad. He had a cool dog called Champ, whom I liked almost as much as my dog Tiger. Dan also owned a guitar, which would be the first real guitar I'd ever touch. He rarely let me handle it, but I knew once he started drinking (and before he started threatening Goodie with his shotgun), he'd say, "Boy, get me my guitar, so I can pick." That was my chance to feel those appealing contours in my hand.

I'd always played music—or played around with it—when I was in school. But now it was summertime and school wasn't in session, so the few minutes it took to get the guitar and carry it over to Dan were almost sacred. I wasn't allowed to play it, which, as every kid

knows, made me want to more than anything. That said, it wasn't
worth a blast of rock salt in the backside—which he threatened me
with occasionally.

AT THE END of the summer of '65, my mother and Bobby came by
car out to L.A. and took an apartment on Pico Boulevard, in a
building called the Westchester Arms. Bobby wanted the entire
family to reunite under one roof because Beverly was expecting.

Unfortunately, this plan was also another scheme for kicking—
Mom had gone back to being a full-blown addict. They brought my
brother Bunchy along, and I moved in, too.

I wanted to live with Beverly and Bobby more than anything,
and would accept any living conditions, and so I left my dogs behind and settled into the bizarre Westchester Arms. The building
had the feel of a New York City apartment building. It was at least
six stories high, a veritable skyscraper for that section of L.A.

We felt right at home. The building was full of our kind of
people, a haven for low-level law-breaking entrepreneurs. The residents were mainly drug dealers, pimps, prostitutes, bookies, and
robbers. I loved living there. I no longer had to worry about the
gangbangers who plagued me in Watts. Other than the ones who
lived in our building, there weren't many kids around at all. And of
those, all of us were friends—and all my new friends were girls.

My new young female friends were extremely savvy and couldn't
wait to tutor me in the ways of their world. Their leader was Stephanie, a physically overdeveloped thirteen-year-old. Stephanie, who
must've grown her huge breasts and five-foot-eight-inch frame
when she was around eleven or twelve, was the ghetto version of
Anna Nicole Smith.

Next in the chain of command was thirteen-year-old Deborah.
She was breathtakingly desirable, but was the physical opposite of
Stephanie. Stephanie was extremely fair, because her mother was
white and her father—who was not in her life—was probably a

light-skinned black man, while Deborah was the color and smooth-
ness of the underside of a Hershey chocolate bar. Her skin was
perfect. Not a single flaw or blemish.

Deborah took my virginity. Well, "took" is not even close to
accurate. I surrendered like the runt of the litter. Though she was a
year younger, I was clearly outmatched. I didn't even know what to
do, but she was in total control. After some super heavy "tongue
kissing," as she called it, she took my penis in her hand, shifted her
body around, then gently put me inside her. "Wow, oh my God," I
whispered to her. My body felt completely weak and liquid, as if it
had no bones. I may have been crying. It was like being high, only
better. I felt like I was flying.

Deborah and Stephanie were women, regardless of the dates on
their birth certificates. It was so different to have girls as my best
friends and leaders. A woman commandant is amazing, especially
when she conducts the mission better than a guy. In the black community in those days (please forgive my generalizing and political
incorrectness), women typically ran the show, and these girls were
teaching me the way our world really worked.

FRESH GARDENIAS and apricots scented the evening air as I walked
down Third Avenue and onto Pico Boulevard. There were lots of
flowering trees directly next to the Westchester Arms, and it was
easy to imagine what the place could have been. Once upon a time,
maybe it was glamorous.

When you walked into the building's lobby, there was a desk to
the right of the elevators, where the rental agent sat. Our apartment
was a one-room flat, equipped with a kitchenette and a double
Murphy bed that pulled down from the narrowest wall of an almost
square room. I slept on the couch.

Once a week there was a big card game at the Westchester Arms.
The responsibility to cook rotated amongst the participants. Today
was my mother's turn. She was going to prepare a huge banquet

with enough food to last the length of the marathon casino tournament. While she was in a friend's apartment talking about her plans for the night, a guy named Bang-Bang, new to the building and the card game, introduced himself and offered to help.

Bang-Bang had earned his nickname because he was a hit man for hire. He had killed lots of people, with many different techniques, but his preference was to shoot them—hence, Bang-Bang. He would introduce himself by saying, "Hi, my name is Bang-Bang, but my friends call me Bang!"

He was the cousin of the building's manager and had just finished a stint in prison, where a number of cons had tried to kill him in his cell. They waited until he was alone, threw an accelerant on him while he was lying in his bunk, and set him on fire. He was so hated that even the guards let him burn for some time before they rang the alarm. As a result he was scarred all over his body, from head to toe.

Everyone at the Westchester Arms knew of Bang's reputation as a cold-blooded killer, except my mother, because she said with a laugh, "Bang-Bang, what kind of name is that?"

"What's so funny?" Bang-Bang said in his intimidating baritone.

He was a hulk of a man and his severely deformed face completed the terrifying effect. Only my mom didn't seem to notice. "What were your parents thinking?" she said.

Incredibly, the contract killer backed down. "Yeah, you're absolutely right," he said in a conciliatory tone. "If my parents had given it to me, it would be silly, but it's a nickname."

Instead of being kind in return, Bev hit below the belt. "Well, I don't know why you kept it. So I guess it's not your parents who were silly, it's you!"

"Who do you think you're talking to?" Bang said, again losing his temper.

"My name is Beverly," Mom shot back. "I'm truly sorry that I don't have a more colorful name like Pop-Pop or Fizz-Fizz because I take too many Alka-Seltzers. I'm just plain old Beverly. Nice meet-

ing you, Bang-Bang. Or do I call you Mr. Bang-Bang?" And with
that she turned and walked out of her friend's apartment and into
the elevator, leaving the killer speechless.

From that moment on, Bang-Bang had to have Beverly. He'd
never met a woman with such chutzpah and wit, wrapped in a
package so lovely. Bang became obsessed with winning Beverly's
love. He knew she was married, and to a white man, but he treated
her husband with the utmost respect.

He also gave me lots of money, every day in fact. I spent it on
my girlfriend Deborah and her friends. He would even babysit my
baby brother, and treated him well. He was my mother's adoring
servant, at her beck and call. Once he gave my mother the keys to a
brand-new sports car, and she couldn't even drive. She said, "Bang,
I can't accept this. Besides, I'm married, what would it look like,
you giving me presents that Bobby can't afford?"

"Well, the car is yours. If you don't want it, give it away, you can
even give it to Bobby, but the car is yours to do what you will with
it."

"Bang, I don't want to hurt your feelings, and I'm truly grateful,
but I can't accept it." And with that she returned the keys, a rare act
of sanity in a clearly insane arrangement.

BOBBY HAD MOVED BACK to L.A. because he wanted so badly to
bring the family together. Ironically, the arrival of his newborn son,
Bobby Glanzrock Jr., who was now getting most of Beverly's attention, unhinged him with jealousy. He was soon back to using heroin
(which they'd actually kicked on the cross-country road trip).

Pretty soon Mom and Bobby were on the skids again, and
brother Bunchy was sent back to New York. Little Bobby was the
only child Beverly actually planned to have, and her whole world
revolved around him; strangely enough, this was the best time Beverly and I ever spent together. Not only was I not jealous of little
Bobby, I adored him; together we took great care of him.

Mothering Bobby actually made Beverly a better mother to me. Her cute figure had returned in record time, along with her naturally independent attitude. But her constant fawning over her baby was, in Bobby's opinion, "not very groovy." The family he so wanted had completely alienated him from Beverly.

Bobby and Beverly had always had a somewhat open relationship, so it was cool with her when he started dating other women. After a few months, Bobby even stopped sleeping at the Westchester. He'd just come in the morning to dress for work. He had taken a new job at a high-end haberdashery in Hollywood. His new girlfriend was the wife of a successful black real estate broker who approved of their relationship, because, as he said to my mother, "all I care about is my wife's happiness." Meanwhile, Mom took a boyfriend named Charles. Charles was small-framed and light-skinned like my mom. He was really nice, like all of Mom's paramours, and also lived at the Westchester. We'd all become friends as a result of the card games and the daily comings and goings. Everybody and everything was cool.

What was not cool was Bang. Bang was disgusted by our family's salacious romantic free-for-all. Things started to spiral out of control during one of the weekly casino nights.

The evening had begun as just another ordinary night of card playing. There was the usual feasting, joking, and reverie, but then Bang jumped into Charles's face for no reason. To everyone's surprise, the skinny pretty boy wouldn't back down. Charles, much like his girlfriend Beverly, was small but quick-witted, and he verbally kicked Bang's butt, shutting him down with a virtuoso round of the dozens.

Bang had given Bobby a pass because he was Beverly's husband. In Bang's funhouse morality, that counted for something. But Charles was just a side piece. Bang wasn't about to let him get away with sleeping with Beverly, especially after he humiliated him in front of her.

The next morning, while Bobby was in the shower and Charles was eating breakfast with me in the tiny kitchen, Bang knocked on the door. When Beverly answered, he whispered the following threat: "If you don't stop fucking that skinny bitch-looking motherfucker, I'm going to kill him. I mean it, Beverly."

Until then Bang had always been a complete gentleman. But he was totally deranged by Bev's fling with this light-skinned pretty boy with naturally straight hair like Super Fly. Her open sexuality and this cat's good looks were too much for Bang to deal with.

Both Bobby and Charles left for their respective jobs, and I went to school, leaving my mother home alone with baby Bobby. And that's when Bang went completely berserk. He returned to the apartment and pushed his way in. He pulled out his gun and put it on the arm of an easy chair. He went to my newborn brother Bobby's crib, picked him up, walked over to the window, and dangled him outside. Mom was hysterical, but she steadied herself. She told Bang that she didn't love Charles and that she would quit him. She was just "going out with him because Bobby had gotten a new girlfriend" and for all intents and purposes had moved out. She begged him not to drop little Bobby out the window.

Bang brought the baby inside, put him back in the crib, and in one motion swept everything off the coffee table with his massive arm. He ripped off my mother's clothes and raped her, while her baby lay unattended and crying through the entire ordeal. In this one violent attack, Bang was trying to pay her back for everything he was feeling. In his own psychotic way, I think Bang believed he really loved her.

"Now, you remember what I said, because I mean every word," he told her when he finished. "Quit that nigger or I'll kill him, and any other motherfucker that looks at you now," as if the rape had consummated a bond between them.

My mother attempted to collect herself. She wasn't sure Bang's wrath was done. Beverly had no choice but to break up with Charles that very night to save his life. Charles was completely blindsided. She never told Bobby about the rape or about his young son being held out the window. Bobby didn't seem to notice Charles wasn't around the next morning when he came to shower and change for work. He left for the office, and Mom let Bang and everyone else in the building know that she and Charles were no longer an item. Bang was satisfied that Beverly was starting to act right and had come around to his way of seeing things.

Later that day she casually told Bang she was popping out for a pack of cigarettes and told him she'd get him a pack. Instead, she caught the bus to Lenora's house. She called my school and spoke to the principal. She told them to summon me to the phone. She didn't tell me about the rape, but told me not to go back to the apartment under any circumstances. She said, "Please come to Lenora's."

This might have worked had it not been for the fact that I couldn't imagine not seeing my thirteen-going-on-thirty Deborah. I thought of her every waking moment. I'd never had sex before her and I wanted it every day. Not fully understanding, and knowing Mom's flair for the melodramatic, I followed my hormones and disobeyed.

By now Beverly had been away entirely too long just to get a pack of cigarettes. Bang knew something was up. He also knew how bright Beverly was. He couldn't outwit her, so he played the only game he had a small chance of winning: the fear game.

I was in our apartment, doing it with Deborah, when Bang knocked on the door. I reluctantly broke off and opened the door. When Bang saw me, he said, "Oops, sorry to bother you." Now he knew where both Deborah and I were. But since Mom hadn't told me anything about the rape—I wouldn't hear about this until forty years later—I wasn't even remotely alarmed.

Meanwhile, Bang went back to his apartment and phoned Deborah's mother. Bang knew Deborah's mom and my mother were best friends, so he told Deborah's mother to call Beverly "and tell her if she wants to see Nile alive again, she'd better get her ass back." He also told Deborah's mom that he was holding her daughter at gunpoint, too. None of it was true. After the call, Bang returned to my place and proceeded to treat us nicely. Deborah and I took advantage of the usual Bang mix of cash, gifts, and the best pot in town. Ultimately he let us go. We never knew we were prisoners.

As soon as I left I nonchalantly headed to Lenora's to meet up with my mom, who dropped the news that we were never going back to the Westchester, "because Bang is a bad man." Really? I still found this hard to believe.

Mom quickly got us a place near the University of Southern California, and I transferred to yet another school. I adapted like I always did, though I longed to be with Deborah. Masturbating quietly after Mom fell asleep in our studio apartment was no substitute. A few weeks later, I visited Deborah, and Bang spotted me and followed me back home. The next day, after I left for school, he showed up at our new house. He hadn't counted on finding Beverly there with her mother, Goodie.

This unexpected plot twist allowed Beverly to gain the upper hand. "Bang, my mom's here and Bobby's coming over," she told him, thinking on her feet. "How about I meet you tomorrow for dinner?" Bang told my mother he wanted to take care of her in a manner that she deserved, while trying to hang a very expensive watch on my little brother Bobby's wrist. He told her he'd gotten it off the body of a pawnbroker he'd killed who was about to turn state's evidence on the mob. "All I want is to be a part of your family," he pleaded. Then he made her promise that she and Bobby would come to his apartment for dinner the next day.

Beverly had him exactly where she wanted him.

Soon after he left, there was a knock at the door. A tall, somber-looking guy introduced himself as Detective Klatanoff, "from Homicide," he said. He showed his badge to my mother. "We're trying to track down"—here he used Bang's government name. "We've been to the Westchester Arms and everyone says if we find you we'll find him." The detective had been told of Bang's infatuation with Mom. "They're all afraid of him," he added, "with good reason. We'd like to move you to the Capitol Motel on La Cienega, so we can set up a stakeout here. We found you and believe he'll find you, too."

Beverly told Detective Klatanoff they'd just missed him and about the dinner rendezvous she'd promised Bang the next night. All of this was still hard for me to believe. Despite the cops' arrival, I still didn't take the Bang threat seriously. But I had to do what my mom said. So we moved to the motel for what we believed would be a couple of days at best. As usual, things didn't go as planned.

The cops hoped that once Beverly and Bobby didn't show for dinner, Bang would return to our apartment. Instead, Bang left Mom, Goodie, and me alone and returned to the Westchester Arms, where, for reasons not entirely clear, he started shooting up the building. He and one of the guys from the weekly card game exchanged fire, and both men were wounded. Though Bang was hit in the thigh, he managed to escape—and to start a high-drama run from the law worthy of Bonnie and Clyde.

Bang had a female friend who happened to be a nurse. He paid her to hit the road with him. They robbed various establishments all across the country, while she tended to him. He never went to a hospital, where it's mandatory to report gunshot wounds to the cops.

And Bang was still obsessed with Beverly. He'd lifted her address book from our apartment, and he'd been calling and bribing people for her whereabouts. Fortunately, no one knew where we were; she knew better than to tell anyone. While Bang was at large, the cops moved us from place to place for our own safety. One day Mom called my brother Bunchy's father, Graham, from the shelter that we were now living in. The always dependable Graham said, "You'll never guess who showed up at my house last night."

"Who?"

"Bang."

"You've got to be fucking kidding me."

"No, he believes you're here in New York."

"Graham, tell me where he is. He's fucking crazy." Bang had given Graham the dead pawnbroker's wristwatch. Maybe Graham was afraid, or he just wanted to honor a deal, so all he would say was, "He's in the most obvious place."

My mother got it right away. She knew Bang had never been to New York. Harlem was the one place he'd blend in. Knowing he always had to have the best, he was most likely at the Hotel Theresa. In the interest of protecting Graham, she called the front desk herself.

"I believe he might be staying there under another name," she said, asking permission to describe her adversary. "He's tall with dark skin, might walk with a limp, and . . ." Before Mom could finish her Sherlock Holmes act, the desk clerk said, "Oh dear God, he's here, and I am so afraid of him. Whenever those two—"

"Two, what do you mean two?" interrupted my mother.

"He has a woman with him most of the time. He is a very scary individual."

"Thank you so much. Please call the police right away if he checks out."

And with that Mom hung up. She called Detective Klatanoff, and he called the NYPD. Then about two hours later he called Mom back.

"Beverly?"

"Yes."

"This is Detective Klatanoff. I'm coming over with the biggest bottle of champagne I can find. We apprehended the son of a bitch and you deserve a medal. We couldn't have done it without you. You and your kids don't have to hide anymore."

I never saw my beloved Deborah again.

six

In Search of the Lost Chord

WITH BANG IN POLICE CUSTODY, WE WERE AT LONG LAST FREE TO LEAD normal lives, no longer on the run or trapped in hotels. Of course, "normal" for us was always relative. Since Bobby now had a new girl, job, and lifestyle in Los Angeles, my mother decided on another cross-continental migration. She would return to New York to live with Graham. I would stay behind in Los Angeles with Lenora.

I felt abandoned—again—but this time I was pleasantly distracted by my new friends and appetites. Mom had two distinct sides to her personality. Though she was the ultimate hip nonconformist, she also respected collegiate strait-lacers. And she believed that by living with my strict grandmother, I'd have a better chance of leading a normal life. My mother didn't know that "normal" for me had changed dramatically since I'd started getting high on hallucinogens, inhalants, and Deborah. I was fifteen years old, and sex and drugs were now my total preoccupations. All I needed to make my transformation into a black hippie complete was rock and roll.

The James A. Foshay Middle School in South Central, Los Angeles, had a solid music program that was classically based. We had a halfway decent orchestra, with a deep European repertoire. We performed everything from Brahms to Tchaikovsky fairly well, even though outside of school no one dared listen to anything that was not vetted by the tastemakers at KGFJ, the local R&B station. I played clarinet in the orchestra's woodwind section, and handled it competently. Like my homeboys, I loved James Brown, but, at least in the safety of the orchestra, I could rock out to J. S. Bach, too.

Lenora told everybody she was my mother, which I resented. I particularly disliked it when she told the officials at school. Maybe she had legal reasons for doing so, but she never shared them with me. I wish I had told her how conflicted this fiction made me feel. Instead, I buried my feelings and rebelled passively, especially after I got a taste of hippiedom.

Lenora gave me everything I wanted that she could afford (including a tiny Sony portable TV that kept me company all night), if it didn't conflict with her religious beliefs and practices—but her religion's traditions changed arbitrarily. For as long as I could remember, we couldn't eat meat on Friday, then suddenly one day we could. Mass, the Catholic church service, was always in Latin, then one day it wasn't. Things like that further alienated me from her devout belief in ceremonies that were obviously man-made. Like my mom, I gravitated more toward science and things that could be proven.

It saddens me now when I think of how happy I could've made Lenora. All I would have had to do was pretend to go along with her religiosity and call her Mommy, regardless of what I thought. The trouble was, I never even called my real mother Mommy.

At the time, Lenora had a terrific boyfriend named Emmett, whom she really mistreated. Maybe he tolerated it because he was aware of the painful life Lenora had led. At any rate, I guess he truly loved her, because he put up with the abuse. Emmett was exceptionally nice to me and taught me to drive in his sporty white Chevrolet Corvair Monza with a stick shift. He worked as a maintenance worker at the Van Nuys Airport, the hippest general aviation airport—for private planes and the like—on the planet. He took me to work with him and gave me a portion of his salary. More than that, I got a firsthand glimpse of the high life. The same way my vocabulary expanded after a day with Dr. Timothy Leary's acid freaks, my word power increased dramatically while working at Van Nuys. Words like *thermals, Lockheed JetStar, Learjet, Cessna, Piper Cub, updrafts,* and *tips* became part of my lingo.

Yes, I said *tips.* That word had an important new meaning. People started giving me tips, not just cash tips, but tips about life.

At the airport many of the faces I'd see were familiar to me from movies and TV. I'd regularly see folks like Dean Martin, Sammy Davis Jr., Gene Autry, Frank Sinatra, and a host of other A-list celebrities. For the first time, I felt like I was in the presence of genuine aristocrats. Most of them were kind and generous. Some had their own airplanes, and when it was convenient, they or their pilots would take me up and let me see the world from a different angle.

My life as a neo-black hippie jet-set wannabe was quite a contrast to my grandmother Lenora's world. She worked as a domestic. Translation: She cleaned up small spaces for white people. Her boyfriend Emmett was a maintenance worker. Translation: He cleaned up large spaces for white people. I, on the other hand, was somewhat delusional about my own occupation. It was manual labor, but with some enormous unlisted benefits. It was the early days of the jet age in general aviation, and I cleaned Frank Sinatra's Learjet, *Christina II.* It had a tangerine-colored racing stripe, and its tail number, N175FS, resembled my name, if you stood alongside the pilot's window looking back. All of the people I met there had one thing in common: They were all in a line of work that fell under the general heading of "show business." This world felt comfortable and familiar to me. After all, I was raised on TV, music, and film.

* * *

EMMETT, ALONG WITH some other airport workers, told me one special story that truly put me on a path to overachieving, or at least always trying to do my very best. It went something like this:

One smoggy afternoon, an airport in Southern California had poor visibility and a low ceiling. In spite of those conditions, a private plane pressed on and landed there because its passengers absolutely had to perform a concert that night. The plane was owned by the blind musical genius Ray Charles. Ray Charles was like a god in my house since my childhood, but this flight proved that the beloved blind singer truly had divine powers. As Emmett told me, beaming with pride: "Brother Ray can take the controls and fly the plane himself; he's absolutely fantastic."

I knew Emmett well enough to know he wouldn't tell a big fish story just for dramatic effect. He said that Charles had brought the plane in via radar ILS (instrument landing system) while the pilot called out the instrument panel readings. But the facts didn't matter. What mattered was the message. In my mind I now saw Ray Charles as the person who saved the plane, the passengers, and the show. It was a complete revelation. Proof that special people can truly bend the rules.

That story flipped some kind of switch inside me. After that I walked into every plane that returned and cleaned it more thoroughly than ever. I increased my duties and doubled back and checked every area that we'd already cleaned. My work ethic permanently expanded. I started to pay closer attention to everything and everybody. It didn't take long before I started intersecting with various cross sections of Van Nuys Airport people, moving in circles beyond my custodian's job. The fact is, I committed to propelling myself toward show biz. Service and success—to me they were one and the same. It was what the hippies and show business people had in common: performing, helping, and sharing.

WHEN I WAS FIFTEEN, Grandmother Lenora was feeling ill and had taken a few days off from work, but she had her own formidable work ethic, and the show must go on even for domestic workers—especially when there are bills to pay. Moreover, Lenora owned the company; her client had to hire a temp to fill her spot. She had to get back on the job. So when she still felt ill after a few days, Lenora called Goodie and asked that she and Emmett accompany her to the hospital. Her intention was to get a doctor to confirm she'd been sick and give her a note explaining her absence to her employer/client, the Franklin Life Insurance Company, which by now had become the only place she was cleaning. It was critical that she remain in their good graces.

After the doctor examined Lenora, he asked Goodie if they could speak in private. The doctor told Goodie that Lenora was in the final stage of ovarian cancer and had a very short time to live. All they could do was make her comfortable and give her the best quality of life for the remaining time she had.

Since the disease had progressed so far and Lenora had never suspected her sickness was cancer, they decided not to tell her she was dying. They also never told me. Goodie and Emmett wanted us both to remain as upbeat as possible during Lenora's final days. They asked me to leave her alone so she could rest. As a result I only went to the hospital once. I never saw her alive again after that. Her passing came as a complete shock. The grief was too much for me to bear.

Goodie called my mother and Lenora's other family members. I don't remember anyone showing up for a funeral, nor do I remember attending one. I have no other memory of the subject except for the day her eldest son, my uncle, showed up at our house to settle Lenora's affairs. His name was Demetrius Clare, and he was my biological father Nile's half brother. (Mom dropped the following family bombshell on Thanksgiving Day, 2010: Demetrius was most likely Lenora's son—and brother. The result of her being raped by her father.)

DEMETRIUS MOVED INTO what used to be Lenora's and my home. When she was alive, I lived by her rules, but they were nothing like my uncle's. He was extremely narcissistic, with a touch of no-

nonsense arrogance. Despite that, I really liked him, and I'm sure he was just doing the right thing, but it felt like he showed up only to liquidate our assets. And he did so in relatively short order.

Within a few days, Demetrius had hooked up with a pretty girl who was at least six months pregnant. I believe he met her when she answered a classified ad offering our furniture at a very good price. She got it for an even better price. I remember her moving in and having lots of sex with Demetrius. (I peeked a lot, I admit.) I'm pretty sure that was the payment for the furniture. It wound up being a turn-key deal, because she moved in and rented the house.

Demetrius got all of Lenora's insurance money by masquerading as her sole heir; their surnames matched and she didn't have a will. We quickly grabbed a familiar Greyhound bus and headed back to New York.

Demetrius lived in the South Bronx. He was balding, dark-skinned, and fairly good-looking, despite his extremely pockmarked face. By the time he was about thirty or so, he also had a complete set of false upper teeth, which he could pop in and out of his mouth using only his tongue. Given the pockmarks, the premature hair loss, and the toothlessness, it was a little surprising to me that there was an endless parade of girls in his world, all of whom to me seemed way out of his league. But he had his own explanation: When we were just sitting around, he'd pop his teeth in and out and tell me how women couldn't resist his toothless cunnilingus.

Like my dad, Demetrius was a remarkable musician. He was tall, with a huge booming voice, not unlike James Earl Jones's or Paul Robeson's, and sang on a few small doo-wop hits with a group called the Popular Five. When Demetrius (everybody pronounced his name "Da-me-tree") wasn't preaching Black Power or bragging about his sexual prowess, he was singing. Musical talent was second nature to him, and to my father. I'd developed a knack for picking up many different instruments, as I bounced from school to school, but compared to them, my skills were rudimentary at best.

* * *

I'D NEVER EXPERIENCED culture shock like the kind I felt back in the South Bronx. The new hood made South Central look like Beverly Hills. Our street was filthy with litter; we lived in the front and the train thundered directly past our windows on Park Avenue and 161st Street. But it wasn't totally miserable. In fact, it was partly because of this odd living arrangement that I became a professional musician. We actually lived with one of my uncle's paramours, who had a son named Butch. Butch played the drums, and had a band. He also had a gorgeous sister. She was completely unattainable, a fly sister who wasn't digging my fledgling hippie affect. I was dying for her to like me, so when Butch and company needed a guitarist for their band, I lied my way into an audition for their group.

As I said, my time playing in the school orchestra had taught me how to get a tune out of most instruments. I had a false sense of confidence, somehow believing that even though I didn't know how to play the guitar, a miracle might occur. That I'd get into the band, and into Butch's sister's pants. But when I picked it up, it didn't take long for them to see that I wasn't anywhere close to a real guitar player. "That's the worst shit we've ever heard," they told me. Needless to say, I was crushed. But the gauntlet had been thrown down: Now I had something to prove.

AFTER THIS HUMILIATION, I convinced my mother to let me come live with her and Graham. Having kids around cramped Graham's partying style, but I was fifteen now. He was my brother Bunchy's dad, which made him sort of like my stepfather. He was a lifelong family friend and still would do anything for Beverly. He lived in the same old house in the industrial neighborhood where we moved when she left Bobby nine years earlier. My mother and Graham were living a druggy, one-dimensional, dysfunctional life.

But I, on the other hand, was focused. I convinced them to buy me a guitar for Christmas. The last orchestral instrument I'd learned to play in school was the clarinet, and I had music books with tons of études.

I went out and bought some guitar books and saw that the guitar had the same written range as the clarinet. Since I could play the clarinet, and knew what the music sounded like, I'd just try to replicate it on guitar. It didn't work. So I went out and got a Beatles songbook (they were one of my favorite bands) and practiced every day. But it never sounded anything like the song I was trying to play. On the clarinet, if you don't have the correct embouchure (the positioning of your mouth), the instrument doesn't sound right. I thought the same concept was true for the guitar. I followed the finger chart perfectly, thinking that I'd soon get the positions right, and then I'd practice my études and master this instrument.

One day Graham came home and heard me trying to play. "Pud, let me help you," he said. He strummed the guitar once. "Wow, this is way out of tune." Oh. Graham judiciously turned the pegs while saying, "You got this tuned like a violin or something."

He finished retuning. He handed it back to me. I looked at the finger chart and put my fingers in the positions that I had been methodically practicing. I strummed, and a perfect G–major chord rang out. I switched to the next position and strummed a D major. Sir Edmond Hillary, reaching the summit of Mount Everest, must have felt something similar to what I felt at that moment. This was more blissful than anything I'd ever experienced. I played the next chord and it sounded like the right chord in the progression. I started the song again. With utter confidence I sang, "I read the news today, oh boy," then strummed an E minor and dropped to the seventh, "About a lucky man who made the grade." There are no words to accurately describe what this felt like. What's the greatest feeling you've ever had? I hate to cheapen the moment by likening it to drugs, but the truth is I got a narcotic rush. Not just any rush, but a "first time" rush, the same as acid, dope, glue, booze, orgasm, or any number of things that I'd done at the time, or that I would subsequently overdo. There's really never been anything like it.

I played all day and all night. I got out my clarinet études. If I went slowly, I could read the music and play it on the guitar. At that moment I decided that I'd stick to just one instrument for the rest of my life.

* * *

IT WAS MID-FEBRUARY 1968. Though winter's end was in sight, I was gloomy. Life with my mother at Graham's had its considerable downside. There were no other houses nearby, only factories. The memories of how bad it had been to live here washed over me like a huge wave, sucking me into an undertow of depression. This was the house where I'd first wet the bed in '59 and where I'd developed severe insomnia. This was where I accidentally hit my brother Bunchy near the heart with a dart when we were kids. This was the loneliest house in the world. All of these traumatic memories became more vivid when the lights went out at bedtime.

At the time, I was going to a mostly white high school, Christopher Columbus, one block north of Pelham Parkway in the Bronx. So my sense of isolation there was much worse than it had been when I was younger. At fifteen I had a more developed sense of identity, and I didn't need other teens to tell me that I didn't belong. So one day I decided to run away.

I grabbed my guitar and retreated to the place where I'd felt safe when I was younger: the subway. I started sneaking out of the house with my guitar strapped to my back and would ride the trains until dawn. For the first time in my life, I'd found an environment that matched my natural sleeping pattern: waking up every two hours—about the length of the longest subway line ride. I slept like a baby. Bums, sexual predators, and other assorted New Yorkers rode the trains with me, but mostly we ignored one another.

IT WAS ON ONE OF THESE RIDES that I met James Irwin, who would, for a time at least, become my dharma-bum hippie guru, and change the course of my life as much as that well-tuned guitar. As I was getting onto a train—an older car—thank God, because for some reason the heat worked better in them—I noticed a tall man, maybe twenty-one years old, about six foot seven, sitting in the corner. He had on a poncho and an Australian digger hat, but to me the most interesting thing about him was that he was a hippie who wasn't wearing blue jeans.

Our eyes met as I entered subway car number 9521 (I remember that number because it's the year I was born, if you make the last number first). I sat across from him. The train was elevated, and every time the doors opened at a station, the temperature dropped thirty degrees because there was a blizzard that night. While waiting to fall asleep, I let my mind wander through scenes of different films that took place in cold climates: *Ice Station Zebra, Doctor Zhivago,* and *The Lion in Winter.* At one particularly cold station, tons of snow blew inside the train car when we stopped, and I started laughing.

"What's so funny, man?" he said.

"The snow blowing in re-minds me of the flick *The Fatal Glass of Beer.*"

In tandem we recited an impression of W. C. Fields's classic line: "It's not a fit night out for man nor beast." And we each grabbed a handful of snow that had blown inside and threw it on the subway door's window, as if it were W. C. Fields's face, mocking the film's repetitive sight gag (an off-screen stagehand throws fake snow in W.C.'s face whenever he opens any door). We laughed so hard we could barely catch our breath. There was an instant chemistry between us, me and my older hippie brother.

"Man, it's too cold to stay in the twenty-cents hotel. You wanna go to a crash pad I know?" he asked

"Absolutely, dude, why not."

"Thing is, we have to give 'em some bread, man."

"Bummer, I don't have any," I said.

"Don't worry, we can panhandle it up on Eighth Street."

"Cool. That'd be far out."

Which is how I started my new career as a professional panhandler.

I'd never live with my mother again, at least not for more than a few days at a time. I was fifteen years old.

"WOODY'S COMMUNE" was on Avenue C and Fifth Street. It was situated just a few blocks from where I'd lived when my stepfather Bobby had his first near-death overdose. It was part commune and part crash pad.

The members of the commune cleaned, cooked, and shopped, while the people who just crashed there had to pay around two bucks a night for a bed, a gourmet meal (Woody's partner Dave was a former chef), and whatever drugs were scored with the leftover money. The first night I crashed there, it was crowded, with maybe thirty people in residence.

Outside was cold, but inside Woody's pad it was nice and warm, even hot. The rooms we slept in were filled wall-to-wall with mattresses. We all smoked weed from a giant hookah, and the smell of it was thick in the air. Up until then I'd never felt completely comfortable anywhere, unless I was alone. But I felt so relaxed at Woody's that I slept as well there as I did on the subway.

Everywhere I looked, people were balling like crazy. Even I, the newcomer to the commune, balled a chick that was "splitting for the coast in the morning." A few days later my penis was oozing puss and burning like lava was flowing through it. I soon found out it was gonorrhea, which was "really common" and easy to treat, according to James. "Hey, man, that's the clap. You just get a shot of penicillin, and in a few days, you'll be back in business."

The man was wise. James Irwin and I soon became inseparable. We were certainly an odd couple. He was a big and tall white guy from Evansville, Indiana, and I was a skinny black hippie from the Bronx by way of L.A. and the Village. But odd couplings were a way of life for me at that point.

James taught me how to panhandle in ten languages (even sign language) and generally became my mentor. He was very attractive to women, even though he wasn't especially good-looking (or at least I couldn't see it). In fact, he was filthy, a street person's street person. But he was smart, and I don't mean your run-of-the-mill average-genius smart. I'm talking next-level, Stephen Hawking smart, but in the hippie's way: He didn't believe in adding specialization and discipline to his genius. He just knew a lot about everything. I've rubbed up against many people with exceptional abilities in my life, but James may be one of the five brightest people I've met.

He had Svengali-like power over me, but I was cool with it. He also had a kind of Messiah complex, but he was generous, loving, and munificent. And when it came to me, his munificence was boundless. Under his tutelage I got politicized, socialized, and sensitized. His liberal ideology tapped into the person that I always was.

At fifteen my appetite for knowledge and growth was insatiable. And with James as my guide, I started dabbling in a myriad of political organizations, from the antiwar "flower power" groups to the Yippies and the Black Panthers, not to mention religions, philosophies, and different martial arts disciplines. And all the while, I was adding to my panhandling income by earning some decent money playing the guitar around town. Not enough to make a living, but enough to keep going with it.

I BECAME AN EMANCIPATED TEENAGER, which meant I mostly slept on the subway and in crash pads. I learned many survival tricks that allowed me to live a prosperous life. For instance, if you finessed the rotary dial on pay phones just right, all the coins emptied out like hitting the jackpot on a slot machine. I was studying Hung Gar Kung Fu under Grand Master William Chung, and a guy I knew from my temple was part of the security at the Fillmore East, and he let me in with a phony press card. I saw any show that I wanted, including opening night in March '68: Big Brother and the Holding Company, Tim Buckley, and Albert King, whose performance moved me unlike any I'd ever seen. I remember the base of my neck getting goose bumps and tears streaming down my cheeks when I heard Albert play the guitar. His instrument called to me like mythological sirens called homesick sailors at sea. Everything in my life was finally starting to make sense.

But life wasn't all fun and games. On April 4, Dr. Martin Luther King Jr. was shot, and just two days later young Black Panther Little Bobby Hutton was shot and killed. Riots broke out, but most of the demonstrations were for the most part peaceful. After the cycle of grieving and protest concluded, hippie life returned to "normal," again a relative term.

STREET LIFE WAS CERTAINLY a lot more exciting than living at home with Beverly and whatever guy she was with at the time. She had left Graham's house and started to date a fan club of guys that helped to support her and little Bobby, and me on the odd days when I'd come home. This typically happened after I had a bad acid trip or got sick. Like on the afternoon of June 3, the day Andy Warhol and I wound up in the same emergency room.

I'd been enjoying the last days of spring with a fair-weather (or weekend) hippie named April. She lived at home and we'd just met that night, Tuesday, June 2, at the hippie musical *Hair.* After the show we went to hang out at the Bethesda Fountain in Central Park, when two guys approached us and said they were on leave from the military. "Can you help us score some grass?" they asked. We took them to a few of our East Village haunts and partied until the wee hours. Then they invited us down to a pad in Little Italy.

While there, they somehow slipped STP (a very powerful hallucinogen, called DOM nowadays) into one of my drinks. I started tripping my brains out and didn't know why. I was quickly losing control. Given I was an old hand at tripping, I initially thought this was one of those fabled flashbacks I'd heard about. But it wasn't—it was much stronger than most heavy trips—and I started freaking out and ran outside. The heartbreaking part is, I later found out that they gang-raped April after I left her alone in the apartment. I'd later find her living on the street because she decided to run away from her parents' home after the incident. I think she was ashamed to face her folks.

I don't remember how long I ran around tripping that day, because I was fading in and out of reality. At a police call box near the corner of Second Avenue and Houston Street, I phoned the cops. I was taken by ambulance to Columbus Hospital, a few short blocks away, panic-stricken and rapidly going mad. Even in my extreme psychotic state, I noticed dawn had just broken. I looked down at my arms. My skin had the texture and color of a lizard's. So like any self-respecting reptile, I spread my fingers wide and tried to catch flies with my tongue.

The atmosphere in the ER was almost festive. The doctors and nurses seemed to be having the time of their lives. There were few if any other patients. Hours passed in the blink of an eye, and it was now the afternoon. Suddenly, apropos of nothing, I was whisked out of the way as a gurney smashed open the ER doors; it was bearing the body of a bloody Andy Warhol, by now one of the most recognizable and important figures in the Village scene. A crowd of people surrounded him and I became irrelevant. Though my head was still a little twisted, my heart told me Andy needed help more than me. I later read that Andy actually died on the operating table, but emergency surgery brought him back.

After the drugs wore off, I called my mom, and was released to her a little after midnight. Sober now (sort of), I felt angry about being kicked out of the ER bash.

(I actually got this resentment off my chest years later, at a dinner party where I was seated next to Andy. I shared this story with him, and he couldn't have been more gracious. Later that night he wrote very flattering words about meeting me in his diary, which you can read after finishing my book.)

* * *

FOLLOWING THE LIZARD/WARHOL INCIDENT, I moved back to the Bronx with my mom. Hippie James moved in with us, too. Two days later Bobby Kennedy was shot and killed. That Saturday there was a peaceful gathering in Central Park in sympathy for Bobby, Martin Luther King, and Bobby Hutton. The climate in the country was hot. People were protesting, rioting, rebelling, and organizing. From my teenage perspective, it felt like something important was happening in America, and I felt the need to help. Oppressed groups were finding their voices, and I was finding mine.

James and I grabbed the D train to Columbus Circle, where people had started gathering. I was happy to be back with my ever-growing hippie family and to be part of this thing called the Movement. I wasn't sure which affinity group would ultimately win my soul, but I knew this would work itself out in time. For now, I was happy to be with exciting, motivated people who felt like family. You don't usually get to choose your family, but I did and I chose wisely. Finally I fit in. I went back to living on the street. Back to crash pads, panhandling, jamming, demonstrating, balling, tripping, and the Twenty Cents Hotel, until I panhandled from a woman named Cinda Firestone.

Cinda was an heir to the American tire empire, and she had a heart of gold. So much so that she let many street people live in her Park Avenue pied-à-terre. One of those people was me. Cinda was an artist with a political consciousness. She made the film *Attica,* which documented the infamous prison massacre. Cinda proved that the Movement touched people in every class. What was happening in America was happening on every socioeconomic level.

My first dive into full-fledged activism came when I joined a unique section of the Black Panther organization: the lower Manhattan Section of the Harlem Branch of the Black Panther Party for Self-Defense. My entry into the group was another case of hippie happenstance.

In Greenwich Village there was a group of guys who dressed "in uniform" and called themselves Panthers. They used intimidation to collect small amounts of drugs and money from tourists and fair-weather hippies. They relied on the media portrayal of gun-toting Black Panthers to coerce their victims. I'd seen these Panther-looking guys in the community, but I didn't know about their crooked extracurricular activities. They preyed on my idealism. They got me to give them money and get donations from the various peacenik and antiwar groups that I was affiliated with. They enlisted me. I thought it was really cool that these guys wanted a hippie in their ranks.

One day a notable article appeared in *The Black Panther* newspaper. It said all Panthers in the New York area had standing orders to show support for the widow of Malcolm X, Sister Betty Shabazz, at a rally in Harlem. I asked the bogus Panthers what time we were going to the rally. They told me they had direct orders from the Central Committee to stay underground. But I followed the orders in the newspaper.

When I arrived at the Harlem Branch at 2026 Seventh Avenue, I told the officer-of-the-day, Jamal Joseph, I was from the Greenwich Village Panthers. He assigned me to a detail. On that detail I saw people whom I knew to be real Panthers from my neighborhood, and they asked me what section I was in. I told them. They instantly realized it was the crooks they'd been trying to track down, so I led them to the shakedown artists. We issued them a cease and desist. I soon won favor of the section and was not only welcomed, but promoted to subsection leader.

Our HQ was a beautiful Twenty-first Street Chelsea town house located next door to the home of actor Anthony Perkins (*Psycho*) and his girlfriend, my future photographer and friend Berry Berenson. Our colorful ranks were comprised of mostly biracial brothers, if that is the current politically correct term. At the time we called them mulatto.

Most of the brothers were from the Village and had white mothers and black fathers. Some claimed more elaborate heritage: The section leader told us his Sioux name was Yellow Kidney. We knew him as Andy Steed. Our group was more dedicated to community service than armed revolution. We worked doubly hard at everything. We marched when we could have taken the train; if we had to paint the storefront, brother Steed actually art-directed and painted the Panther logo.

We were model Panthers. We studied the literature diligently, and worked overtime on the "Breakfast Program." There was credible information that hungry children were at a disadvantage in school, so we fed them. FBI head J. Edgar Hoover deemed it "the single most dangerous program in America." Ironically, the program was eventually adopted by public schools nationwide.

Though I only stayed in the party a few months, my tour felt much longer. It was during the height of the FBI's successful initiative to destroy the Panthers, called Cointelpro, an acronym for the illegal "counter-intelligence program" that would ultimately crush the organization and result in my leaving. The party was infiltrated with a number of agents (who interestingly enough have since apologized and become lifelong friends with many of the Panthers they set up).

IT WAS 1970, and in a very short while I'd gone from being a wide-eyed hippie to a wide-eyed, ex–Black Panther seventeen-year-old servant of the people. Then, on one truly eventful night, a needy member of "the people" turned out to be my father.

I'd just attended the Marx Brothers Film Festival at the Thalia Theater with my then girlfriend, a radical Israeli activist named Ilana. When we left the theater, a crowd had gathered to try and help a man who was lying on a phone booth floor at the corner of Broadway and Ninety-fifth Street.

I recall making my way through a crowd and seeing the man's feet extended out of the phone booth into the gutter. I looked up from his feet to his face and realized the man lying in the street was my dad. I was completely shocked by my father's condition. He was a total derelict. Had he been a complete stranger, I'm sure I would've been twice as effective at comforting him until the ambulance arrived. Instead, I recoiled and returned passively to the crowd and listened to his familiar babbling about my mother's wedding day desertion. I was so traumatized by this scene recurring that I shut down emotionally and became completely detached. But not so detached that I didn't take note of the ambulance and the name of the hospital he was being taken to.

Ilana never knew I had any connection to the guy.

Most of the incident was subsequently tucked away in that place where I have stored many things too painful to fully recognize. Almost forty years later, though, as a result of working on this book, I started thinking about Ilana and how much I'd love to hear her account of the story, knowing it would probably be very different than mine.

I always say that there are no coincidences in life—only the appearance and illusion of them. On June 25, 2009, Michael Jackson died. I'd just finished doing an interview about my relationship with the deceased King of Pop for the BBC News, when I looked down at my BlackBerry and saw a message via my website from a woman living in London, who identified herself as—you guessed it—Ilana. She had seen me on the evening news and had no idea of my whereabouts or my career in show business until that moment.

We caught up on our last four decades and I found out Ilana's version of this story. She never had the slightest idea that the man lying on the street was my dad, because I had detached myself so well at the initial incident. She told me that she actually remembered being at some hospital, but didn't remember the story I told her about how I found out that my estranged father was even hospitalized.

When I was much younger, I watched a television show called *The Naked City*. The tag line was, "There are eight million stories in the naked city; this has been one of them." Out of the eight million people living in New York at that time, what were the odds of me running into my father on the street twice, ten years apart, in a similar alcoholic situation? My father gave me a present every time I encountered him. I believe the biggest present he gave me was his gift for music. The day I found him lying in the street, he gave me a stronger suit of emotional armor. David Bowie once told me something like "If you come from art, you'll always be from art." I assume one could apply this simple existential statement universally. (If you come from shame, you'll always be ashamed; if you come from fear, you'll always be afraid, etc.) I came from a great many things.

Though the father I'd come from gave me disappointment on that day (maybe in myself as much as him), many times before, he'd given me kindness, open-mindedness, and music.

A few months after I found him in the gutter, he would die, and I'd turn pro.

IN 1970 I WAS SPENDING time playing in a band called New World Rising, which I'd started with another Black Panther guitarist named Tom Murray. He went to the famous Stuyvesant High School, where I'd been going (though not officially) since I ditched Columbus High. In those days certain city high schools were "liberated territory." A popular slogan of the times was, "The streets belong to the people" ("and so do the sidewalks!" I and my group of Stuyvesant radical friends added). Under the United Federation of Teachers, so did the schools. Teachers had solidarity with students. We were treated more like the way I believe college students are treated. If you wanted to learn, they wanted to teach.

Since I'd picked up the guitar twenty-four months before, I'd been playing all the time, and there were teachers all around me. The night I ran away from home, my guitar escaped with me. Many hippies played guitar and I picked up lots of tips from them, and my technical faculties had improved exponentially. By the time I met Tom, I'd become a fledgling composer. We needed an ensemble to perform our compositions, so Tom and I put an ad in *The Village Voice* for other musicians, and New World Rising/Smoking Gauge (our name when we played purely blues) was formed.

NWR was a good band. In mid-August 1970, our first manager, Graham (my brother Bunchy's father), set up a showcase gig for us at an Upper West Side club called Ungano's. Graham was hooked up. He had personality, pretty young girls, music connections, and lots of drugs, especially coke, which was more cherished than platinum in those days. He knew the club's owners because he was a skilled carpenter who'd done a lot of work for them, and they owed him a favor or two. Though Ungano's regularly featured unknown bands, this payback was a huge opportunity for us because we'd be playing four nights straight. We thought this was our big chance to break out—we knew there'd be a ton of music industry people in the house.

While setting up our gear, we were told that the Stooges would be stopping by and their friend Alice Cooper would be there, too. I hadn't heard very much of Alice's music at the time, but lunchroom gossip had it that he was the reincarnation of a witch with the same name. This gig was starting to feel really important. We were so excited we couldn't set up quick enough.

Out of the clear blue sky, the Ungano brothers, who owned the club, insisted that we sign a management contract thicker than *War and Peace* before they'd let us play. We refused. "We don't think our situation is quite that complex," we more or less told them.

"Well, take your stuff and get the hell out of here," we were told. "We're doing you a favor."

They thought that they'd called our bluff, but we weren't bluffing. Graham couldn't jeopardize his relationship with the Unganos, so our de facto managers, White Panther members Mike Kleinman and "Famous" Toby Mamis (Toby later wound up managing, of all people, Alice Cooper), phoned Mickey Ruskin, who owned a bar called Max's Kansas City on Park Avenue around Eighteenth Street, to see if we could play there instead.

They convinced Mickey that their unknown band had some devoted followers who'd guzzle beers all night and told him the band would play for free. Somehow fate was on our side, because most nights during this period the Velvet Underground would be performing, but not that night, as this was the last week of their run.

We half packed the house, and our energy was strong. We played all night and I'm pretty sure we made some sort of history. The fact is, I'd been going to Max's for ages to eat the free food at happy hour (our drummer went to the School of Visual Arts, and Max's was like an SVA annex). Most of the acts I'd seen there were duos and trios. The Velvet Underground had the most people (four) I'd ever seen on Max's stage until New World Rising played. Though the evening didn't set the world on fire, it was successful enough that soon Max's started to feature larger bands. Mickey booked the room as "Upstairs at Max's Kansas City." Alice Cooper even played there a few weeks after us!

You won't see New World Rising's name in rock-and-roll history books. We didn't become famous, but we were among the first wave of jazz-blues-rock-fusion electrified bands in the Village.

Clubs like the Electric Circus, Café Wha?, the Dom, and Generation (which became Electric Lady Studios), as well as artists like the Fugs and the Blues Project (with Danny Kalb), were turning Village audiences from collegiate beatnik folkies into drop-out psychedelic acid freaks, who literally "danced" to this music. A new crop of larger groove-jazz-influenced bands started appearing on the scene: Elephant's Memory, Blood, Sweat & Tears, Ten Wheel Drive, and many others.

OUR BAND WAS QUICKLY gaining a nice little rep and played gigs for audiences from hard-core bikers to softhearted peaceniks. In those days our broad range of music had something for everybody. We even survived a week at the Gold Lounge, in Harlem, where a triple homicide occurred the first night we played there. But we stuck it out, even though it was a just a "fifteen center" (fifteen dollars a night per band member). By now it was clear that the rock-and-roll bug had bitten me, and its infection had specific delusional symptoms: Every gig was Woodstock, every girl was a model, and every paycheck was a fortune. I pursued show business like the conquistadors pursued gold in the New World. We advanced at an unprecedented pace, soon making as much as thirty-five dollars a man(!), and I was becoming one of the known cats. We were on a mission to capture the hearts, minds, and souls of the city's toughest crowds. While the war in Vietnam was raging, our battle for New York was just beginning.

I was in the thick of the hip alternative music scene and gigged or jammed more or less every night.

ONE EVENING THAT SAME YEAR, I wound up at someone's loft that doubled as a recording studio. When I got there, a platoon of musicians were jamming, and I plugged in my guitar and started wailing. I had just dropped orange acid and was tripping pretty heavy. I hadn't even turned eighteen, but already knew of most of these musicians personally, and I add their names here for the hard-core music history cognoscenti, for whom this list should be a revelation. Our group that night included Chip White, a popular jazz drummer; George Braith, a brilliant saxophonist who played two horns simultaneously; Calvin Hill, bassist extraordinaire who had just joined McCoy Tyner; Ned Liben, who later became tech-pop superstar EBN; Velvert Turner, a good friend and musician who palled around with Jimi Hendrix.

And then I turned and noticed Jimi himself, who'd been in town a lot lately as he was building a studio of his own.

That night the collective meshed together. We moved and grooved like a flock of birds, each flying on our own power but somehow heading in the same direction and always winding up in the same place, as if by some internal programming.

The studio was thick with cigarette and cannabis smoke. We were drinking from flasks filled with Almaden wine. There must have been girls there, but I don't remember a single one. I was temporarily in a world where the only people were musicians. "Hey, man," I said to the cat playing next to me, who I knew was the studio's engineer. "Are you feeling what I'm feeling?"

"Yeah," he said, "this is beautiful." I know we were all very high, but we were keenly aware of our senses and surroundings. Acid can sometime heighten the way you experience everything. I was taking in all the sounds.

"Did you hear that?" someone said, reacting to a riff. "We might find the lost chord [hippie slang for musical nirvana] tonight."

Then I said, "Man, this is the greatest stuff I've ever heard in my life."

After what felt like a millennium, our number reached a crescendo. Then we slowed the tempo and backed the volume down to complete silence. We knew we'd just experienced a once-in-a-lifetime event. The collective's total was much greater than the sum of its individual parts. We were exhausted and fulfilled. The voices in my head and the hallucinations faded. A hint of daylight crept under the door. The room was silent except for our breathing.

Then suddenly a familiar voice broke the silence. It was Jimi speaking for the first time all night—or maybe the first time I could hear him.

"Hey, man," he said, sheepishly. "Uh, did anybody record that, man?"

We'd been so caught up in the moment—and of course so high—that no one had thought to roll tape!

Which is why my teenage jam session with Jimi Hendrix in the house lives on only in the memories of a small band of survivors who've laughed about this night with me many times over.[*]

SHORTLY AFTER MY EVENING with Hendrix, I had another bad acid trip and moved back to the Bronx with my mom, who now lived at 1744 Clay Avenue near Grand Concourse. At this point in her life, my mom didn't keep one steady boyfriend. Instead, she kept a large number of them to help her make ends meet. She'd soon become pregnant with her last child, from one of the Italian guys. His son is my youngest brother, Dax. True to form, Big Bobby gave Dax his last name: Glanzrock. For most of his childhood, Dax believed Bobby was his biological father.

* * *

[*]Woodly Valsuka, an early video art pioneer, is believed to have recorded a portion of the jam session. But I've never heard it.

ATTEMPTING ONE LAST GO at formal education, I checked into William Howard Taft High School. My life felt so rich, and so much had happened to me, but I still wasn't old enough to graduate.

Around this time I met a girl whose family had a significant impact on me: Connie Rodgers, a stylish, hip, jazz-fed white girl with a voluptuous figure. She was a student at Taft and totally out of my league, but somehow we ended up together.

Connie's stepfather was a famous upright-bass player named Ray McKinney. He was her younger brother Chris's dad, and he was black. Having Chris around was like having a new little brother. In a strange way, our families were cut from similar cloth. Connie's mom, Betty, mostly dated black jazz musicians, so her daughter dating me wasn't much of a stretch. Betty, like my white stepfather, Bobby, was beyond cool. It was she who would introduce me to my future partner, Bernard Edwards. They'd worked together at the post office's main branch, Grand Central Station. Connie's mother let me move in with them, when out of the blue my mom suddenly decided to go west for good.

EVEN THOUGH I STILL WORE freakishly large (but trendy) hippie glasses, I was a jazzer at heart, because jazz was the music of choice in my beatnik parents' household. I loved it, too. My guitar playing was progressing naturally and had gotten much better. It was around that time that I started studying with two very important teachers: Ted Dunbar and Billy Taylor. Billy Taylor, a living legend, was the director of the Jazzmobile program, which was dedicated to teaching young people jazz (which he called "America's classical music"). It was located in Harlem at public school I.S. 201, where I studied as if my life depended on it.

During the time I studied there, I got more subbing gigs than any other guitar student. Ted Dunbar taught the guitar class at Jazzmobile, and I also took private lessons from him. Ted played with his thumb like Wes Montgomery, and was a master of harmony, and that rubbed off on me. I was getting better and better.

I needed to expand and I started studying traditional classical guitar with Maestro Julio Prol, in Greenwich Village. This too was a
natural fit. Throughout my childhood, classical music was the one
class in school I always looked forward to. My skill at reading music,
which I acquired from jazz and classical training, helped me get more
professional gigs, even though I was mostly substituting for the name
cats. I didn't see it at the time, but the puzzle pieces of my scattered
life were starting to link together. During improvisation lessons, Ted
Dunbar used to constantly yell, "Nile, connect your shit!"

On one of my very first subbing gigs, I ran into a Van Nuys
Airport alum named Wes Farrell, the record executive, who was
married to Christina "Tina" Sinatra. In classic airport fashion, he
gave me a nice "tip" that night, which would lead to a host of musical jobs: TV and radio commercials, recording sessions, as well as a
gig playing in the backup band for an act on his label called New
York City. My shit was starting to connect.

I HAD FUNDAMENTALLY QUIT public school but was hardly giving up
on my education. Actually, my goal, now that music had become so
central in my life, was to enroll in a college-level music program. I'd
been an indifferent high school student at best, and of course lacked
a diploma. My classical guitar teacher wanted me to go to the exten-
sion division of the Juilliard School, which had recently relocated to
Lincoln Center. I was also interested in the Manhattan School of
Music, which had moved into the space vacated by Juilliard, across
from Columbia University.

One day, when I was visiting the Manhattan campus, trying to
decide which place was best for me, John Moody, a bass player
friend of mine, said auditions for *Sesame Street*'s theatrical road show
were being held there in one of the practice rooms. They were
looking for a guitarist.

I was in the right place, at the right time, playing the right instrument, and I got the gig.

I wound up touring all over the country with the *Sesame Street* band and, for the first time in my life, made a real living playing the guitar. The job changed my life, and marks for me the day I truly became a professional musician. It changed my mother's life, too— from that day forward I've financially subsidized her lifestyle.

IT TURNED OUT that one of the stars of *Sesame Street,* Loretta Long, who played Susan, was married to the guy who managed the Apollo Theater in Harlem.

One day Loretta's husband told her about an opening for a guitarist in the Apollo house band. The current guitarist, Carlos Alomar (whose wife, Robin, would later sing on my debut hit single), was leaving to join David Bowie's "Young Americans" tour. They needed a guitar player who could read music and learn the repertoire fast. Loretta told them about this guy with weird hair (at the time I had a big electric Afro that was corn-rowed until showtime) who was really good. She got me an audition.

I arrived at the Apollo proudly wearing Landlubber hip-hugger bell-bottoms that I'd embroidered with psychedelic flowers and patches. On my feet were natural-colored python-skin platform boots.

The Apollo was all about traditional black music, and I was more into Country Joe and the Fish than I was into Joe Tex, but had big love for blues and jazz. The songs I played for the audition were "I Put a Spell on You," from blues legend Screamin' Jay Hawkins, and "Clean Up Woman," by Betty Wright. The latter arrangement was in F sharp, about eight or nine pages long. Guitar players are by and large notoriously bad sight readers, but by then I could read my skinny black hippie ass off.

I didn't miss a note, but I had a strict interpretation of the chart. I didn't understand R&B-style interpretation of the notation yet, which was definitely not cool, but I could follow the conductor very well and that made up for my lack of soul. They auditioned me because of Loretta, but I earned the gig with my playing. (This skill also helped me get hired as a studio musician. If you're over forty, you've likely heard me play classical guitar on a popular Savarin coffee commercial from the seventies.)

A typical show at the Apollo featured a variety of artists. The first artist on the bill for my maiden night was Screamin' Jay. The music director knew that I could sight-read right through the show, so he told me I didn't have to make Jay's rehearsal. I just needed to be backstage an hour before the curtain.

I used this free time to casually tour this familiar part of Harlem. Urban renewal was in full effect. The Apollo was just two blocks from the old Black Panther office, and around the corner from the Gold Lounge, where my old band had been overshadowed by a triple homicide. I walked east on 125th Street to Seventh Avenue and saw the New York State Office Building (President Clinton's future office site). A few months earlier, we community protesters had closed it down; now it was buzzing with construction workers.

I reminisced about my activist days. Now I was here to do a different type of community service, playing at the world-famous Apollo Theater. The last time I was on this block, I was marching "in formation" and would jump at the orders of Kathleen Cleaver; today I jumped to a different voice.

BACK INSIDE THE APOLLO, the stage manager screamed over a cheap little loudspeaker. "The half is in, the half is in," he said, which was code for "Thirty minutes to showtime." The whole place operated with the precision of a combat submarine. The stylish Ebony Fashion Fair audience didn't seem to fit the scarlet-and-gold-colored vaudeville-era theater, but the Apollo broke every rule that I'd been living by. I'd mostly worked for people who appreciated you from the moment you hit the stage, but the Apollo was well known for chewing up the biggest stars and spitting them out. I couldn't wait to show them what the hippie with thick glasses could do. Remember, I was so good I didn't even have to make rehearsal.

Ten minutes before the curtain went up, I took my place on stage in my designated chair. All of the old-timers were used to the routine, and for them it was just another show. But I could hardly be nonchalant about playing on the same stage where James Brown had recorded one of the greatest live albums ever. Where Ella Fitzgerald, Billie Holiday, the Jackson 5, and so many musical gods had gotten their start. Even Jimi Hendrix had won the fabled amateur night contest, and delighted its intolerant crowd, with his acrobatic guitar-playing virtuosity in 1964.

I was so nervous thinking about all that history, and pleasing the folks on the other side of that closed curtain, that I didn't really pay attention to the coffin that was on the stage off to my right. As the conductor put his hands up to cue the band, the curtain went up, and out of the coffin popped Screamin' Jay. His face was made up to look like a skeleton, and it scared me half to death. I jumped out of my chair, screamed, instinctively pulled out my guitar cable, and ran stage right.

The entire audience burst into uncontrollable laughter while Screamin' Jay chased me around the stage. Then I realized the whole band, if not the entire management, was in on it. It played great to the crowd because I was genuinely afraid, and they all knew it. My nervousness and complete shock caught me by surprise, and for this experienced kung fu practitioner, flight took over, not fight.

I finally got it together and returned to my seat to thunderous applause, and the show went on. The "youngblood" had passed a trial by fire at the Apollo. Needless to say, Screamin' Jay was a smash that night, and after that, all the old-timers became my friends and personal faculty of R&B, funk, and soul. The first thing they taught me was how to interpret R&B notation. Though the music looks the same as jazz (and sometimes classical), you don't feel it the same way. The band's members had played with everyone from wannabes at the infamous amateur night contests, to the current crop of one-hit wonders, as well as superstars like Stevie, Aretha, and Diana, giants so big you need only mention them by their first names.

They schooled me to always be on my toes and expect the unexpected.

* * *

THE APOLLO WAS LIKE the black Colosseum: it was thumbs-up or thumbs-down, and you were shown no mercy if you couldn't cut the mustard. By the time I'd finished my stint at the Apollo, I had played with artists on every rung of the R&B ladder. I was now ready to go after the brass ring and what was to be the most wonderful school of hard knocks on this planet.

And believe me, you needed to be prepared for the Chitlin' Circuit.

part 2

Roam If You Want To

seven

Chic Sh*t Happens: The Rise and Call of the Disco Revolution

It was an early fall Friday night at the Fairtree Lounge, a Bronx hot spot that featured live music for a slick crowd straight out of the latest Blaxploitation flick. These were the early seventies, and polyester shirts with long flyaway collars, large-brimmed hats, and double-knit wool suits with Missoni patterns were standard dress.

I'd been recommended by a guitarist friend as a last-minute substitute for the guitarist in Hack Bartholomew's better-than-average pick-up band. As a sub, I didn't know a soul on the stage, but they were playing an R&B song called "Sissy Strut" in the key of C, and I hopped right onstage with my arch-top jazz guitar and joined in.

Bartholomew's band wasn't top shelf, but Hack's trumpet playing had soulful flair and he gigged with Joe Simon, a soul chart-topper. Hack was a solid front man and knew how to put on a good show: something you had to know to work at the Fairtree, a mid-level gig on the infamous Chitlin' Circuit, a string of black night-clubs that stretched from Buffalo, New York, to South Florida. The same way Jewish entertainers had the Borscht Belt, soul musicians had the Chitlin' Circuit. Most R&B acts east of the Rockies worked it on some level. There would be no Commodores, Impressions, Marvin Gaye, LaBelle, Hendrix, or Funkadelic without it.

Playing these clubs, which ranged in décor from ghetto-fabulous versions of the bar in *Star Wars* to tin-roof shacks in the Bible Belt, was the mainstay gig for most of the musicians I knew at the time. This was our equivalent of Class A baseball. You had a long way to go to get to the majors, but it was a necessary step. It may have been the minors, but the Fairtree had a tough crowd that was used to see-ing quality acts, some of whom would go on to become big stars. If a patron called out "Chocolate Buttermilk," "Pusher Man," or even "I Want You Back," the band had better play it and play it well.

On any other night, I would've already filed the proceedings under "just another gig." Only there was something special about this band: the bassist, Bernard Edwards. We'd actually spoken over the phone a few months earlier about gigging together, and we hadn't hit it off. Bernard was not impressed with my avant-garde classical-jazz-rock-fusion ideas and told me in no uncertain terms to lose his number. But once we started playing together that night, well, it was like we each telepathically knew what the other was thinking. The two new dudes took command of the unit, and the quality of Hack's show jumped up a few notches. Now we came off like a fully rehearsed band.

If someone didn't know the material, Bernard and I called out the changes. We instinctively formed a temporary partnership for the sake of keeping the band tight behind Hack, so he could con-centrate on being the show's star. Little did we know that this was to be our primary role for the rest of our lives.

THINKING BACK ON THAT FIRST NIGHT, I can still vividly see and hear my future partner's traditionalist soul-brother swagger. Nard was dressed stylishly, but conservatively: He wore silk slacks with back flap pockets, playboys, and a bly. Playboys resembled Hush Puppies with one-inch-thick rubber soles, and blys, if that's how you spell it, were knitted shirts with elaborate patterns. I was in my usual hippie ensemble. We were as different as night and day, but like night and day, you couldn't have one without the other.

We became inseparable. If I got hired for a gig, I worked hard to get Nard added, and vice versa. For the next couple of weeks, we did a few consecutive boogaloo gigs (which meant the set list was comprised of current R&B pop songs) before getting another call from Hack and moving to a more upscale Italian nightclub where the set list was expanded to include standards. I don't recall the club's exact name for sure (I think it was Delmonico's), but it was on Morris Park Avenue in the East Bronx, a sparsely populated section of town that I'd lived in at various times in my life, with Beverly and Graham.

It wasn't exactly instant fame and glamour, but it was nicer than our Chitlin' gigs. For me, alas, it was short-lived. I was fired from Hack Bartholomew's band our first night there, because my girlfriend Connie came to see me. According to management, they didn't like the way she was dressed. Bernard saw the trouble coming. "Yo, man," I remember him warning me when he noticed her entering the club, "Connie's headlights are on high beam." My girlfriend had come to our gig wearing a very revealing low-cut designer dress. Picture a reverse wool corset that laced up the front from her navel. The opening widened the whole way up, until it reached her breasts. Very Sophia Loren. I got sacked and wound up getting paid for a half night's work. "Hey, man, we can't have that here," the white club owner told me. He never explained what the "that" was that they couldn't have there, but he didn't have to. It was the last time I'd work with Hack, and the beginning of a lifetime working with Bernard Edwards.

Nard and I gigged together on the Chitlin' Circuit up until 1977.

From the back of the bandstand, we learned the fundamentals of how to build a successful music production business. In 1973 Nard landed the gig that would change our lives. He became music director for a vocal group called New York City, which was known for its Philly-sounding soul, despite its name. NYC was signed to a label called Chelsea Records, which was owned by Wes Farrell, who was married to Tina Sinatra. They were both Van Nuys Airport people, an irony I didn't bother explaining to my friends. We took the name the Big Apple Band as NYC's backup band.

New York City scored a hit record, "I'm Doing Fine Now," by producer/songwriter extraordinaire Thom Bell, who was best known at the time for his work with the Delfonics, the Stylistics, and the Spinners. We'd soon be gigging all over the world. And for a while, we were on a hot streak. We played large venues with a diverse group of headline R&B acts such as the O'Jays and Parliament-Funkadelic; we even did some dates on the American leg of the Jackson 5's first world tour. NYC's Philly Soul sound was very happening. Thom Bell was at the top of his game, and his slick, sophisticated soul dominated the R&B and pop charts.

Though the Big Apple Band didn't play on Bell's recordings, we played the music live very well. Bernard and I always tried to make live music faithful to the records, as we'd done in Hack's pick-up band the night we initially played together. But this was my first taste of playing in front of people in big-time situations. With *Sesame Street,* I played in the orchestra pit and was basically hidden. Now I was twenty-one years old and things were changing quickly.

WHEN I STARTED WITH NYC, I only ate organic food (preferably macrobiotic). I didn't drink, smoke, or take drugs. I was wholly dedicated to practicing guitar and embraced a monklike celibacy. My personality caused some discomfort between me and my New York City bosses, because they thought I was gay. Of course that could be the only explanation for my strange habits as far as these brothers were concerned.

In retrospect, I can sort of see their point. The band had many willing girls throwing themselves at us, but I wasn't interested. I just wanted to read books and practice every chance I got. I was very shy on stage, almost to the point of being introverted. I kept my head down and never looked at the people in the audience. New York City wanted to fire me, but Bernard convinced them to keep me.

Slowly but surely my situation forced me to change. I remember the exact day it happened. We were back on the Chitlin' Circuit, as some time had passed since "I'm Doing Fine" was on the charts. We were in Raleigh, North Carolina, when the tour bus pulled into a McDonald's and I ordered a fish sandwich, thinking, Well, at least it's fish! Next, we hit Myrtle Beach, South Carolina, and I had a one-night stand with an army girl who snuck me into her motel room through the window. Before we had sex, she asked me inquisitively, "You're really from New York, right? Do you know any Jews?" I replied, "Millions of 'em." I enjoyed the punch line as much as the sex.

To keep costs down, the band shared rooms on the road, and my roommate was the drummer. He had a constant trail of girls and I'd sometimes get the overflow. I dated a number of hot flight attendants and I started to drink wine—but only with my meals! Yes, I was becoming more like the other dudes in the band. I was also becoming much closer to Bernard. Though he never criticized my odd proclivities to my face (other than to joke around), he constantly worked at redesigning me into a soul man. Nard wasn't the only one giving me the Pygmalion treatment. I had another muse in Miami Beach, Marsha Ratner, leader of a pack of fabulous people in that town's wild party scene. She was also a single mom who reminded me of my own mother.* When she first saw me perform, she wondered why I kept turning my back to the crowd and from that point on committed to helping me come out of my shell, and,

---

*Her young son, Brett, grew up to be a popular film director. Brett is like my brother, friend, and son. Our identities were both formed in the color-blind world of art—and he's as comfortable with Mike Tyson and the Wu-Tang Chan as I was with the B-52's or Duran Duran.

slowly, it started to work. My final act of transformation also took place in Miami, but this one was musical.

One day, following a gig in Miami, Nard got me to trade in my prized jazz guitar, a hollow-bodied Gibson Barney Kessel, for a sleek solid-bodied Fender Stratocaster, the six-string equivalent of trading in a Range Rover for a Porsche. The local act that opened for us played on our equipment, and their guitar player sounded better than I did on my own amplifier. Nard convinced me it was the guitar that made the difference. His soul-man makeover plan was working. He came to my room to admire my new guitar and showed me the style the other guy had played on my amp. He fingered the chords with his left hand, and his right hand would continuously play sixteen notes to the bar while accenting the main parts of the rhythm. He called it "chucking." Bernard used to be a guitar player before he switched to bass, and one lesson was all I needed. For the next few nights straight, while my roommate pursued all manner of trysts, I was having a love affair in the bathroom with my new ax. In just a few days, I'd emerge as a chucking funk guitarist who knew more jazz chord inversions than most of my R&B counterparts.

Around that time I met a girl named Karen who fit my soulful transformation like a Temptations sharkskin suit. She was one of those girls who was so fine, people just wanted to be around her. She knew everybody from Nicky Barnes, the famed New York gangster, to DJs like Frankie Crocker, Vaughan Harper, and scores of other local radio personalities. With Karen as my girl, a Strat as my guitar, and Bernard as my bandleader, I started to fit into the R&B scene more organically. Karen's friends became my friends and Nard's music became my music.

New York City was our main gig, but the Big Apple Band sometimes played without them. Truth be told, the Big Apple Band was only one of many monikers we worked under. While NYC was losing its popularity, the backup band was developing a following. Our name changed based on the gigs that our various agents and managers landed. About the only thing that remained consistent among every version of the band was me on guitar and Bernard on bass. (We also had the good fortune of regularly working with two talented up-and-coming young singers: Luther Vandross and Fonzi Thornton, both of whom I'd known ever since the *Sesame Street* days, and who would appear on records with Bernard and me for the rest of our lives.)

By then I'd been working with Nard for about three years. We were as close as two people could ever be. Our level of artistic trust was high. Every relationship that I've had with an artist is a slight structural variation of my relationship with Bernard. We taught each other how to believe in each other's artistic ideas; we also taught each other how to fight for ideas when we thought they best served the project. And we'd serendipitously created a production technique that would be the foundation for every project we'd do until our last breath. We called it DHM, or Deep Hidden Meaning. Our golden rule was that all our songs had to have this ingredient. In short it meant understanding the song's DNA and seeing it from many angles. Art is subjective, but if we knew what we were talking about, then we could relay it to others in various disguises while maintaining its essential truth.

BY THE MIDSEVENTIES, the New York club scene was exploding, and the once trendy Apollo, which used to be the be-all and end-all for R&B musicians, was quickly becoming a musical dinosaur stuck in the black music culture of the fifties and sixties.

Meanwhile, there was a mighty storm organizing on the horizon, called disco. My downtown stomping ground was the leading edge of this revolutionary movement. History has reduced this glorious and complex period so badly that it's often dismissed as a one-line cinematic throwaway—the *Saturday Night Fever* or Studio 54 era—but it was so much more than that, especially for me.

A new way of living, with a new kind of activism, had emerged, and my new crew—girlfriend Karen, music partner Bernard, and myself—embodied it. As founding members of this fledgling counterculture lifestyle, we held our meetings and demonstrations on the dance floor.

Karen and her stylish comrades all danced their curvy asses off. For them, the movement, in every sense of the word, was as open and communal as the forces driving the hippies of my youth. Karen was black from Staten Island, but her friends were a rainbow coalition from every cultural background and neighborhood. I'd say they were even more expressive, political, and communal than the hippies before them, because they bonded through their bodies, through dance; they were propelled by a new kind of funky groove music. Dance had become primal and ubiquitous, a powerful communication tool, every bit as motivational as an Angela Davis speech or treasured as that eighteen-dollar, three-day Woodstock Festival ticket.

All revolutionary movements are fueled by a desire for change to an unsustainable status quo. This revolution's warriors were engaged in a battle for recognition. "Sex, drugs, and disco" was the new battle cry. The underground, now ethnic and more empowered than ever before, was becoming mainstream.

For the first time since Chubby Checker separated dancing couples with "The Twist," it was now cool again to touch your dancing partner. A whole slew of touchy-feely dance moves were introduced into the mainstream clubs—a consequence of gay sex coming out of the closet and onto the dance floor. People enjoyed intimate interaction with multiple partners, often with the same sex, while still maintaining the appearance of dancing. The names of some of the new dances revealed the new openness of the times: the Hustle, the Freak, and the Bus Stop. Think about it: a "hustle" is a drug deal, con, or a hooker's transaction; a "freak" is a sex or drug addict; and the "bus stop" is where it all took place. It was all a far cry from the foxtrot or rumba.

THE FUNKY DISCO MOVEMENT was spreading through the atmosphere like volcanic dust, and everybody was dancing all around the world.

Unfortunately, the music that we played with New York City was no longer happening. We were on the road gigging when the band decided to break up, the result of its second album failing to produce any hits. Karen also decided to break up with me while I was on this tour. NYC played our final show in England. My hotel room had been broken into the night before the band was to return stateside. It was a Friday night and my passport was gone. Since I couldn't go to the U.S. embassy until Monday, my bandmates left me behind and headed home.

I was cool with all that. Since Karen dumped me, I'd been seeing a girl named Carey, a hostess at a prestigious London club called Churchill's. We'd met at the London gig where New York City played on this last tour.

Carey had London on lockdown. She knew everybody, especially all of the newly wealthy Arab oil sheiks, who were the most dominant force in the London social scene since the Beatles. Because of her blond cover-girl Swedish looks and status as a Churchill's hostess, we had carte blanche at every trendy spot. The combination of London and Carey was so exciting that even after I got my passport replaced, I decided to stay.

One atypically clear London night, Carey took me to a club to see a band that I'd been hearing about, but had never actually heard. They were called Roxy Music. Coincidentally, they were playing at a venue called the Roxy. Their glamorous fans looked like a cross between the fashion, music, art, and sex industries. My old band NYC's last few gigs were mostly on army bases that were spread throughout Europe during those Cold War times, but this was nothing like those gigs, which felt like extensions of the Chitlin' Circuit. The combination of crowd, setting, and music blew me away. I hadn't seen anything quite like it. It was as mind-blowing as my first acid trip back in L.A.

Roxy Music's front man, Bryan Ferry, was suave and oozed elegance. Their music was a diverse offering of eclectic rock with changing time signatures and ethereal textures. Though I'd never heard them before that night, I could hear their sound was evolving.

It was a totally im-
mersive art experi-
ence that felt like I
was absorbing more
than just music.

After the show
Roxy Music's songs
stayed in my head
for the next few
days. I needed to
hear them again. I
bought their last
two albums, *Stranded*
and *For Your Plea-
sure*. When I pulled
the two LPs from the record bin, the sight of Playmate of the Year
Marilyn Cole and London jet-setter Amanda Lear on the respective
covers gave me a eureka moment: The visuals of the covers were an
essential part of the band's imaging and marketing, almost as important as the music itself. After seeing the records, I made a 360-degree
connection and had my first glimpse of an idea that would ultimately result in my band Chic. I was closing in on our DHM.

After I picked up the Roxy Music records, I called Bernard at
home and simply said, "I got it." "Got what?" he replied. "The
concept for our next band." We both knew we'd have to make a
living sans the luxury of New York City's regular paychecks. He
was surprised that I was still in London. I explained how I'd been
living in a hotel and Carey was picking up the tab. I was sitting in
with different acts at a string of clubs and superimposing my
chucking style over everyone's music, which instantly made them
sound funky. I had quickly become the talk of the town—well,
sort of. Carey's influential friends had taken a liking to my style
and thought maybe I could be the funk version of Hendrix. Music
industry types wanted to link me with some of the local artists and
create a new London-based R&B funk rock unit.

Funk rock had just made its way across the pond, and bands like Ian Dury and the Blockheads and others were starting to reflect the influence. The leaders of the current wave of London tastemakers, who'd seen me sit in with the likes of General Johnson ("Give Me Just a Little More Time") and others at a club called Gulliver's, thought I could be the next big thing. But I knew that whatever I was going to do musically, it had to include Bernard. Since he was married and lived in New York, I took the next plane out.

ALMOST AS SOON as I touched down, the Big Apple Band started to make our sophistofunk rock dream a reality. In a scene straight out of *The Magnificent Seven,* we hunted down willing musical gunslingers. First to join up was a drummer named Tony Thompson, who'd just finished working with the all-female funk-fantasy-fusion act LaBelle. Tony could play all styles. He had great technique that was very aggressive, not ideal for the slick stuff, but smoking on our rock-flavored songs. I'd known Tony from pick-up gigs on the then hip Persian scene, which included artists like Jamshid Alimorad, Aki Banaii, and superstar Googoosh.

Next we added keyboardist Rob Sabino, one of the truly underreported heroes of our funky jazz-rock sound, and a solid pillar in our new organization. It was mostly he who played all those brilliant acoustic piano parts in the small openings in between Bernard and me chucking later in Chic.

Finally, we added an outstanding male lead singer named Bobby Cotter, who had just finished a stint in *Jesus Christ Superstar.* Bobby was a great front man, handsome with incredible vocal range and abilities. We were ready to rule the world, or so we thought.

Our new unit gigged regularly and eventually recorded a hot demo, which was produced by *Saturday Night Live*'s music director, Leon Pendarvis. The music got a lot of attention from the labels, but no offers after they saw we were black. Bobby's voice was supersoulful, and before they saw us, they were probably imagining we were like a funkier Queen or Journey. The demo's sound leaned more to the rock-funk side rather than the smooth-groove side, so the labels assumed we were white. It was clear after months of meetings that our funk-rock formula didn't work, so we went back to the drawing board.

We knew many local bands. Our keyboard player was friendly with one particularly odd new group called KISS. They wore whiteface makeup onstage and looked like deranged superheroes. At some point we started checking out KISS's live shows. There was something very cool about the way their theatrical whiteface roles were so defined onstage, and that nobody had any idea what they looked like offstage.

One auspicious night a lightning bolt of an idea hit me: "What if we played the faceless backup band professionally?" I asked Bernard. It wasn't crazy to me. Actually, it made a lot of sense. The Big Apple Band originally was the faceless backup band for the

vocal group New York City, who were the stars. Though we had hired Bobby Cotter to be our singer, he was clearly our band's front man. He looked like a star and we looked like his band. This faceless role fit us perfectly. We knew we didn't know how to come off like stars even if we tried. When we had meetings with record labels, they'd direct the questions to our keyboardist, Rob. They assumed he was the leader simply because he looked white! He was Puerto Rican and always used to tell the execs, "Hey, I just got here, it's their band. Talk to them!"

Taking our cue from the few KISS shows we took in, Nard and I started to reason everything out. We didn't look like our music. The labels all loved us until they saw us. We weren't stars—but our music was! The answer had been right in front of our faces: KISS! We realized KISS's art direction was just as important as their music, much like Roxy Music. Both bands presented completely immersive theatrical experiences, albeit in diametrically opposed ways. How could that translate to us? Nard and I thought it over and came up with some answers via "band logic," not to be confused with actual logic:

KISS's onstage characters were faceless offstage. *Faceless.* Check! We could do that.
Roxy Music was slick and suave. *Slick and suave.* Check! We could do that.
Their art direction was as important as their music. Check! We could do that.

Then Bernard and I tried to figure out how to mesh KISS's anonymity with Roxy Music's musical diversity and sexy cover-girl imagery. This concept stuck in our minds no matter how many survival gigs we had to take in the meantime. For the next few months, we were consumed with this.

Nobody around us had any idea what Bernard and I were obsessively up to. Even our drummer, Tony Thompson, couldn't see the big picture of what we were trying to do. And who could blame him?

KISS and Roxy Music were rock bands. No matter how inspiring they were conceptually, they were clearly rock. But musically, I found my inspiration in jazz. Many of my jazz heroes were enjoying hit records—only they were doing it by making R&B dance music. Roy Ayers, Herbie Hancock, Joe Beck, the Jazz Crusaders, Norman Connors, and others were topping the pop charts. So we developed a new sound that was a fusion of jazz, soul, and funk grooves with melodies and lyrics that were more European influenced.

Just when we thought we had everything together, things started falling apart. Our lead singer suddenly left. Then another group called the Big Apple Band put out a phenomenal disco reworking of Beethoven's Fifth Symphony. It was an instant smash called "A Fifth of Beethoven," by Walter Murphy and the Big Apple Band (who were also faceless). Our phone started ringing off the hook with congratulatory messages from our studio musician friends. Problem was, they had the wrong Big Apple Band. Walter was a New Yorker, born within a couple months of Nard and me. He gigged on the same circuit, doing R&B covers, but his Big Apple Band got a hit record first.

We had no choice but to start over with a new name—and try and connect our small but reliable mid-level-bar-band following to it. In those days word of mouth was exactly that, one person to another, and if you weren't a signed act with a press agent it could take months before folks got the news. Back when I'd originally talked about Roxy Music's style, Bernard suggested we call the group Chic. Tony and I laughed and shot him down, but we had the luxury of being the Big Apple Band, and were doing gigs! Now, because of Walter's hit record and the loss of our lead singer, we had to call ourselves something different. "Chic" still sounded funny, but I decided to at least give it a try.

Bernard thought of the name, so as the group's main writer at that time, I did my part and wrote the first song, "Everybody Dance." Only a handful of bassists on earth could play the bass line I wrote for the song, but a few years had passed since the night Nard and I had met in the Bronx, and by now I knew what he was capable of. The jazz-influenced song was really complicated: It had a mixture of harmonically extended chords, and the latter half of the progression incorporated two strict chromatic movements in the bass. I compensated by writing an insanely simple hook: "Everybody dance, do-do-do, clap your hands, clap your hands." I sang it to Bernard, and he liked it, but asked me, with great earnestness, "Uh, my man, what the fuck does 'do-do-do' mean?" I responded with equal seriousness, "It means the same things as 'la-la-la' motherfucker!" I've never laughed as much in my life as I did with Bernard.

As I said earlier, the band had acquired a little following, and our ex–lead singer Bobby had a friend named Robert Drake, who'd become one of our biggest fans. Robert was a true audiophile who owned a personal recording studio and worked as a maintenance man at a larger professional studio called Sound Ideas. He booked our first session as the new band there. We worked at the studio after hours when it was supposed to be closed, and the only person we had to pay was the elevator operator, ten bucks, to keep his mouth shut about the secret session. Robert engineered the record and also charmed the studio's assistant engineer to kick in her time free, too!

The backbone of this life-changing session was our four-man Big Apple Band rhythm section, but we also reached out to some good friends to help make the song sound more like a record. Luther Vandross brought along his crew of singers; Eddie Martinez (Run-DMC's "King of Rock") played the guitar overdubs with me; and two top jazz studio cats, David Friedman and Tom Copolla, played the vibraphone and clavinet, respectively. This crew of thrown-together friends became a template that has never changed for the Chic Organization's productions. Luther's vocal arrangements of my basic song taught us what to do and how to do it from that point on. We had never produced a record before that night and didn't realize we were producing one then. I was the composer/arranger/orchestrator/guitarist, and Bernard was the bassist/bandleader, and we acted accordingly. In this setting Robert Drake was the session's engineer/producer, if you will.

We all had done enough sessions to know to let the engineer get the sounds first, and after he'd done that, we'd rehearse, then we'd record. It quickly became apparent that the two people who were most in charge were Bernard and me, despite the fact that we were not calling ourselves producers yet. It was clear I had written the song, and he was directing the musicians. We started changing and rearranging parts based on the ensemble's interpretation of the music.

Nard changed his bass line to a chucking part, so I simplified my original part because it complemented his. Prior to that session, only I had actually played the song, but now we were all playing it together and this new arrangement took the song to a higher level. After we knew we had the arrangement exactly right, we started recording.

From the first downbeat, we knew it was hot. I had fully orchestrated the lengthy song, which was a series of different instrumental sections, highlighted with "breakdowns." A breakdown is accomplished by taking out major parts of the composition and featuring the basic elements of the groove, then adding more instruments until finally the whole band is playing again. The concept is to deconstruct the song and rebuild it in the listener's ears. I knew that this formula worked at live R&B shows, and believed it would work on records. We completed the entire song in one night. Mind you, the first incarnation of "Everybody Dance" had no lead vocal, only Luther's choral arrangement of my hook. Robert did a rough mix at the end of the night, and what happened next is too weird for words.

We did this recording session before cassettes existed, so the only time we got to hear the song was when we listened to the playback a few times after recording it, very late that night. I didn't hear it again until three weeks later, when I got an "emergency" phone call that demonstrated the effect that our faceless breakdown music had on people.

By 1976 there was a new social and cultural phenomenon that Americans were just becoming aware of—buppies (black urban professionals)—and their stronghold was New York City. The musical engineer on "Everybody Dance" was also the DJ at one of the city's hottest buppie clubs, the Night Owl, which happened to be in Greenwich Village.

At this time I was temporarily living in the Flatbush section of Brooklyn, at my then girlfriend Rosalia's apartment. We'd met a few weeks earlier on a gig I was doing near the Brooklyn Navy Yard. I had written "Everybody Dance" at her crib, because she had a day job that allowed me to compose alone uninterrupted. A mere three weeks after we'd recorded it, Robert, who had made a few lacquers (lacquer records that could be reproduced quickly), made an "emergency" call to me because he was DJing and had to be sure he'd get me between records. "Hey, Nile, you've gotta come over and see this," Robert said.

"See what?"

"I can't explain it, you just have to see it. Come to the Night Owl, and when they stop you, tell them you did 'Everybody Dance.' "

The fact that I'd be stopped was inevitable. The Night Owl catered to an upscale black crowd that adhered to a strict dress code. I didn't have the duds or the dough to get in, so I asked Robert, "What do you want me to do?"

He repeated his instructions, then emphasized, "Tell them you are the one who did 'Everybody Dance.' That's all you have to do, no matter who stops you. You got it?"

"OK, cool. See you in a couple hours."

I'd started dressing while still on the phone because the curiosity was killing me. I ran to the subway and rushed to the club to see whatever it was that I had to see. As soon as I got to the door, the huge bouncer said, "Hey, man, you can't come in here dressed like that."

"I'm a friend of Robert Drake."

"I don't give a damn if you *are* Robert Drake, you ain't getting in here dressed like that."

"Oh, I almost forgot. I did 'Everybody Dance.' "

" 'Everybody Dance?' Brother, let me shake your hand. What's your name?"

"I'm Nile."

"Yo, this is Nile. Let him in," the bouncer told another bouncer inside, working the ticket booth. I took the elevator up. The door opened, and the next bouncer said, "Hey, you can't come in here looking like that." Right away I said, "My name is Nile, and I did 'Everybody Dance.' "

" 'Everybody Dance?' Damn, no shit? Come in, brother man. Can I buy you a drink? Hey, Tom," he shouted to the white owner of the black club, who was smoother than a gravy sandwich. Tom was the seventies version of my stepdad, Bobby: sartorial perfection, slick rap, and an appetite for sisters. "This is the dude that did 'Everybody Dance.' "

"Hey, man, my name is Tom, and this is my place. You can come here anytime you want and it's on the house."

This all seemed like Robert was playing a practical joke, because I'd never met any of these people and they were treating me like I was the man. Tom and I chatted for about ten minutes about his new club in my old hood, and then he escorted me through a heavily cigarette-smoke-clouded room over to the DJ booth. Robert was talking to a beautiful buppie hottie who worked on Wall Street.

"Yo, Nile," he said as soon as he saw me. He didn't spend any time with idle chitchat. He screamed over the music, "You've got to check this out," and started laughing.

The stylus dropped onto the lacquer, and after Tony's opening drum fill, Bernard's killer bass line came in. I hadn't heard this for almost a month, but I knew the song right away because I'd written it. The Night Owl patrons let out an almost bloodcurdling "Owwwww." Then my guitar entered along with Rob's piano, David's vibes, and Tom's clavinet. The room filled with voices—"Everybody da-ance, do- do- do, clap your hands, clap your hands." A frenzied crowd of dancers, playing air guitar and air bass on the dance floor, lasted through seven continuous replays of Robert's two lacquers— approximately an hour of the same song. I'd been into dancing and nightclubbing since my days with my ex-girlfriend Karen, and I understood why DJs played a popular record repeatedly to keep the dance floor hopping, but this was ridiculous. *An hour of the same song, and it was my demo!*

Did I really just witness this? It was so overwhelming that while I outwardly pretended to accept it, inwardly I questioned it. But I reasoned that Robert couldn't have staged this, and if he could, why would he? Everything was feeling completely absurd.

To further highlight the absurdity of the scene, Robert said, "Now watch this," and played the No. 1 record on the *Billboard* chart that week in October 1976, "A Fifth of Beethoven," by none other than Walter Murphy and the Big Apple Band: the group who just a few months earlier had forced us to change our shared name. All the people started booing and threatening to leave the dance floor. Robert replayed "Everybody Dance" at least another four times before the crowd would accept "A Fifth of Beethoven." How ironic was that? While Walter's record played, I ran to a corner telephone in the club and called Bernard, who was at home asleep with his wife and kids. I said, "Get up and come down here. You've got to see this."

"See what?"

"I can't explain it. You just have to come down to the Night Owl. Oh, and remember to tell them at the door you did 'Everybody Dance.' " A little while later, I saw Bernard's puzzled face as he approached the DJ booth in the smoke-filled room with the club's owner, Tom.

THE REBUILDING OF our new band had begun. But as positive and fantastic as the Night Owl was, it would take quite some time to get a Chic album deal. We'd bring many industry people to the Night Owl to witness the crowd's reaction to our breakdown music, but it never went anywhere, so we just kept working at it.

Bernard and I liked to gig together, but that wasn't always possible. Bernard got a gig, playing bass on a session with a producer/ arranger/musician named Kenny Lehman, who was also introduced to us by Robert Drake; the song was a sappy but hooky single called "I Love New York," or something like that. In those days singles had to have an A and B side in order to be sold. Typically B sides were filler, but every now and again you'd get a song like Gloria Gaynor's "I Will Survive," which might be the biggest B side of all time. Kenny just had the band jam and would finish the filler song later.

At that point I had been the sole writer in Chic, so Kenny came to me with the B-side jam, whose musicians were Jimmy Young on drums and Bernard on bass. Based on a number of factors, including the originality of the bass line, Kenny and I agreed we should bring Bernard back in as a writing partner.

I had written a hook that went, "I just dance, dance, dan-dan-dance, all of the time. I just dance, dance, dance . . . all the time." When Bernard heard it, he said, "That's too complicated." He suggested we change it to "Dance. Dance, dance, dance."

From that moment on, Bernard was my official songwriting partner. It was his very first song, and it was right. Nard was a bandleader and was accustomed to changing parts to bring out the best in everyone for live shows. When he became a songwriter, he did the same thing. His philosophy was simple and pragmatic: Fix it now, so we don't get booed off the stage later. It's really why we worked so well together. I would always overwrite and he'd always simplify it. Countless times he told me, "Damn, you've got the whole album in that song." He had a knack for understanding what a song was trying to say, then getting the song to say it.

I had already written the song's verses more or less, and after Nard simplified the hook, we thought it was ready to record. Once again we hired my old *Sesame Street* friend Luther Vandross as the vocal contractor. In the seventies we followed the professional rules of recording, even if the gigs were nonunion. The unions had established pay scales, and people were paid according to their responsibilities. The leaders or contractors of a group of musicians were paid higher fees and had greater responsibilities, primarily hiring, conducting, and filling out the contracts.

After Luther and his crew had recorded the song, the chorus was a little too simple for me, so I wrote the phrase "Keep on dan-cing," following the pattern of rewriting in the studio that we'd established working on "Everybody Dance." This completed the chorus and the song's vocals. Kenny Lehman did the orchestral sweetening on "Dance, Dance, Dance," and my original hook was relegated to the role of a secondary counterpoint melody, played on a Micromoog synthesizer during the verse. We used every complex musical idea that I had written for the song, but we rearranged them according to Nard's sense of balance and logic, which perfectly checked and balanced my impulse to overdo it.

"Dance, Dance, Dance" was our first complete song. We had discovered our formula for operating as long as we called ourselves Chic, a name that was slowly growing on me. We wrote more and more songs together based on our own golden rule: Every song had to have Deep Hidden Meaning. Bernard agreed. Armed with our new concept, we went out to conquer the world again—one dance floor at a time. There was a method to our madness: We felt that audiences would be more receptive to multilevel messages, just as long as they liked the groove. We also loved showing the essence of our grooves, by breaking down. Chic lived to break down. We used to have an inside joke between us that went, "A song is just an excuse to go to the chorus, and the chorus is just an excuse to go to the breakdown."

It took the record business a bit longer to pick up on the joke. But eventually they got it.

ATLANTIC RECORDS IN NEW YORK had started out as a pure R&B label, with artists like Ray Charles, Ruth Brown, and Aretha Franklin, but by the time of Woodstock, they had many cutting-edge rock acts too, including powerhouse groups like Cream, Led Zeppelin, Yes, and the Rolling Stones. If you were a New York recording artist, you wanted to be on Atlantic or Columbia, the top of the food chain.

Through our growing group of connections, we'd made contact through intermediaries with all the New York–based labels. The entire A&R staff of Atlantic Records passed on "Dance, Dance, Dance" because they didn't believe the song would play well on the radio, owing to its longer-than-average breakdown. That opinion was shared across the board.

One day one of our executive producers, Tom Cossie, finally got the record to the president of the label, Jerry Greenberg.

After hearing it only once, Jerry said, "Cossie, it's a smash. I got to have it."

There was just one small problem: We had already gotten a deal. We were technically signed to Buddah (*sic*) Records, a label best known for teenybopper pop acts like the 1910 Fruitgum Company. To make matters worse, Tom worked at Buddah and he'd gotten us signed there. So why were we out shopping for a deal? Buddah had contractually agreed to get our single "Dance, Dance, Dance" out in time for *Billboard* magazine's big annual disco convention. Tom knew this was the place to break our song. For whatever reason, Buddah missed the pressing date, and it looked like they wouldn't get our record to the convention in time.

Tom Cossie was an old-school promotion man and there was no way he was going to miss the heat the convention could provide. So he took a second-generation copy (magnetic tape loses fidelity when it's copied) of the master to Atlantic. He told Jerry, "If you can get the record out first, it's yours." Never one to turn down a challenge or a smash, Jerry commissioned the Warner/Atlantic helicopter to fly the pressings back from the plant the same day, and had limos deliver the records throughout the eastern region, all the way up to Boston (ah, the good old days of the record business). This was a huge contract breach, but it was worth the risk to both Tom and Jerry.

Not only did we make the convention (the song was pumping out of every conventioneer's hotel suite), it was also playing in the important (chart-reporting) clubs, with Atlantic's label on it. We had added the name of one of the top DJs at the über-disco Studio 54, Tom Savarese, as the mixer (in truth he did an edit that we never used), which was an important move because Studio 54 was the center of the disco universe. And with that, we were off and running.

By the time Buddah got wind of it, it was too late; they could only play catch-up. "Dance, Dance, Dance" was the hit of the disco convention. And that second-generation master is the version Atlantic put out. As they used to say, "If it's grooving, who cares what it sounds like?" Buddah had the high-fidelity master, but Atlantic had the momentum. Clive Davis, then an exec at Buddah, called

Jerry up and asked him, "Hey, Jerry, how can you do that to us?" So Atlantic agreed to let Buddah put out the single out of goodwill, and to avoid a lawsuit. We went gold on both labels but only got paid for the Atlantic sales.

We'd certainly taken a circuitous route, and it was far from overnight, but we'd finally achieved everything we wanted. Back then, most R&B acts wore flamboyant clothes, but we created believable alter egos: two men in impressively labeled but subtle designer business suits, which effectively gave us the anonymity of KISS. We put sexy girls on our album cover, which was suave like Roxy Music, and we tooled a new form of Euro-influenced R&B that also still passed the smell test of my jazz police friends. Then we put together a corporation that would manage and develop this entity and its future enterprises, the Chic Organization Ltd. We were born out of the studio, but now that we were real (at least contractually and on records) we had to (1) go out on the road and prove this was an immersive artistic experience and (2) demonstrate that the two young ramrods at the helm could make this a viable new business.

"Dance, Dance, Dance" was formally released to radio in the summer of '77 and started climbing the charts. It was an instant hit and gig offers were coming in fast and furious. Atlantic picked up our album option, and we created one very quickly. We wrote four more songs* and put vocal verses on "Everybody Dance," and had an album literally in a matter of days. Bernard and I were signed as individuals, and had agreed to provide the services of an entity we called Chic.

We set out to cast the lead role, a sexy female, and we were going to be the suave backup band. If it worked out, to the public we'd look like a corporate version of Rufus featuring Chaka Khan.

We had hired a lead singer who wasn't part of the New York studio scene, Norma Wright, her obscurity further adding to our

*My ex-girlfriend Patty translated one of them ("Est-ce Que c'est Chic?") into French for extra sophistication.

mystique. We got her to insert her middle name, which happened to be Jean, to pay homage to the real name of legendary movie siren Marilyn Monroe. We then formally hired our drummer Tony Thompson to role-play. He was very handsome and looked good in anything. Though he'd take our first press photo with us, he'd only wear a sport jacket; he wasn't feeling the suit thing because he saw himself as a rocker. But he loved playing with us and went along with it as best he could.

Tony still didn't believe this concept was going to work, even after we'd made the album and were paying him a salary. When we told him to get ready for rehearsals for a tour, he responded with, "Really? What songs are we gonna play?" It may seem odd now, but in his defense it's important to remember that Tony didn't even play on "Dance, Dance, Dance," and wasn't part of the initial Chic experience.

Bernard and I always tried to sound as close to records as possible when playing live (unless we changed it intentionally). So we hired Luther Vandross, one of the people who sang on the record, to come out on tour with us. Luther brought along Alfa Anderson from his own group. (Bernard and I were in Luther's backup band, playing at Radio City Music Hall, the night we made the ten-dollar recording of "Everybody Dance.")

Norma Jean and Tony hadn't participated in the song that had gotten us the deal. They weren't involved in any of the decision making or art direction. Had they been, maybe one of them would have stated the obvious: Hire two girls to headline Chic to match our art direction. We'd only find out this was a problem after doing our first few live gigs after our debut album was everywhere.

"Dance, Dance, Dance" was clearly two girls singing lead, and our album cover featured two hot female models. Since Chic was a new group, it wasn't a giant leap to think the two cover girls (one of whom was early black supermodel Alva Chinn) were singing. On the road playing with us, we had Luther's crew, two keyboard players, string and horn sections, and we sounded perfect, but we didn't look like our music. We made it through the first tour okay, but we soon recognized that people thought they were being short-changed. This had to be fixed *tout de suite*. We needed to bring in another front girl.

Norma Jean introduced us to a friend of hers named Luci Martin, and she and Norma worked the front line together. Finally we looked like our music! We'd successfully become a completely immersive artistic experience. Our art direction would remain as important as our music, and our next two album covers would prove this definitively, so much so, we even got Mr. Hard Rocker Tony to wear a suit.

When Norma left the group to go solo, Alfa, who'd been singing with us since the first tour as part of Luther's crew, took on Norma's role. Alfa and Luci became the two girls who'd be most associated with Chic, mainly because of the huge success of our next record, *C'est Chic*. It netted Atlantic their only six-million-selling single, and one of the only two records to go No. 1 on the *Billboard* chart three times, "Le Freak." For a brief period, Chic was volcanically hot.

IN MY HASTE TO TELL YOU about us, I've skipped over what was simultaneously happening to me. Our first show to promote our debut album was at a large nightclub in Atlantic City called Casanova's. It was dimly lit and the crowd was very receptive. We'd broken on radio in that region and were greeted like family. That was a relatively easy experience to handle. Our very next gig, on the other hand, was on the West Coast as part of a summer festival, for which Chic was about to play its first stadium. We'd gotten very big, very fast—and now we were facing some seventy thousand people in Oakland, California, in broad daylight. I was racked with terrible stage fright.

I was backstage, literally shaking with fear. The sight of this quaking mass of humanity was unlike anything I'd ever seen before, at least not from this point of view. Sure, I'd been to huge rallies and every manner of hippie tribal celebration, but I'd never been on this side of the microphone. I'd had a nice trail of professional gigs, but I'd always been in the backup band; I was not prepared to address seventy thousand people. Fortunately, a cure was at hand. My roadie said to me, "Hey, boss man, try this." He passed me a Styrofoam pint-sized cup of Heineken. I gulped down that beer, and all was suddenly right with the world. I felt a warm wave of confidence spreading over me.

I ran onstage, faced the crowd, and screamed out, "OAK-LAND!!!!!!!!"

The crowd responded with "CHIIIIIIIIIIIC!!!!!!!!"

It's a cliché. I know it's a cliché. I was a musician beginning his downward spiral into alcoholism. I was an addict—I mean, I'd been sniffing glue since I was old enough to cross the street, and had dropped acid before I started high school. I loved drugs. I'd grow to need alcohol daily. I won't drag out the suspense—for a lot of my adult life, drugs and alcohol were there; a lot of my adult experiences took place while I was under the influence of one mind-altering substance or another. I loved them. They nearly killed me. But I couldn't have done it any other way.

Back in the dressing room after the show, I instructed my roadie to always have a drink on stage for me. I'd started out that first day with just one cup of beer. By the end of the tour, Heinekens encircled the drum riser in a beautiful symmetrical pattern of bio-regrettable white cups. This functional sculpture's elixir helped me play a new role, that of an accidental rock star—designer threads and shoes, a guitar over my shoulder, and alcohol coursing through my veins.

Our greatest early ally at the label was our PR person, named Simo Doe. We'd do extensive promotional tours that she'd arrange and for which she showed us how to reduce detailed answers to sound bites. At first it made us feel like liars, but then we learned that sound bites were all they wanted. This was a medium that had only small openings in their programming schedule for human-interest stories. "Make them short and sweet," is what Simo taught us. Our success required us to replay this jovial spin game. In order to overcome my shyness, I started to drink before every interview, then during. I became accustomed to hearing myself talk on TV and radio, and would even go to DJ booths and shout out to the crowd on the dance floor.

Though Chic rarely played clubs (which couldn't accommodate a band of our size), clubs all around the country welcomed us with open arms as guests. This was not just limited to the hip clubs of New York, where new ones seemed to open nightly; club life was spreading around the world like nuclear winter. Our music was crossing over into every sector of society. We played in places that didn't usually have live black acts. One town we played in hadn't had a public pop concert (black or white) since Elvis had caused a riot two decades earlier. Chic not only played there, we got a police escort. I couldn't believe how almost everywhere I went, once people found out I was the guy from Chic, they'd treat me like a rock star.

And where does a fledgling rock star hang out? Back in the seventies, there was only one place that fit the bill: Studio 54.

THE FIRST TIME I WENT to Studio 54, I was not treated like a star. My music pumping on the dance floor, the supermodels on our album's cover, DJ Tom Savarese (who had mix credit), and my then girl-friend Nefertiti were the stars. Nefi had graduated from the presti-gious Fashion Institute of Technology. Many FIT people partied at Studio, and I was Nefi's guest. The club had only been open a few months, but it was already the hottest spot on earth.

It made sense that I wasn't treated like a star that first night, be-cause no one knew what Chic looked like, and Studio was all about who you were and how you looked. Nefi was really into how to achieve the look; she was a stylist who could design and make cloth-ing. It was she who taught me about high fashion. Before I met Nefi, I'd never heard of Fendi, Fortuny, or Fiorucci. I learned about haute couture and met many top designers, like Calvin Klein and Roy Halston, at Studio.

I had many great nights in Studio, but none as important as the night I tried to get in without Nefertiti and failed: New Year's Eve, 1977.

BERNARD AND I rounded the corner at Eighth Avenue onto Fifty-fourth Street. The first thing I saw was a massive mob, herded like cattle onto a sidewalk that couldn't possibly contain them, and spilling onto the street. There was a good explanation for this may-hem: If those people could be anywhere in the world, this was the place. I can still picture the redecorated hallowed halls of what used to be CBS's broadcast studios: coke-carpeted bathrooms, flat-black-painted walls, elaborate neon disco lights that dropped from the ceiling, ear-assaulting speakers, and churning sex nooks. And over the next nine years, I became a part of the club's inner circle.

By the end of '77, everyone in the club world was talking about our new breakdown sound, and we had become so popular that Grace Jones, who was a huge star at the time, had invited us to Stu-dio for her show on a freezing New Year's Eve. Grace told us to go to the stage door. But for some reason, we were turned away by the doorman, who promptly told us to "fuck off!" (Funnily enough, the guy contacted me about thirty years later on Facebook to apologize!) After he slammed the door in our faces, we decided, Oh, maybe Grace left our names at the front door. It took us forever to swim through the crowd and get the attention of the soon-to-be-famous front doorman Marc Benecke.

Bernard and I announced that we were personal guests of Grace. He told us, "Yeah right." When we politely yet urgently asked him to please check the list, he actually stopped, looked it up and down, scanned all the pages (which seemed courteous and respectful), and then said, in a clear, precise, definitive voice, "I looked, and you aren't on the list." He returned to scanning the crowd for notables. We knew that was the end of the negotiation. We were dressed to the nines, but after contemplating our options, we just sloshed through the snowy streets, around the corner to the cozy apartment of our DJ friend Robert Drake. I was living there while he was gigging in Rome.

We downed a few bottles of vintage Dom Pérignon, and a little coke, which I'd started snorting while touring on the road. I picked up my guitar, started jamming on a guitar riff and singing the words that the stage doorman had said to us earlier, "Fuck off," and Nard added, "Fuck Studio 54—aw, fuck off." He grabbed his bass and we played this over and over, grooving and laughing. We developed the groove and even wrote a bridge, then came the chorus again: "Awww, fuck off—fuck Studio 54—fuck off."

"You know, this shit is happening!" Bernard said, while pulling his sunglasses down his nose in order to achieve genuine eye contact with me. He did this whenever he was serious, because almost everything was a joke to us.

"We can't get this song on the radio. 'Fuck off' is pretty hard-core for Top Forty," I said, laughing. But Bernard was serious. And I'd learned to listen to him when he was serious. He had a great ear for hooks, and realizing that this little riff and chant sounded good, we changed "fuck" to "freak." "Awww, freak off," we sang energetically. It was horrible, but we tried to make it work.

"Hey, man, this is not lifting my skirt," I said to Bernard.

"Yeah, I know what you're saying," he responded.

Suddenly the proverbial lightbulb went off. "Hey, man, we should say, 'Awww, freak out.' "

" 'Freak out'?"

"Yeah, like when you have a bad trip, you freak out."

That wasn't the best reference for Bernard, since he was the last person who'd take LSD. So I quickly added, "Like . . . when you're out on the dance floor losing it, you know you're freaking out."

"Yeah, plus they have that new dance called 'the Freak.' That could be the DHM," he said, referring to our flare for Deep Hidden Meaning, now a must for the Chic song formula.

"Yeah!" he added, his voice rising with excitement. "It would be our version of 'Come on, baby, let's do the Twist.' "

Bernard was really into it, and we were in sync. After playing and singing for a while, Bernard made it completely ours by adding, "*Le freak, c'est chic*" in place of "fuck Studio 54." Maybe the reason why this came to us so quickly was because we were composing the songs for our next album, which was basically finished until we came up with this off-the-cuff ditty. Chic released "Le Freak" in the summer of '78. It featured Luther Vandross along with our signature double-female-lead-vocal sound, this time performed by Alfa Anderson and Robin Clark. It was a worldwide hit, and we got our first seven-figure check for the label's only triple-platinum single (six million in those days). The Zen of it was, by not getting what we wanted, we got more than we ever imagined.

THE MASSIVE SUCCESS of "Le Freak"—approximately twelve million units worldwide—set Chic officially on fire. Suddenly the money started flowing like water, and our lifestyle changed forever. One day Nard and I were walking down Park Avenue, fresh from our business manager's office, still processing the scale to which we'd struck it rich, when we happened upon a Mercedes dealership. The store was filled with the entire range of that year's models; their metallic finishes shining from the showroom stung our eyes. All the browsing customers were white male executive types, except us.

Make no mistake: We didn't look like vagabonds. We were in the latest designer suits because we always attended every business meeting in character, creating the Chic mystique. We couldn't imagine KISS ever showing up at the record company without donning their costumes, nor would we!

A salesman charged over to us to try and delicately shoo us out of the store. It was clear to him the likes of us couldn't afford his wares. "Um, can I help you, ah, *gentlemen*?" he said in a condescending tone, putting an extra bit of cynical sting on the word.

Bernard, who always had a gift for saying the right thing at the right time, didn't even look at the salesman; instead he walked over to the mirrored wall of the showroom. While panning himself up and down, he said, "I'm not sure. Which one of these cars goes with a brown tie?" He walked around the showroom and added, "I think that one matches, what do you think?" It was one of the three most expensive cars in the showroom, a 450 SEL. The salesman told him the price to scare him off or just give him a reality check. Bernard retorted, "Well, in that case I'll take that one over there, too!" It was a two-seat blue sports car. I did my best not to laugh. Finally I couldn't hold back anymore and started cracking up. Bernard bought both cars on the spot just to make a point. Still pissed off, he sternly said to the salesman, "Be courteous and cool to everybody who walks in, because you never know who they are, or what they're capable of doing." He finished the paperwork, made them prep the cars, and we drove them both away, unbalancing their carefully styled showroom.

I DIDN'T BITE THAT DAY, but I certainly did my share to prop up the economy. I was flying pretty high. It was exciting to have money and I figured it would always be that way for the rest of my life. I'd keep writing songs—they were coming easy to me and Bernard—and keep getting big checks. My first two post–"Freak Out" purchases were a Porsche 911 and a Cigarette deep-V ocean racer. Given what we were earning, these toys were hardly extravagant, but for NYC residents in 1978, let alone a former hippie like me, they were *waaaay* over the top. After all, most people in New York City didn't even drive. I reasoned it was just part of the job, part of creating the mystique.

Meanwhile, I took the boat out every chance I could. I concentrated on learning the foundations of seamanship, including dead reckoning and celestial navigation. We didn't have GPS back in those days, only radar and depth finders, so going on trips to ports unknown was very exciting. The racing paint job on my first boat was amazing; it made the vessel look like it was gliding across the water when it was sitting still. The sight of my Afro blowing in the wind while I was speeding around the tristate waterways must have been quite a vision. Another attention grabber was my boat's massive sound system. It was supplied by my gadget-guru DJ friend Robert Drake and was audible over the Cigarette's twin engines. I once took Debbie Harry and Chris Stein of Blondie out in a fog so thick you couldn't see two feet in front of you. I had to use radar and listen for the bells on the buoys to pinpoint our location. When we finally got back to port, they were the happiest people in the world, and I was as cocky as Captain Quint in *Jaws*. Break out the blow, baby!

I also spent a lot of money on clothes: I took the band's name seriously and elevated my wardrobe accordingly. My garb came from a mixture of cutting-edge high-end stores like Charivari and Maud Frizon (they've both long since closed), as well as Skin Clothes and Ian's (two shops that catered to show-biz punk rockers).

Drugs and alcohol were also a big part of my budget. I had an extremely high tolerance level and never seemed to get drunk, something I now know is an ability most alcoholics have. By that point I was boozing and doing coke all day, every day, but I wasn't reckless—quite the contrary. Even though I lived life on the edge, I was in total control. For the moment.

* * *

STUDIO 54 QUICKLY BECAME my number one hangout. We were homegrown heroes who'd achieved international pop success. I soon became part of Studio's inner circle of diverse superstars, like David Geffen or Truman Capote. Once I'd achieved that exalted status, I hung out in one of four areas: the basement, the balcony, the women's bathroom on the ground floor, or Steve Rubell's office (the ultimate sanctum sanctorum). I spent most of my time in the women's bathroom—which came to be known as my office.

The women's bathroom at Studio 54 was the first thing you'd pass after entering the club's main entrance. I can still remember how exciting it was the first time a girl brought me inside. I was afraid that the women would freak out and call a bouncer, but most didn't even notice, let alone care that I was there. Women's bathrooms have long lines and I thought that a guy taking up a valuable stall would be frowned upon, but you see, I had lots of blow. I was never asked to leave, which made me feel very special, so special I'd often spend the entire night in there. All my drinks were brought to me; all my friends met me there. Typically, I'd secure one stall as if it were my own private space. If someone had to use the toilet, I'd let her come in, and she'd pull up her skirt or drop her pants and just go in front of me, even if we were total strangers.

It may seem highly unlikely today, but inside Studio there was a Dionysian sense of belonging and trust. Nothing was taboo. Usually I'd give my visitors a hit of coke if they wanted it. Sometimes we'd have full-on sex, or maybe one or more girls would give me oral sex. If I sound casual about it, it's because that's just the way it was. There was never any pressure to do or not do anything other than what one wanted to do. Under the broad category of partying, people could accept or demur based on their proclivities. Nothing was frowned upon. I don't remember a single girl ever asking me to leave the stall to do her business.

Studio's basement looked like a modern version of ancient catacombs, scary and secluded. It was restricted to all but the inner circle and employees. In the relative safety of our underground bunker, we acted like lunatics just because we could. There were storage rooms aplenty because the building was CBS Broadcasting's theater and studio (hence the name "Studio 54") before it was a club. Many of these rooms resembled the jail cells called holding tanks. When I was downstairs, I acted cool but was always looking over my shoulder. I knew about the vampires who fed off the patrons' blood—in exchange for keeping the club owners forever young, or so the story went. From the look, feel, and odor down there, any sane person could believe it was true.

The balcony may have been the most mind-blowing, maybe because it was open to anybody. Here they did what the inner circle did behind closed—or slightly ajar—doors for all to see. It reeked like a Tijuana brothel. My first time up there, I caught a major movie star partying to the max. I won't say her name because later she became a good friend, but I saw her balling in the balcony. Compared to my hijinks in the bathroom, this seemed way over the top. I don't know why it was so shocking. I guess I'm not as cool as I thought I was.

Rubell's office was the ultimate VIP room, mainly because it had its own bathroom. Even though I did anything I wanted in my "office," I had the freedom to ascend to another level of hang when I disappeared inside his private bathroom. One night hit songwriter Paul Jabara (he wrote Donna Summer's "Last Dance" and many others) and his constant companion, who I assumed was his wife or serious girlfriend, were in the tiny bathroom doing coke with me. In a typically casual way, I peed while we were partying. Paul said, "Nile, you ain't gonna waste that on no bitch?" Talk about being caught off guard. Not only did I not think he was gay, but his girlfriend (or wife) was scorching hot in her skimpy body-hugging outfits. The way he'd said the word "bitch" had a hint of disdain, adding to the situation's awkwardness. I don't remember the words I used to decline his obvious advance, but I kept the spirit cheerful and we all laughed it off. A few years later, he died of AIDS, as did many of the Studio crowd. But in those early free-love days, we rolled like the Roman Empire before the fall.

Yes, 54 might have been home base, but in an odd development it started to fail my increasingly ravenous appetite. Happening clubs seemed to be opening almost weekly, and I had to be there. One night as I was leaving Studio to check out a new club, I ran into a friend's wife, who was flying solo. This was odd: She and her husband were one of New York's then "It" couples, and they were always seen together. She was gorgeous and trendy; he wasn't just a handsome, muscle-bound sports star—he was as nice as he was popular. I dug them a lot!

"Do you trust me?" she asked. I didn't get what she meant, but she wasn't high and the statement wasn't out of character. I thought she was going to tell me something about her strangely absent husband.

"Of course I trust you," I said. Then she told me to open my mouth and close my eyes. She placed a tablet on my tongue and said, "You belong to me tonight."

I didn't want to look like a chump in her eyes, because I admired her so much. She looked like an exotic cross between film starlets Dorothy Dandridge and *Black Orpheus*'s Marpessa Dawn, only more brown-skinned. She was impeccably adorned from head to toe in the latest haute couture, and she spoke perfect French and Italian, because she'd been a European runway model. As stunning as she was physically, it was her Mensa-level intellect that made her unique. Standing before her, I felt overmatched and somewhat afraid.

"What did you just give me?" I asked.

"X."

"Ecstasy?"

"Yeah, ecstasy," she said.

"Oh wow, I haven't done that in years." She held my hand, then kissed me in a reassuring way and said, "This is really good stuff, and I've been saving it to do it with someone special." And with that she turned me around and took me back inside Studio. That's all I remember her saying. We headed straight out to the floor and danced until the X kicked in. How do I explain the feeling of X? It's hard, but soon I was enveloped with that familiar feeling that I'd not felt since my teens, like everybody in the world was my best friend. I had absolutely no fear. X always made me feel like I was standing on my tiptoes, seeing above the crowd. I felt like I could look over anyone's head no matter how tall, my view unobstructed.

Then she took me to a friend's apartment. Maybe she felt this was less illicit than the balcony, bathroom, or catacombs of Studio. We made coke- and champagne-fueled love until the next morning. I don't remember what time I went home, or how I even got there, but we never spoke of the incident again. As sexy as this was, something about sleeping with a friend's wife made me feel like my moral compass had been reset, and not in a good way, and I started doing things that before that night I would never have done. I'd soon break up with my wonderful girlfriend Nefertiti, after I'd fallen hook, line, and sinker for her best friend, Michelle. I even dreamt the entire Chic song "I Want Your Love" while lusting after Michelle in my slumber.

DESPITE ALL MY PARTYING, things were getting better than ever with my day job. The hits kept coming. Over the next two years and a few months, we'd released six albums featuring some enormous hits: "Dance, Dance, Dance," "Everybody Dance," "Saturday," "Having a Party," "Sorcerer," "Le Freak (Freak Out!)," "I Want Your Love," "Chic Cheer," "He's the Greatest Dancer," "We Are Family," "Lost in Music," "Thinking of You," "My Feet Keep Dancing," "My Forbidden Lover," and "Good Times." Most of the singles and all their parent albums were gold. Many were platinum and multiple-platinum.

We were living and thriving in the most progressive and financially lucrative period in the history of art in America, and we knew that to do it, we had to play by different rules. Our Deep Hidden Meaning (DHM) allowed us to be artists, knowing most would at best see us merely as technocrats. We were bards who self-imposed a deceptive masquerade architecture on our lyrics. I'm not trying to make more of our songs than they were. They simply were more than most realized. We were proud and welcomed the challenge, but envisioned a future that we knew would come one day.

We shared Afrobromantic dreams of what it would be like to have real artistic freedom. Freedom—to combine the right words with the right music, to paint the right picture—to represent the brilliance of complex simplicity. We wrote for the masses, but worked tirelessly to make sure there was a deeper kernel that would appeal to the savvier listener.

Let me give you a sense of what I mean:

Paul Simon did it like this:
Why am I soft in the middle?
The rest of my life is so hard.

James Brown did it like this:
Thinking of losing that funky feeling?
Don't.

David Bowie did it like this:
Let's dance. Put on your red shoes, and dance the blues.

We had to do it like this:
He wears the finest clothes, the best designers, heaven knows,
Ooh, from his head down to his toes.
Halston, Gucci, Fiorucci.

Only the hippest folks knew who those three fashionistic names were and what it meant to use them as lyrics at the time. Today, using designer names in pop songs is somewhat commonplace.

We had to be trendy, but there was always an extra level of insight dedicated to our subjects; it was never one-dimensional. It was like the old joke about the educated slave who drove a buckboard through an intersection because the penalty for literate blacks was death. When the cop stopped him after his action caused a huge accident, he said, "Nigger, are you blind? Are you a goddamned idiot or something, boy? Didn't you see the stop sign?" The slave answered, "I'm sorry, boss. Do you mean that red and white hexagonal thing?"

WHILE I WAS BUSY CELEBRATING my success, some heads-up record companies started noticing that Chic had captured the magic of Studio 54 in our music, and they thought they wanted to bottle it. One was Jerry Greenberg, the president of Atlantic Records, who thought we could work that same hit-making mojo with other superstars on his label. He offered us everyone from the Rolling Stones to Bette Midler. We were flattered, but since superstars were already superstars, we knew that if we wrote and produced hits with them, no one would know what we did. We also knew only one way of working, which was, Do exactly what we say! This might not go over well with stars. So we suggested instead that they give us a lesser-known talent, so we could prove that we could make our own superstars. Greenberg told us about "a group of sisters that are like family to the label," he said, adding, "they stick together like birds of a feather." They were called Sister Sledge. After our meeting we went home and glanced at our notes.

The record exec had delivered almost verbatim the lyrics to "We Are Family," one of the biggest hits of all time. It seemed like a perfect situation to link to our hit-making technique. We had two concept albums under our belts by now, and we were developing the process and quickly becoming proficient. We agreed and started to conceive what this sister act that we hadn't even met should be. Their song "Love Don't Go Through No Changes" had been a popular R&B song, but we knew DHM-based breakdown songs could take them all the way to the top of the charts. Our confidence grew with every song we penned, though by now we'd come to expect we'd make a lot of changes once we got with our band, so basically everything was just a thumbnail sketch. Even our string arrangements would often change on the spot.

The first time we met Sister Sledge was also the first time they ever heard the song "We Are Family." When they walked into the studio, we were still writing the song as it was blasting over the loudspeakers. This had to be markedly different from what they'd expected, but it's how we worked. We didn't have to have it done, because we understood the song's DHM and we intrinsically knew what the song had to say. Once we had finished, we gave it to them and basically said, "Here it is and here's how it goes!"

Our aim was not to be tyrannical, but we only knew that way of working. A song remained malleable until we felt it was right, even if that meant the sisters just had to sit around and wait. Pound for pound, I think *We Are Family* is our best album hands down. But our method caused some friction between us and the sisters.

The best example of this friction was with the lyrics of their first single, "He's the Greatest Dancer." They were religious girls and took offense to singing, "My crème de la crème, please take me home." They thought clean-cut girls would not have a one-night stand. We explained, "The song is not about you, it's about him and the power the greatest dancer has over you." They suggested we change the lyric to "Please don't go home." This was in direct conflict with the song's core truth. We insisted that the lyric stay as we'd written it. They reluctantly sang it (though you couldn't tell that from Kathy's breathtaking delivery), but there was a wedge between us because we would not negotiate. After all, this was supposed to be their record. And it was (from our point of view).

Their record came out and went to the top of the charts. The album *We Are Family* is the best example of DHM perfection. We knew who they were (or certainly who we thought they should be) and crafted a production that revealed that reality on every song. Contractually we didn't have creative control, but we had it musically, and we were dedicated to protecting our music. This philosophy would ruffle feathers, but sell millions of records.

DURING THE HEIGHT of Chic's success, I never quite realized how big our music had gotten, mainly because we more or less lived in the

studio. When I wasn't clubbing, I was recording or watching movies. That was my entire existence. We rarely did live shows. But
when we did, well, they were something to remember. If there's
one live gig that captures what Chic was capable of onstage, it's the
show we did at the Padres' stadium, in San Diego, during a festival,
when we opened for Marvin Gaye.

Rick James and Marvin Gaye were backstage in Marvin's dressing room. According to Rick, who told me this story—he was a
good friend before drugs took him out—Marvin was getting ready
to go onstage and the two of them were partying, laughing, joking,
and having a blast. Marvin lifted his glass to take a drink and all of a
sudden an earthquake hits. Earthquakes are not unfamiliar in California, so Marvin did what he instinctively knew to do during this
type of emergency: He dove under the nearest desk and screamed to
Rick, "Come on, man, get the fuck down here!"

Rick starts laughing. "That ain't no earthquake," he says,
"That's just Chic."

"What's chic?" Marvin says.

"The band Chic. You know, your opening act. Chic, muthafucka. Chic. Damn, where you been?"

Marvin regained his composure, put on his performance clothes,
and waited to be summoned to the stage.

Meanwhile, we're in our dressing room drying off, trying to
come down from the rush of performing. Those of us who did
drugs started doing drugs. All of a sudden, there was a loud knock
at the door, loud enough to compete with the noise of the
still-cheering crowd. Cops. We quickly hid our illegal substances
and opened the door. It was the sheriff's officers and the stage manager. But instead of arresting us, they said something totally unexpected: "We need you to come back and do an encore. If you don't,
there's going to be a lot of trouble."

How could there be any trouble? we thought. We'd fulfilled our
contract. They didn't see the drugs. We figured everything was cool.
Then the cops explained why they were so insistent. "You have to

do something or there's going to be a riot, and I'm sure you don't want people to get hurt."

We had no choice but to go back onstage. The minute we did, the earthquake started again. I remember looking out at the upper deck. You could see and feel the entire concrete structure swaying like a palm tree in a light wind. The entire crowd was performing the vocal chant from our song "Chic Cheer." It basically just goes "Chic-Chic" endlessly, over the groove.

But there was a problem: We were still a relatively new band at that point, without much of a back catalog. We only had a handful of songs and we'd played them all. That was that.

We hadn't gigged much as Chic, but were seasoned enough entertainers to know the golden rule of show business: It's better to leave them wanting more than to leave them wishing you'd stop. Besides, we had way too much pride to repeat a song. Nor did it help that Luther—our main background vocalist—and the rest of the crew had already gotten onto the bus for the drive back to L.A. It was just Bernard, our two front singers, Luci and Alfa, our drummer Tony Thompson, and me.

So here was the dilemma: We couldn't play, and standing on the stage blowing kisses wouldn't calm down the crowd.

Bernard and I had a quick little plebiscite with our team and we found a solution: We asked a groundskeeper to bring out the golf cart that ferries the pitcher in from the bullpen during a baseball game. We proceeded to ride around the perimeter of the field, waving to the people like a bunch of popes and queens of England. We drove around until it got stale to us; truthfully, we felt a little foolish, so we returned underneath the stadium to our dressing rooms.

We figured that was it. This still didn't quell the crowd. The cops came back and asked us to please do it again. So we did, as stupid as the stunt felt. There are so many things in my life that I can't explain. Marvin was an international superstar, a personal hero of mine, far more famous and important to pop culture than Chic will ever be, yet many people booed him. He didn't do anything wrong, in fact he didn't get a chance to. I don't think that booing was about Marvin at all, it was about Chic being the flavor of the moment. (And don't worry about Marvin—many more people cheered him on, as always. He was still Marvin Gaye.) We could only imagine what Marvin was feeling. (Ironically, a similar thing happened to us a few years later when a brand new hip-hop artist called Kurtis Blow opened for us.) We were the new kids with the hot new sound, and we took another awkward victory lap. People who saw that show still catch me off guard to this very day. When I least expect it, a stranger will come over to me, shake my hand, and say with a knowing expression, "I was in San Diego." I feel like I'm part of some clandestine funk society whose underground members are waiting for the signal to rise up again.

IN TWO SHORT YEARS, we'd forgotten how special it was to sell a million copies of a single song. It wasn't because we were arrogant; we were just on a hit-making treadmill, with no time to savor the accomplishments. Within a few years, we'd learn just how important the gold and platinum records were, because for Chic they'd stop coming.

There's a line I like from the film *Highlander:* "There can be only one." Truer words have never been spoken. Around the time we found ourselves too busy to pick up yet another platinum record (yawn) for our latest hit single "Good Times," there was another song tracking neck and neck with us. It was a catchy ditty called "My Sharona," by a new band called the Knack. "Sharona"'s meteoric rise in the summer of '79 happened to coincide with a circus-like novelty event called Disco Demolition Night, in which the participants lost control and almost destroyed the Chicago stadium where it took place. It all started as a prank by a DJ from a local radio station who'd been fired when they changed the format from rock to disco, and morphed into a movement called Disco Sucks.

Now, I love silly gags and satirical entertainment and enjoy cheap thrills. I'm liberal, understand the right to protest, and am open-minded, with a pretty good sense of humor (I sound like I'm a beauty pageant contestant), but what happened during the Disco Sucks phase was astonishing to me.

Bernard and I always believed that most pop music fits into the broad category called rock and roll. Rock and roll was ever changing, and this art form had different genres of classification for the benefit of consumers, like sections in a library or bookstore. Once any genre—folk, soul, rock, or even some jazz—reaches a certain position on the pop charts, it does what's known in the music business as crossing over, and gets played on the Top Forty stations. That's the reason so many of us own songs by artists from genres we normally wouldn't—their hit songs crossed over into the pop Top Forty mainstream.

When a genre repeatedly crosses over and comes to dominate the Top Forty, what had originated as an insurgency becomes the new ruling class. This was the path disco had taken—from the margins where it started, a weird combination of underground gay culture and funk and gospel-singing techniques and, in the case of Chic, jazz-inflected groovy soul. But it was basically all rock and roll, historically speaking, as far as we were concerned.

But the media and the industry pitted us against the Knack—the disco kings in their buppie uniforms versus the scrappy white boys. But we never saw it that way. We thought we were all on the same team, even if our voices and songs followed different idioms.

Boy, were we naïve.

And boy, did things change.

I would love to say things went downhill just because our records weren't good enough, and I do think our later work wasn't as commercial (or good) as our earlier work. But Bernard and I always fought our battles with our music itself. Since we were not stars, this wasn't an easy battle to wage. The Disco Sucks campaign started gaining momentum, and the Knack (through no prompting of their own) were positioned as the saviors of rock and roll. Chic, on the other hand, were the enemy of it. It was like we were in some Gothic tale of elves, dragons, warriors, and monarchs. One group would continue to befoul the throne under the dark rule of Disco (the music of blacks, gays, women, and Latinos), and the other would try to return it to its rightful rulers (the white guys).

We didn't realize this war was industry-wide until a party one night in 1979. *Cashbox* was a music-trade publication like *Billboard,* chock-full of sales figures, charts, and stats. Bernard and I were invited to the magazine's annual soiree, though most attendees were businesspeople, not artists. The party was in a restaurant that had two rooms, one of which was used as a nightclub. This was the perfect place for a music industry shindig in '79. After a sumptuous meal, we'd all dance and party well into the night. Our industry was very healthy at that time. The music scene in general was robust, but it was especially great for an artist who specialized in dance music.

Donna Summer, Anita Ward, Samantha Sang, and Andy Gibb singles routinely outsold the legendary rock giants of the pop industry. It was a magical time. There was one Cinderella story after the next; check out any reference guide that gives you record sales statistics. Little-known groups like Taste of Honey and Chic could compete head-to-head with the big acts. In fact, at that time the biggest-selling records of artists like the Rolling Stones and Rod Stewart were dance records. Dance music was inclusive music, because it was more about the music itself than rock's often-bloated cults of personality, and this naturally resulted in a larger sales base. Example: A person who normally wouldn't buy a big Bee Gees record like "How Can You Mend a Broken Heart" would buy "Night Fever" in a heartbeat. The latter song was even played in underground clubs. The music reached across all social, racial, and political boundaries.

By now, just around thirty months after the release of our first single, Nard and I had collected seven singles that were certified gold (one million units), six that were platinum (two million units), three that were double platinum, and one that was triple platinum. Those are only domestic numbers; typically in our business you'd double that to get a good indication of your worldwide sales.

The magazine's party was in full swing. Everybody was packed into the restaurant side of the establishment, and no one was in the nightclub room. This was our first *Cashbox* party, and Bernard and I thought folks wanted to stay in the restaurant and talk about business. After about an hour or so, the restaurant had become unbearably overcrowded and ridiculously hot. We couldn't figure out why nobody was going to the nightclub, which seemed to be the logical thing to do.

"Maybe they're not going in because they're nervous?" Bernard ventured.

"What?" I said.

"You know, like kids at a party waiting for someone to get the courage to be the first to ask a girl to dance."

I responded, "OK, let's be first." We thought if we led the way everybody would follow. No one did! And when I say no one, I mean not one single person.

Nard looked at me and said, "Damn, man, does my breath stink? I know yours does, but I thought my mouthwash was cool."

After hanging by ourselves for about twenty minutes, we knew something stronger than our breath was keeping people out of the spacious, air-conditioned room. Maybe we didn't understand industry protocol, being relative newcomers. So we drifted back to the stifling restaurant to join our friends. We looked back at the nightclub and noticed a small neon sign above the room's entrance. This simple little sign explained why the hip, nonconformist rock-and-roll rebels were terrified to go into the room.

The sign only had five letters: D I S C O.

The Disco Sucks movement and its backlash were so toxic, people in the industry—people who were eating off of the record sales coming from dance music—were all afraid to be associated with anything disco, even the word on a small sign above a door. Something about that really enraged me. Until then I believed I was part of a wonderfully elite group who marched to their own beat. I had worked hard to get there. We were free. We all did what we wanted, said what we meant. We were the music business. Music people gave voices to the voiceless.

Chic never considered itself a disco band. Not because "disco" was a bad word or beneath us, but because it was slightly disingenuous. The accurate etiology of Chic is rooted in bands that more closely share our musical DNA: the Fatback Band ("Backstrokin' "), Brass Construction ("Movin' "), BT Express ("Express"), the Joneses ("Love Inflation [Part 2]"), Crown Heights Affair ("Dreaming a Dream"), Kool and the Gang ("Hollywood Swinging," which was the inspiration for "Good Times"), Hamilton Bohannon ("Foot Stompin' Music"), and so many other jazz-funk and R&B instrumentalist acts that wrote hit records. (One day I'll write the definitive playlist that influenced Chic, a treasure trove of the funkiest grooves on earth.)

Bernard and I defiantly stood in the DISCO room all by ourselves. "Look at the brave rebels," I said to Bernard. I was very disappointed.

I know there is bad music in every genre, but to classify all of it as, well, sucking is absurd. Many of the people at that party didn't care much for classical or Celtic, but they'd never say it sucked across the board. All artists at the top of their art form's food chain are specialists. I'm not a roots music aficionado, but the sheer virtuosity of the cream-of-the-crop bluegrass artists should be obvious and jaw-dropping to anybody.

The anger I felt at the party wasn't because I knew this situation would have an effect on me (I thought the "My Sharona" thing was a singular event) or my career, but because of what this situation looked like to me. What I saw was classic hypocrisy: people who'd been making a fortune off of this music willingly throwing it under the bus, rather than standing up for it when it became uncomfortable or politically inconvenient. To put it another way, they milked it when it was up and kicked it when it was down.

Chic soon lost its footing and we broke one of our promises to each other: Never use our music for direct protest. We couldn't do that very well, because it wasn't what Chic stood for. The statement about the "brave rebels" was the inspiration for "Rebels Are We," the first single from our *Real People* album. At the time, we said we were parodying a satirical Woody Allen song of the same name, but that was only partially true. We were angry.

It didn't matter. Our band was over commercially. We'd no longer be seen as the funky groundbreaking group with clever lyrics and audio-processing magic, thanks to the mega engineers we worked with: We were now a disco band, a band that, like disco, sucked.

I'M NOT COMPLAINING, I'm just sayin'. We always knew that once we'd made it in show biz, our downfall, like that of most groups, was pre-ordained. It was just a matter of when. We tried but we never had another hit with Chic. What we didn't know at the time was that the owners of the Chic Organization Ltd. would go on to make even more hits than we'd had in the early years. Only now we'd be making them for mainly rock acts. And the songs, strangely, were no longer called disco. They were new wave, dance, new romantic, and modern or even traditional rock. I'd learn that altering names to revalue a product hadn't changed much since my grandfather changed his name to Goodman.

eight

The Second Wind

ONE SUMMER DAY IN 1979, AROUND THE TIME THE DISCO SUCKS movement put a bullet into Chic's career just a couple of fast and furious years after it had exploded, I took a long walk along the famous Santa Monica Pier. We had a gig that evening at the Santa Monica Civic Auditorium—a very special gig, as it would turn out—and I had about an hour to kill before sound check.

It was early afternoon when I arrived at the pier, which was as familiar to me as the South Bronx. Back when L.A. was my hometown, the pier, which jutted up from the beach like the trestle in the movie *The Bridge on the River Kwai,* used to be called Pacific Ocean Park (POP), and I'd come here a lot, my young and often addled mind filled with glue fumes and images of the surfer/beach-party films that were shot there. That afternoon Santa Monica felt about ten degrees cooler than Beverly Hills, where I was staying.

When I was a kid, I used to obsess about the final episode of a TV series called *The Fugitive,* which was also filmed there. This was the very spot where the hero, Dr. Richard Kimble, fought a life-and-death struggle with the one-armed murderer on a ride called the Mahi Mahi, high above the pier. I'd gotten so into it that as a kid I used to ride the Mahi all the time. When it reached top speed, you'd be at a ninety-degree angle over the pier, looking straight down about a hundred feet above the ocean, a great view and a perfect symbol for my life back then, when drugs and sex were like flying and suicide all at once.

Now, at twenty-seven years old, I was on a very different kind of ride. Bernard and I had won the lottery. We were living the musician's dream—pretty much everyone in the country had heard our music, most of them had loved it, and we'd gotten rich from it. I could stop working that day and live forever on what I'd already earned if I chose to. It had all happened at warp speed, a real-life roller coaster. But now it seemed like everything we'd worked so hard to achieve was fading away.

Our art—tribal, communal, ecstatic, visceral, transcendent, joyous—was anathema to the culture, just like that. It was as if we'd thrown ourselves into this beautiful thing only to discover that we'd gotten it entirely wrong. No, no, this isn't what people want at all. They'd lost their heads for a minute and embraced our sound, but now they seemed to be saying, "No, please, no more." The status quo had reclaimed its throne.

But the battle wasn't over yet. We weren't giving up and we were far from finished. The insurgency had to go even deeper underground, and do battle like guerillas. Our next campaign was just getting ready to launch.

It all started with an unlikely turn of events back on the East Coast.

I'D MET A LOT of record business people in my life by then, but Suzanne de Passe was like no one I'd ever come across before. Dynamic, beautiful, and bright, she was president of Motown Productions, and Berry Gordy's right hand by most accounts. She was very powerful, and she knew it.

De Passe also happened to be a big fan of the Chic Organization, which was very good for us. Though many show business people had already dismissed us as part of the now-derided disco movement by the summer of '79, Suzanne knew that we were in fact big-thinking jazz-funk rockers who'd gotten a break by conceiving Chic at a propitious moment, and she had a plan to prove it.

Suzanne and Nard and I went way back, though we'd never actually met. We first heard about her in New York at a club we frequently played, called the Cheetah, which she'd booked for a few years in the late sixties. The Cheetah had more than the fabled nine lives of regular cats. It had survived countless trends. It had a hippie rock phase, and was once popular as a Latin club. Under Suzanne's watch, it mainly appealed to the black crowd. While our careers were taking off, so was hers. She came to Motown in 1968 and her meteoric rise soon had her extending the brand's reach into film and television through a new subsidiary called Motown Productions. She was nominated for an Oscar in 1972 for co-screenwriting *Lady Sings the Blues,* a film that revitalized Diana Ross's career. Suzanne eventually rose to the position of president of Motown Productions, a rise that ended with Berry ultimately selling her that entire operation.

Before she moved up, her last order of business at the record label was to reignite the musical career of Motown's top superstar, Diana Ross, and that meant making a radical move by going outside the company. And we were the people she had in mind to do it.

Our first official meeting to discuss the Diana Ross project took place at Chic HQ at 110 East Fifty-ninth Street. The space actually belonged to our attorney, Martin Itzler. It was a penthouse with panoramic views of the New York City skyline. Marty's walls were adorned with photos, awards, and gold and platinum records that he'd amassed over the years, which gave the cozy environment an air of show business importance.

When Bernard and I got off the elevator, we could hear the sounds of laughter and cackling spilling out into the top-floor waiting area, as if there was a huge party going on inside Marty's office. We didn't wait to be announced.

It was my first sit-down with Suzanne, but it felt like we'd known each other all our lives. Then again, maybe there were other factors affecting Bernard's and my mood. After all, these were the days when Bernard and I had the habit of making frequent trips to the bathroom, and not because we'd been drinking too much coffee. We were doing tons of blow, and even though it was top of the line, our resistance was growing; more and more hits were required just to maintain a nice buzz. Call it a sign of the times, but no one ever said a word about what was a fairly obvious drug habit.

And what a ritual it was: On cue we'd both get up in sync, and walk single-file like a couple of soldiers in Gucci suits. Once in the bathroom, we'd go into the same stall together, take out a hundred-dollar bill (it always had to be a hundred during this period of silly status symbols), roll it into a straw, and stick it in the left nostril first and snort a hefty amount. Then we'd switch to the right one and do the same. Then we'd go to the sink and run cold water on our first two fingers and stick them up about a half-inch into our nostrils to make sure there was no trace of coke visible to the naked eye. We'd shake it off, smooth out our jackets, and march back down the hall to our meeting.

At some point during a lull in the laughter, Suzanne seized the moment to get down to business. And just like that, the first link in the chain was forged.

DIANA ROSS HAD RECENTLY come off of a pretty big hit record called "The Boss," which had been written and produced by the husband-and-wife team of Nicholas Ashford and Valerie Simpson, longtime Motown insiders. As big as this record was, it was nowhere near the league of the mega-crossover sales that Chic had tapped into. Suzanne wanted to make sure that Motown was part of this wave of chart-topping black pop, especially since Berry Gordy had perfected the black-crossover entertainment business in the first place. Suzanne was the ultimate consigliere. She was always loyal to the Don and what he'd created, but she also knew that the old ways didn't work the way they used to. If the business was going to survive, it had to grow or die.

The supply chain in the music business was dependent on so many people, places, and things lining up just right, but the Chic Organization rewrote the rules. We got rid of as many outside variables as possible. We started out downsized. Our overhead was low, and the return on investment was very high. Our early investors and business colleagues all did very well indeed. In the beginning we had almost nothing; soon we owned everything we'd created. Monetization of our assets was key to survival in the ever-changing music business.

Early on, our attorney, Marty, used to tell us, "You'll never be big forever, so I'm going to teach you how to always make a living in the music business, even when you're not hot." We'd always felt thankful for Marty, because he helped us in the beginning to get out of the legal mess that was the result of Chic being signed to two labels. He'd also thought of calling the business the Chic Organization Ltd. Though we never fully developed the Chic brand the way artists do now, we were able to do licensing deals, productions, and compositions to order; we even purchased rare stamps and documents. We invested in the then new General Electric technology called the CT scanner and started a medical business called the CHIC Mobile Diagnostic Laboratories, which sent CT scanners to hospitals that couldn't afford to have the million-dollar units in house. Marty and Suzanne were wheeler-dealers and they put a new Chic Organization/Motown deal into motion.

I KNEW SUZANNE was skilled at making things happen, but I had no idea exactly how skilled till she showed up unannounced at our very next gig, Santa Monica Civic Auditorium—with Diana Ross in tow, dressed in full superstar regalia.

I don't remember Diana's exact outfit, but I do remember thinking, Damn, we're onstage singing about being chic and she looks more chic than we do! (Our clothes used to get so saturated with perspiration that it was hard to remain dry, let alone chic. Nard was wearing a tan pastel-colored suit made out of crepe de chine that got so completely sweat drenched that by the end of our shows we called it "crap do shine."

And here was Diana Ross casually dressed in the middle of the day, her signature mane blowing back to expose her face, looking like she'd just finished a cover shoot by Scavullo. A waft of Santa Monica Beach air lifted her hair off her shoulders like Mother Nature's production designer had choreographed the scene for maximum impact.

I'll never forget how I felt at that first sighting. We briefly made eye contact and she was smiling ear to ear as if I was her best friend in the world. She represented the perfect blend of soul and style, everything we wanted Chic to be. Ever since I was young, I'd loved the songs of most Motown acts, but the Supremes were special. The combination of Diana's delicate soprano voice, the way she was styled, and the perfect songs that were chosen for her made her Berry Gordy's Galatea. (The mythological story of Pygmalion wasn't far from Berry and Diana's real story, even down to him fathering a child with his beautiful creation.) As a kid, I was a daydreamer who loved reading, watching movies, and acting out mythological stories. I remember thinking, Wait a minute, is this a dream or an acid flashback? Is Diana Ross really watching us?

Maybe this is real stardom, I thought to myself. Maybe our songs are just that big? After all, it was possible, especially given the chemicals and hormones juicing up my perception. In a few short months, I'd gone from a shy introvert, frozen with stage fright, to a co–front man, thanks to a steady diet of what I called the Killer B's: blow, booze, and babes. I'd never have to play a song in concert that I hadn't composed myself for the rest of my life. From as far back as I can remember, I was consumed with feeling ugly, which had the residual effect of also making me feel disposable and rejected. This new convergence of stimuli made me almost feel attractive, which was different than I'd ever felt before. The battle against disco might have dented our dignity, but here was Diana Ross enjoying my show.

I wasn't the only one who could sense something special was going on: Suddenly people in the audience started noticing Diana too, and their response—it was a capacity crowd, and they were whipped up into a frenzy—made me feel very special. Diana's visit couldn't have come at a better moment: Our songs "Good Times" and "We Are Family" were dominating pop culture (the latter due to the World Series bid of the Pittsburgh Pirates, who'd adopted the song—as many would—as their inspirational anthem).

In spite of the Disco Sucks movement, "Good Times" had gone No. 1 on the *Billboard* pop chart, and this was definitely our crowd.

"Aw, freak out," we screamed in sync with our instruments, the last three beats concluding the song and our set. "Thank you, Santa Monica. We love you people. Get home safe and don't hurt any-body," Nard said in his cool, suave voice. It was the false ending to the show. We rushed offstage and ran back to our dressing rooms to get ourselves together a bit; after all, we expected the crowd to call us back for an encore. But before we could get to our dressing rooms, Suzanne de Passe, who was standing in the stage right wing, said, "Hey, guys, I'd like you to meet Diana Ross."

It was a surreal moment. My blood was still racing from the show, and my mind was already leaping ahead to the encore. Suddenly a goddess wanted to say "What's up?" It was hard to maintain any degree of politesse, but I did my best. Before I could say a word, her perfume spoke first, reminding me that she was a refined pop diva and cool as a cucumber and that I, on the other hand, was dripping in sweat; my silk suit felt like a terrycloth sauna bathrobe on my hyper-thermal body. The glare of the backstage lights, the massive screaming crowd, and the stage manager's frantically trying to pre-pare us for the encore only amplified the surrealism. With a formality that was out of place for this maddening setting, I said, "How do you do, Miss Ross?"

"Did you enjoy the show?" Nard added.

"Call me Diana, and it was really great," she said in a laughing rhythm.

"Thank you so much for coming," I panted, trying to catch my breath.

"It's really nice to meet you."

The situation was almost otherworldly. Two contrasting sound-tracks were clashing in the room: Diana's silkily angelic voice and the frenzied crowd screaming at the top of its lungs. Backstage, it was all decorum and dignity, while out front, uncontrollable insanity pre-vailed. The elegant diva looked like she just jumped off the cover of *Vogue;* our fans looked like they were ready to storm the Bastille. But Diana was perfectly cool with it. A veteran performer herself, she knew we'd have to put our little convocation on hold until after an encore.

"Um, we've gotta go back out to do one more song," I said.

"OK," Diana said, with a little wave as we ran back onstage. "I'll meet you in the dressing room when you're finished. Break a leg," she added with a giggle.

We did our encore and completed one of the best shows of our lives. We'd clearly made a strong first impression on Ms. Ross, and she told us as much when we saw her in our dressing room after we'd finished. There was something in the air that bonded us. She was almost like a sister, and Bernard and I started our typical tom-foolery, making fun of each other's performances. Diana was de-lighted watching the two of us, giggling like a kid watching the "Follow the Yellow Brick Road" sequence from *The Wizard of Oz*. She was ready to join us. Suzanne knew her artist well and had played her cards exactly right.

BEFORE DIANA, THE ONLY ARTISTS we'd produced were Chic Organi-zation–related projects: ourselves, Norma Jean Wright (our former female vocalist in our short-lived one-girl configuration), and label mates Sister Sledge. We'd never worked with a big star, unless we were their backup musicians.

Now we were being given the awesome responsibility of retooling the career of one of the biggest stars in the world. This was what Atlantic Records president Jerry Greenberg had had in mind when he'd suggested we work with the Rolling Stones a few months earlier. We weren't ready then, and maybe we weren't ready now. But Suzanne de Passe believed in us and had made it happen. Thank God for her focused faith.

We were going to need it.

In a little more than two short years, we'd sold more than twenty million units of product, but as I've said, our records were about to stop selling with a thudlike finality. The entire industry would quickly turn against us.

And that was just the half of it: The glamorous project we were about to embark on with Diana Ross would cost us far more tears, pain, and humiliation than our first record deal ever did.

But tonight all of that seemed as unlikely as Richard Kimble losing his battle with the one-armed man, or California falling into the ocean. And among the jubilant crowd in the Santa Monica Civic Auditorium's Pacific Ocean zephyr, there wasn't the slightest ill wind blowing at all.

IT WAS AROUND NOON, relatively early by a musician's time clock, when we arrived at Diana's luxurious New York apartment for the first time. The place was in a prewar apartment building on Fifth Avenue and overlooked Central Park. Her apartment felt like a mansion in the sky: high ceilings, spacious and grand rooms. The décor exuded an understated regality, and my first impression was of how tastefully it was decorated: not too little and not too much—Goldilocks-style.

Although she's a superstar, there is something deceptively normal about Diana Ross. Yes, she's beautiful and glamorous, but she laughs freely. She's regal and rightfully so, but also unpretentious, kind, and generous, and will throw you a homegirl-from-the-projects curveball when you least expect it. She once feigned sickness at a dinner party and asked me to drive her home. We then secretly drove to Queens to get White Castle hamburgers. She's got a great sense of humor, and we quickly found ourselves having a ball with her.

Some of these qualities I detected right away, but I didn't really know her yet and I'd be lying if I said I wasn't slightly nervous. Diana was cordial and made us feel very comfortable, but Bernard and I were just eager to get down to business. We had this golden opportunity, but the storm called Disco Sucks was raging, its funnel cloud trying to suck us up and carry us off into black history. There was a sense of urgency at this meeting, at least on our part.

Before we started composing, our plan was to have a few interview sessions with Diana. We didn't want to misrepresent her, a mistake we'd made to some degree with Sister Sledge. The fact that they'd never heard the songs until the day they came to record—we were still writing them in the studio—hadn't helped either. That was a less-than-desirable way to start a relationship, as we'd learned the hard way.

Determined not to make the same mistake with Diana, we wanted to get a broad range of subjects that she was interested in.

"So, Diana," I probed, "tell us about yourself. What's on your mind? What kind of things would you like to do? What makes Diana Ross tick?" I wanted to start cautiously but she opened up right away.

"This is a time of major change in my life," she told me, "and everything is going to be 180 degrees different from now on."

"What exactly do you mean by that?" I asked.

"I'm going to live here on the East Coast," she told us. "I have a feeling life will be more exciting here. I'm actually looking forward to turning my world around."

Based on that conversation—and, admittedly, a few cocaine pow-wows between Nard and I—the result was the song "Upside Down."

Many of the song ideas for Diana's new album, *Diana,* were transcribed in my childish scribbling during those interviews. I could have come off like a new-wave black Edward R. Murrow in my pre-eighties cutting-edge suits, but I was clearly relaxed and, respectfully, not too prying. (OK, I admit it. I was trying to impress her with my sense of high fashion and knowledge of the hottest new designers, so I wore many hip outfits to this series of interviews.)

"My new life's going to be fun and adventurous," was how our next session started. "I want to do exciting new things." We were just getting to know her, but by now there was a definite story line developing. Although she was upbeat, it soon became obvious to me that Diana Ross was leaving something painful behind. But most survivors possess a gift for looking ahead, and without a doubt, she had it. This interview resulted in a composition called "Have Fun (Again)." We were so impressed (and frankly surprised) by her incredible gentility and kindness, we composed a song called "Tenderness." This record was clearly going to be about the vulnerable and powerful woman we were getting to know. From our point of view, this album was going to be about the complete Diana Ross, a butterfly who'd returned to being a chrysalis, just so she could enjoy the thrill of metamorphosis again.

Even artifacts in Diana's surroundings influenced us. She had a fabulous collection of dolls, stately paintings, and a cute baby grand. It was the baby grand that captured our imagination the most, resulting in the song "My Old Piano."

We paid tribute to Suzanne de Passe and Diana with a song called "Friend to Friend." It was the best way we knew how to say "thank you" to the two amazing women who'd rescued us from becoming a minor footnote in rock-and-roll history. Thirty years later I still cry every time I listen to it.

ONE NIGHT IN THE FALL of '79 while out partying, I made a pit stop at a club called the Gilded Grape, the pinnacle of trendy sleaze, and took in the crowd: transvestites and transsexuals, lesbians and gays, bis and heteros. The place's main attractions were its underground vibe, music, and Hell's Kitchen location (the neighborhood's nickname comes from Davy Crockett, who said the people who toiled in the area were "too mean to swab hell's kitchen"). Even the toughest New York would've felt slightly nervous in this part of town, at this spot, at this hour. For me it was a sanctuary, the wonderful underbelly to snobby spots like the 21 Club, just a few blocks away.

On a trip to the bathroom, I noticed a number of Diana Ross impersonators lined up on either side of me, peeing. I felt like I was in an unscripted *La Cage aux Folles* number. Suddenly it dawned on me that Diana was an iconic figure in the gay community.

"What would it be like," I wondered, "if Diana celebrated her status among gay men in a song?" I shared the anecdote with Bernard, who agreed that it would be a cool idea to have Diana talk to her gay fans in slightly coded language.

"I'm Coming Out" was the smash result. We originally envisioned the song as the opening to Diana's live show for the new album. The horns in the song's intro were a soul fanfare for the pop diva. To this day Diana opens with it. The last time I saw her in concert, I'm sure I had a Cheshire Cat–like grin spread across my face through the entire song. For me, the best feeling in the world is seeing an idea or fantasy become a reality. Since I don't have children, my songs are my children—real creations that I nurture and cherish like a parent.

Diana was a deeply personal project for me, and the songs I wrote for that album were more important than any of the ones that had preceded them. By the summer of '79, I was freed by the knowledge that I'd never have to work again. The royalties from "We Are Family," "Le Freak," and "Good Times" alone confirmed that. I was doing this record because I wanted to do it. I wanted to get it right— to push the envelope. Diana's clout gave us the opportunity to compose bolder songs.

The first single, "Upside Down," was different from anything we'd written before. Its structure was angular and its groove's chords were staccato, this time without a smooth keyboard pad underneath, unlike our past hits. We started the song with the hook, like almost all Chic songs do, but cut to the verse with a modulating chromatic progression. It was a complex but interesting way of performing this unorthodox but simple key change.

We included excessively polysyllabic words like "instinctively" and "respectfully" in the lyrics, because we wanted to utilize Diana's sophistication to achieve a higher level of musicality. Along with the complicated verse, we deliberately made the chorus rhythmically more difficult to sing than the catchier, one-listen song hooks for Chic. We weren't working with talented session singers this time, we were working with a star. We wanted to give her more ambitious, intricate material to work with and interpret, to fill with her own intelligence and skill. Despite the departure from our tested style, we knew "Upside Down" was a monster hit.

Unfortunately, not everyone agreed.

Nard and I considered ourselves seasoned rejection vets. The powers that be had frequently reacted negatively to our music. When we played "Le Freak," Atlantic Records's first reaction was, "Do you have anything better on the album?" "Le Freak" went on to become their only triple-platinum single. But that was then. This was a whole new ball game. We were more seasoned now. We were in the zone, and we'd written our finest work for maybe the greatest pop star of her generation. We never expected to run into problems.

It all started with a guy named Frankie Crocker ("the Chief Rocker"), an influential New York DJ at the urban-music-formatted radio station WBLS. Back then WBLS was the number one station in America, and Frankie was the number one DJ at the station. Diana was eager to give Frankie a first listen, so they decided to meet over dinner. Excited, we made a tight rough mix for her, happily waved goodbye, and said, "Have a nice time and give Frankie our best." I remember watching a mink-clad Diana almost float out the studio door.

About three hours later, when she returned to the studio, her mood had dramatically changed. She seemed to have fallen into some sort of emotional abyss. I mean she was extremely low, I'm talking Marianas Trench low. "What happened?" we asked.

"Frankie said this song is going to ruin my career," she told us. "He was very serious and very worried about what you're doing with me." She paused for a moment and then added, "Why are you guys trying to ruin my career?"

"What are you talking about?" Bernard said.

"Frankie talked about a lot of other records and told me that they had the hot new sound."

We were shocked. Shocked and stunned.

"Frankie's our friend, Diana," I said. "He likes our music. He'd never say that about us. He knows we're not trying to ruin your career, 'cause we'd also be ruining ours!"

I like to believe Frankie's concerns were genuine. And I guess I understand, at least in theory, where he was coming from. "Upside Down" was unlike any song we'd ever written at the time, and it was unlike any song Diana Ross had ever recorded. But we were sure we hadn't lost our compositional magic; in fact, it was getting better. We absolutely knew the record was a tour de force. But no matter how much we tried, we could never fully console or convince Diana.

And to make matters worse, Motown reacted the same way as Frankie Crocker. We expected them to get it, but they just reinforced the negativity. We were about to get torpedoed. On some level, we always understood when white-owned labels didn't understand us, but we weren't prepared for what Motown was about to do to us.

" 'Upside Down' is not a Diana Ross record," said Berry Gordy, "and neither is the rest of the album." And that scorched-earth response appeared to be unanimous at the label. I had no idea what kind of heat Suzanne must have been getting. After all, it was her project. I have to believe that she was continuously raked over the coals by Berry, and probably Diana as well. We actually knew that Suzanne liked the record, but now we couldn't even get her feedback because we suddenly had no further contact with her (after our attorney contacted the Motown brass in response to Motown's sudden change of heart).

We were devastated. This was the most important project since our debut, and everybody hated it—everybody except us. Motown stopped communicating with us altogether. We didn't merit so much as a single reassuring word. Not even from Diana. Then Motown demanded all the tapes back from the session and we finally got it:

We'd been fired.

* * *

EONS SEEMED TO PASS. Then one day a test pressing of Motown's "mix" of our record arrived, which was a completely different aural experience than what we'd intended. It didn't have the same punchy big bottom end and used different edits and vocal composites. We hated it and were furious about what had happened to our masterwork. Between the interviews with Diana and all the meetings, planning, and rewriting, we'd worked harder than we'd ever worked on any record. We simply couldn't fathom how a black label could treat us so disrespectfully. Besides, Diana Ross was our queen, and like loyal subjects, we'd given her our very souls. We tried to rationalize her and Motown's response, and decided that everybody was just afraid to be associated with anything that was even slightly associated with disco. We were certain it wasn't the music.

We played the Motown mixes for everybody at the Power Station recording studio. They loved them. We played it for Gene Simmons from KISS, who was recording next door, and he told us it was great. We respected Gene, but he was dating Diana Ross at the time, so what else would he say? Chic's original engineer, Bob Clearmountain, told us, "Guys, they can't mess this record up. It's impossible. The songs are so good it doesn't matter what they do to them." We still didn't agree. When we listened to Motown's version, all we could hear was what could have been. This hijacking of our work was a travesty. So we held our ground.

Ultimately, Motown decided to put out the record they hated.

ON SEPTEMBER 6, 1980, "Upside Down" hit the No. 1 spot on the *Billboard* charts and stayed there for four weeks, about a year after the Disco Sucks movement. *Diana* went six times platinum in America alone and remains her biggest-selling album of all time.

Ironically, the song that followed "Upside Down" into the No. 1 slot was Queen's "Another One Bites the Dust," which sounded remarkably similar to Chic's "Good Times," which had gone No. 1 a year earlier at the height of the disco backlash. "Good Times" would also go on to inspire INXS's "New Sensation," the Clash's "Radio Clash," Vaughan Mason's "Bounce, Rock, Skate, Roll," and Blondie's "Rapture," among many others. The song's greatest accomplishment may be its role as the bedrock for hip-hop's first mega-smash, "Rapper's Delight," by the Sugarhill Gang. Obviously, disco didn't die, it just grew up and changed its name and address.

DIANA'S SUCCESS REDEEMED BERNARD and me as artists, but Chic continued to spiral downward. We were still stigmatized as an artifact of a now defunct movement. At the same time, paradoxically, we were the serendipitous vanguard of the next cultural phenomenon, hip-hop, through the "Good Times" sample on "Rapper's Delight." This was new and unprecedented territory—after all, there is no "Rapper's Delight" without "Good Times"—and we had to fight a copyright infringement lawsuit to defend

our "borrowed" contribution to someone else's hit. You might be able to "sample" a piece of candy, but we weren't ready to let someone else get all the cash from dining off of something we'd built from scratch.

The mogul at the end of the Sugarhill Records trail was Morris Levy. Levy was about as powerful as they come in the music business. His vast entertainment empire included nightclubs, record labels, artist management, and the biggest cash cow, music publishing. It was our publishing interest in

the song "Rapper's Delight" that we were protecting when we sued to regain our stolen property.

When we went to the CEO of Atlantic to back us in the suit for reclamation of their asset, they declined. They were not willing to take on the man who had sued John Lennon and won. So we had to go it alone against this industry titan. But as luck would have it, our

attorney, Marty Itzler, was one of Morris's ex-attorneys and knew Levy very well. Though we've never discussed this aspect of it, I'm sure Marty hoped that in the end there'd be enough money to go around and that we'd all be able to do business once cooler heads prevailed.

We fired the opening salvo and contacted Sugarhill Records, threatening a lawsuit. Lawsuits are part of almost every successful business, so we continued doing what we normally did, which was make records.

The expected legal formalities followed. But that's when things really got interesting. What happened next is so strange I still don't know who was really behind it.

IT WAS A HOT AUTUMN AFTERNOON and we were in the middle of a session at the Power Station, our home base for years, when the owner burst in and yelled, "I have to get my people out of here!" He instantly stopped the session and forced his employees to leave the room. Before we could say "What the fuck," three large well-dressed black men entered the now empty studio, led by a guy who'd years ago unsuccessfully tried to sign Chic to a major label.

The situation was strange, but since we thought of this dude as a friend, we had no reason to be nervous. The mood changed when the fellow we knew introduced the three large dapper strangers to us as our friends. At some point I realized that the biggest of the four dudes was clearly packing. His tailored jacket was opened to reveal glimpses of his gat. This didn't exactly square with what he was saying, which had something to do with the idea that he was "there to look out for us." Apparently, our "friend" had heard that we were threatening to sue Sugarhill Records. What followed was a lengthy and puzzling diatribe about how things were going to play out if we continued pursuing legal recourse. "Even if you win, you'll lose," he concluded. "Seriously, brothers, we're here to help you." And with that, our new "friends" exited the room as quickly and mysteriously as they'd entered.

We were completely baffled. They were so well spoken, dressed, and mannered, it wasn't clear if they were actors playing gangsters or genuinely concerned citizens who just happened to be carrying concealed handguns. We called our attorney right away and told him about what had just gone down. He gave us a new and worrisome laundry list to keep track of, from hang-up calls to mysterious phone threats. "You've got to be kidding me," I said to Bernard.

What followed was one of the most sober band meetings ever. Someone was trying to intimidate us, and we simply couldn't give in. We decided we had no choice but to go through with the suit. So Marty put in a call to the powers that be and said his clients were not backing down. Could we have? Sure. But all we knew was that it had taken a lifetime of experience to come up with "Good Times."

If someone could take what it had taken our entire lives to create, then what value did any of it have, anyway? If we didn't fight for our art, then why should we expect Atlantic to? Forget about the fact that it was legally recorded property we were protecting in the first place.

In the end I'll never know exactly how much backroom wrangling took place, but at the end of the day we got equal billing on the copyright—and a lot of money.

A few months later, after the matter was settled, we got a call for one last deal point: We had to buy Morris two round-trip tickets to Paris on the Concorde and a pair of his-and-hers Rolex watches. When Marty asked, "Why?" Morris responded with a classic so ridiculous, it was funny even to us. "Come on, Marty," he said. "I gotta fuck ya!"

Talk about an offer we couldn't refuse.

In the final analysis, "Rapper's Delight" turned out fine for us. Ironically, though, given the song's historic influence on music, musicians, and the world at large, Chic never really got the credit it deserved. Hip-hop was rapidly becoming the new black. Despite the major role our song had played in the movement, we still made "live" music, which marked us as creatures from a different generation. The writing was on the wall. Despite our massive string of hits, barring some supernatural act, we'd soon become irrelevant.

I WAS TWENTY-SEVEN YEARS OLD, ancient in the music business in the early eighties, especially for a black male.

Black male musicians can sell as many records and perform with the top white male acts when they're young, but a black equivalent to Elton, Sting, Bruce, James Taylor, Paul McCartney, Billy Joel, Phil Collins, Eric Clapton, Tom Petty, David Bowie, the Eagles, the Stones, Jimmy Buffett, Paul Simon, etc., doesn't exist. Prince is probably the only one who's close. Even a true American legend, Stevie Wonder, doesn't have the earning potential of anyone on that list. My options were limited by the nature of the business.

Atlantic Records let us record every album left on our contract. On some level Jerry Greenberg knew we still had it, and that we'd figure out how to be successful in the anti-disco aftermath. It was just a matter of time. He let me do a solo album called *Adventures in the Land of the Good Groove,* and gave us a movie soundtrack, *Soup for One.* Both were commercial flops by Chic standards, but Jerry hung in there through these experiments. I was searching for something, but whatever it was, it was eluding me.

As I say to vocalists who are singing a little flat, sharp, or out-of-the-pocket, "We're in the neighborhood, but we haven't found the house yet."

David Bowie helped me find the house.

Here I am at five, sent away again: this time to an upstate camp with my cousin Herbert. We lived in the hood, but that didn't stop my mother from dressing me like Little Lord Fauntleroy. *Author's collection*

In Los Angeles, the morning of the day I met Timothy Leary. *Author's collection*

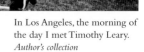

My two grandmothers, Lenora and Goodie, in Watts, along with Goodie's dog, Champ. *Author's collection*

My grandmother Goodie and her man, Dan. Dan's guitar was the first I handled, but he would've killed me if I ever tried to play it. *Author's collection*

Jazz great Billy Taylor was one of my influential early instructors. *Michael Ochs Archives/Getty Images*

Beverly and I in L.A. in the mid-1970s. I was making music and money, but still on the humble. *Author's collection*

With my brothers Bunchy, Dax, and Bobby in the late 1970s. From the fly suit and the flyaway collar, it's clear that the Chic checks were starting to come in. *Author's collection*

Grace Jones performing. She invited us to her show at Studio 54, but we were turned away. We consoled ourselves by writing "Le Freak," the song that would change our lives. *Bettmann/Corbis*

Bernard and I at the Power Station, the longtime home base for the Chic organization. *Allan Tannenbaum*

James Andanson/Sygma/Corbis

Chic at our peak—glamour, fashion, drama, and deep hidden meanings.

Charlyn Zlotnik/Getty Images

Sister Sledge—their *We Are Family* album may have been the best work Chic ever did.
Kees Tabak/Sunshine/RETNA

Bernard completing final preparations on his 'fro before a performance in Santa Monica in 1979. After that show we'd meet Diana Ross for the first time—and by then our exquisite crepe de chine suits had been sweated into "crap do shine."
Cheryl Hong

Alfa Anderson prepping for the Santa Monica show, with Bernard probably talking shit.
Cheryl Hong

At the front of the tour bus in 1979, playing Scrabble with the band. *Cheryl Hong*

Here's our drummer, Tony Thompson, and me at the airport. Even when we were traveling, we kept our fashion game up. *Cheryl Hong*

As a top Motown executive, Suzanne de Passe entrusted the label's biggest star, Diana Ross, to Chic. It was a rocky road to *Diana,* but the album became the bestselling one of Ms. Ross's career. *Isaac Sutton/Ebony Collection via AP Images*

Diana Ross was royalty, but as fun and unpretentious as she was beautiful and glamorous.
Harry Langdon/Getty Images

My brother Bunchie wasn't a rock star, but he was still living the dream.
Darlene Dale

Here I am with the band for my second solo album, filming a video for our single, "State Your Mind." A black man fronting a big-haired white band was a novelty then, but not the popular kind.
David Allen

Working with David Bowie on the *Let's Dance* album transformed my career—and, to some degree, his. *Paul Hardy/GEMS*

Steve Ferrone, John Taylor, Simon Le Bon, and me. I hooked Steve up with the band after they lost their first drummer, Roger Taylor. *John Bellissimo/RETNA*

Debbie Harry was a close friend and an excellent clapper.
Courtesy of Danny Fried; photograph by Dominick Conde

My mother, or "Chic Bev" as her vanity license plate read, having fun in Long Beach.
Author's collection

Me with Brett Ratner and Nick and Julie Anne Rhodes. *David Allen*

Here I am wearing Rick James.
Courtesy of Danny Fried; photograph by Dominick Conde

In the studio with the Thompson Twins, recording *Here's to Future Days*.
David Allen

Even in makeup, hakama, and kendo gloves, I'm not far from my guitar.
Curtis Knapp

The delightful B-52's, whose *Cosmic Thing* album I co-produced.
Andy Freeberg/Hulton Archive/Getty Images

With fellow Honeydrippers Robert Plant and Jeff Beck. *Ebet Roberts/Redferns/Getty Images*

The remarkably talented Vaughan brothers. I first worked with Stevie Ray on the *Let's Dance* album and we remained friends until his tragic death. *Stephanie Chernikowski*

Playing at Live Aid with Madonna, backing up the Thompson Twins.
Courtesy of Danny Fried; photograph by Dominick Conde

At a party at the penthouse of Nirvana's Shyamser Wadude—1980s glamour, decadence, and crazy eyes. *David West*

I fatally messed up my Billy Idol impersonation by turning the fist into a thumbs-up. Otherwise, we're twins. *David Allen*

I became friends with Eddie Murphy while working on the *Coming to America* soundtrack. *Courtesy of Danny Fried; photograph by Dominick Conde*

The downward spiral was in full effect. With my girl-friend Lamya Al-Mugheiry and the actor Jaye Davidson. Jaye was red-hot at the time for his starring role in *The Crying Game*. *Author's collection*

Keith Richards was pivotal, ironically, in getting me into rehab. *Katz/AP Photo*

My first sober show after rehab. I shouted "I belong here!" at the end of the set, confusing everyone, but it had to be said. *Author's collection*

With Bernard and
our interpreter, Masako,
on a promotional tour
in Japan.
Author's collection

Nancy Hunt *(second from right)*,
the head of my charity, the
We Are Family Foundation.
Marc Birnbach

In the wake of 9/11, we gathered to re-record "We Are Family," with a roster of over 200
performers, from Diana Ross and Patti LaBelle to New York City emergency workers.
Theo Wargo/WireImage/Getty Images

nine

Let's Dance . . . Again

On a temperate early autumn night in 1982, I watched the closing credits of *Saturday Night Live* from the mirrored platform bed of my West Side apartment. *SNL* wraps at 1 a.m. In those days, that was when my evenings were just getting started. All I needed to get the show on the road was a bump and a few mouthfuls of vodka.

By '82 I was a full-blown daily drug user, something I'd vowed never to be, given the devastation it had wreaked upon my parents' lives. The drugs were one thing. But I was actually more surprised that I'd morphed into a daily drinker. I was disappointed with myself. Since I was so aware of my habits, I thought I could exercise control over them by setting some ground rules. Chief among them was, *Never drink too much brown liquor, because that's what alcoholics do.* I might have had a taste for the clear stuff, but as a matter of hippie pride, I figured I would never be an alcoholic as long as I kept away from whiskey, the preferred drink of dead-end rednecks and Connecticut gentry in denial.

I headed down the garage ramp to choose from one of four cars I used for club hopping. That night felt right for my 1977 blue Maserati Bora. I slid into the cockpit of its cream-colored interior, the most luxurious to ever grace a derrière, and the perfect ride in this new decade of opulence and extravagance. Wherever I pulled up, the Maserati tended to create something of a minor spectacle, which was the point.

In the early eighties, much like today, most Manhattanites didn't drive, let alone own a car. Little more than a decade earlier, I'd ridden the subways and marched half the length of our fourteen-mile island daily doing community work. But now I rarely walked anywhere. I had a stable of cars and drove everywhere. As a result I'd often find myself chauffeuring a strange variety of stars from club to club. For instance, on this night (technically the early morning), my guest of honor was Billy Idol, who in '82 was at the peak of his celebrity from his smash "White Wedding." He and I used to hit clubs pretty regularly together. To be honest, I can't remember if Billy was actually riding with me or if he just arrived as I pulled up to the Continental. Either way, we walked in together.

THE CITY'S UNDERGROUND CLUB scene seemed to feel a collective responsibility to blow the seventies away. I was with it. I've always been the weird-looking guy in the room, and every decade had an alternative movement that fit me like a glove. I was now planting my freak flag in the eighties art scene, and the Continental was one of the artiest spots of them all. The décor was composed of odds and ends that looked like they were plucked from thrift shops and the Broadway sets of *Pal Joey* or *West Side Story,* but its random-generated eclecticism felt paradoxically futuristic. It was the era of post-punk "Club Kids"—goth music and multicolored hair were all the rage. This colorful menagerie, somewhere between Théâtre de l'Absurde and Dadaism, was the new normal in the early eighties New York demimonde, which would introduce styles in fashion, art, and, for lack of a better word, *lifestyle,* that the mainstream would eventually rip off and domesticate.

ANYWAY, AFTER BILLY AND I walked in and my pupils adjusted to the club's dim light, I noticed something strange enough to catch my eye, even in this den of weirdness: David Bowie was sitting at the back bar, all by himself, soaking up the bizarre scene. Bowie, who'd spent the last decade dressing as an androgynous alien, a harlequin, and an albino "duke," seemed almost mundane in this environment. Even for someone as cool as David Bowie, it was probably a strange brew.

After saying hello to some friends, Billy finally noticed David. I'd been clocking the rock legend all along but pretended to be cool about it. Meanwhile, Billy, never what you might call a wallflower, shouted, *"Fuckin' 'ell, that's David Booooowiiiieeeee!"* and started heading in David's direction, his progress only slightly slowed by a violent spasm of vomiting. Billy wiped his mouth on his sleeve and marched on.

In the dim light, Bowie's hair looked darker than in any picture I'd seen of him. He was quietly sipping orange juice. Compared to the rest of us, he looked laid-back and only mildly interested. I could tell his artist's brain was taking it all in and filing away anything that was worthy of occupying space in his vastly rich conceptual vault.

I studied him for a while. He looked to be in good shape for a dude his age and seemed proud of it (I'd later find out he was taking boxing lessons). I wasn't intimidated by his legend and it wasn't his celebrity that drew me—at that point I'd worked with Diana Ross, clubbed with Andy Warhol, and sold millions of my own records with Chic. But to me, Bowie was on the same level as Miles and Coltrane, James Brown and Prince, Paul Simon and Jimi Hendrix, Joni Mitchell and Nina Simone. In other words, he was a genuine creative artist, doing what I called "that real shit."

I walked up to the bartender, Scotty Taylor, and asked him to introduce me to Bowie. He silently mouthed back, *I don't know him.*

This was odd because Scotty had been a popular bartender since the early days of Studio 54, and he knew *everybody*. I was on my own. I walked over to Bowie and sat on the stool next to him and just started talking. Before I knew it, we'd spiraled into a passionate conversation about music. Just then Billy arrived, none the worse for wear for his eventful journey across the club. I can't recall if he shook Bowie's hand with the one he wiped his mouth with, but it didn't matter; everything was cool. I guess it's a British thing: Drunken barfing is all in a night's hang. At any rate Billy couldn't get in a word edgewise because David and I had already locked into such a heavy conversation.

"Damn," I said, "I had no idea you were so seriously into jazz." Bowie had just recited a veritable who's who of cats that he was into, including Lester Bowie (no relation), the trumpeter from the Art Ensemble of Chicago.

"Nile, I grew up in England, where we have BBC Radio," he said. "They played everything that was popular—soul, blues, jazz, R&B, and rock. We don't separate the music on the radio by race or genres." We wound up talking all night about all sorts of music. I don't remember anyone ever bothering us; we were like old friends sitting on a couch in someone's living room. The wide-ranging, reference-heavy, autodidactic rap made me feel like I was back in the mix of the beatniks, hippies, and jazzers of my youth. At some point I must have given him my phone number, but I don't remember doing so.

SOMETIME IN THE LATE SEVENTIES, I bought a house in Westport, Connecticut, and I was renovating it at the time. One day I went up to check on its progress and Al, the general contractor, told me, "Hey, Nile, some guy pretending to be David Bowie called up. I knew it was a prank, so I hung up. He kept calling back, so I kept hanging up." I laughed and didn't take this seriously at all. Then, out of the clear blue, I got a call from Bernard Edwards. Nard and I were a little on the skids at the time. Chic's sales were dwindling with every release and I was working on my solo album, *Adventures in the Land of the Good Groove*. Nard and I knew that my going solo meant the beginning of the end of Chic, and the phone conversation between us had a very uncomfortable tone.

"Yo, man," he said, speaking very quickly, "David Bowie called my house and after he talked to me for a while I realized he must have thought I was you. So I gave him your telephone number up at the crib in Westport, and I figured that the shit was probably cool."

I just said, "Yeah, it's cool." Then we hung up.

Our relationship was clearly changing. Nard, who was always the stronger one, seemed to be more affected by the industry's snubbing. The person who'd always been the bandleader was becoming more and more unreliable. His drug habit made him a hermit. In retrospect, I think he was afraid of failing, so he did everything not to finish our records. I felt like he didn't believe in me anymore, so I set out to prove that I was better than ever and worked at a pace that he simply couldn't match. Of course, I had an unfair advantage—most of our song ideas started with me (and the best ones ended with him), I was an insomniac, a bachelor with no kids, and thrived on anxiety.

I reflected on the abrupt phone call and the distance growing between us, took two heaping hits of blow, and then shouted from my balcony down to the construction crew:

"The next time that dude calls saying he's David Bowie, *give me the phone.*"

Eventually, Bowie called again.

DAVID AND I AGREED to meet at the ritzy Bemelmen's Bar at the Carlyle Hotel. When I mentioned I was meeting Bowie, my then girlfriend and her friends insisted on planting themselves in the bar just to get a glimpse of him.

To be honest, I was a little excited, too.

This meeting was the flip side of our first. We weren't in the dark and throbbing Continental at 5:30 a.m., but at the elegant Carlyle in the middle of the afternoon. The sudden shift in context must have thrown us, because we each walked in and sat silently, a few barstools apart, for at least twenty minutes. I'd gotten there a couple of minutes after our scheduled rendezvous time, and I truly didn't recognize the thin white man at the bar with his head down.

Eventually I walked out to the lobby pay phone and called David's office.

"What time is he getting here?"

"He's been there for at least half an hour."

At which point I went over to the only sort of Bowie-looking guy in the place and introduced myself. We shared a good laugh at the absurdity, but our missed connection only made me like Bowie even more. It wouldn't have been racist or odd for Bowie to assume the only black man in the exclusive Carlyle bar that afternoon was Nile Rodgers. After all, we had scheduled a meeting. But David must have thought there was just another young black man at the Carlyle, since in my designer day clothes I didn't look like the Nile Rodgers he'd met at an after-hours bar.

I CALL BOWIE THE PICASSO OF ROCK and roll (much to his embarrassment and discomfort) because of his prodigious creativity, but also because he looks sort of like Picasso drew him. Famously, one of his eyes is blue and the other gray-green. He's extremely handsome, of course, but his features are slightly unbalanced and draw you to him, with a touch of vulnerability or danger in his otherwise aristocratic mien. He changed me, helped me, and supported me almost as much as Bernard did, but more dramatically: With Bowie my metamorphosis was accelerated and compressed, and came about, improbably, at a moment when the music industry considered me unworthy of working with an iconic figure in the business.

This time around, unlike my run with Diana Ross, my partnership with musical royalty would be even more blasphemous: The sovereign was a white rocker.

* * *

ONCE WE CLEARED THE AIR at the Carlyle and exchanged some small talk, Bowie made his proposition. "I'm wondering what it would be like to do a record together," he said.

Bingo. I'd been thinking the same thing. At the time, I was deep into my own experimental new record and assumed our musical ambitions were perfectly aligned. The concept of my new album had taken me a little out of my comfort zone—and for the first time, I didn't have a partner to work through it with me. I leaned into Bowie, feeling like I'd found a kindred artistic spirit. "Yeah. I'm trying to develop new ideas like I did when I started, and I have a young engineer and we're working on altering music in new ways, creating new sounds," I said.

Bowie responded that he'd always felt the freedom to be flexible and do music the way he wanted. He was never afraid to change, and never wanted to limit himself to a certain audience, class, or sound. David's position felt artistic without a hint of egotism. It almost sounded as if he had no choice. He was *compelled* to find what was beyond the horizon. His words were literally music to my ears—just what I needed to hear to carry on my experimental solo project with gusto.

Which is not to say that I didn't already have a healthy sense of the importance of my solo work. By the time I'd met David, I hadn't had a hit since Diana Ross, way back in 1980, but I was feeling self-assured. Bowie's bravery seemed to come from being clear-headed and sober, but it was drugs and booze that gave me the confidence to take chances again after five flops in a row. I believed my mission was to get everybody to see music my way. "A kite flies highest *against* the wind," I had read when I was younger, and time had proven it out. Almost all my commercial success had been a struggle. I'd always managed to find the guts to embark on the things I was most afraid to tackle. Whenever I had to screw up the courage to do something risky—but right—I repeated to myself a famous movie line:

"Courage is being scared to death—but saddling up anyway."
—JOHN WAYNE

So while I knew instinctively that I had to keep following my own vision, David's independent spirit was infectious and helped me refocus.

Unlike Diana Ross, David Bowie didn't have a record company to answer to, because, believe it or not, *he didn't have a record deal* at the time. And I didn't have Chic. While we were in the middle of working on our seventh studio record, our record company decided not to renew our contract. So Bowie and I were in the same boat, both a bit lost at sea. We'd have to figure it out together—but without a record company breathing down our necks, everything could be done on our terms. I'd always loved collaborating. And because I hadn't learned how to edit consistently yet—to keep the good and toss the bad—the Bowie project came at the perfect time in my artistic development.

I was in *heaven*. A new liberator had entered my life. Just as Diana's pedigree allowed Chic to compose pop music on another level, Bowie's history, innovation, artistic brilliance, and white-English-rocker status bestowed upon me a freedom that was almost unimaginable. For a while I started to think like him, compelled and committed to change and transform.

IN THE MINDS OF THE MUSIC INDUSTRY, Chic's technical facility was below that of rock artists, or at least that's the way it felt to me. Maybe it's because we weren't flashy or because we played so effortlessly. Or maybe it was just because we were considered disco, which most people experienced in a club, played by a DJ, not by a live band swinging their instruments around. But where did they think those records came from? The whole thing was full of irony. Many of rock's biggest superstars can't even play the basic chord changes on our very *first* record, "Everybody Dance," because they don't understand the fundamentals of harmony and chord theory, let alone the countless jazz inversions on our later compositions. Still, we were deemed musically inferior to most three-chord rock musicians by music critics. But not by Bowie.

He respected what I did and, more important, what I thought. David decided to fund our project himself. A few days later, he came over to my apartment at 44 West Sixty-second Street, a building called Lincoln Plaza Towers, and we started formal preproduction, which typically involved conceiving, writing, and arranging the material. At the time, Bowie wasn't especially theatrical looking, a far cry from the redheaded, heavily made-up bloke who appeared on the cover of *Scary Monsters*.★ His day-to-day appearance was natty but unassuming, which helped me get used to dealing with him as a friend and partner, not a rock icon. After a few meetings, this new guy in the nice suits was just . . . David. His seemingly casual appearance was actually the flowering of his next drag: He was delving into the eighties metrosexual world of high fashion, a precursor to what's called "Executive Realness" in vogueing competitions, where men sashay down the runway in a stylized version of the archetypal businessman's suit.

There was one thing I noticed about David's appearance that was a little freaky: a tattoo on his lower leg. When I asked him what it meant, he said, "It's the Serenity Prayer in Japanese."

I said, "What's the Serenity Prayer?"

"It's how I remember to stay sober."

I thought to myself, Wow, he has to be seriously committed to that concept to have it inked on his body for the rest of his life. So out of respect for David's sobriety, I changed my behavior around him—as best I could.

★ ★ ★

★Ironically, my next-door neighbor was Tony Visconti, a producer who'd worked on a number of Bowie records, including *Scary Monsters*. His office/apartment was in my building, which had thirty-plus floors and at least five units per floor. But his was directly next door! What are the odds of that in a city of more than eight million people?

DURING ONE OF MY MANY MEETINGS with David at my apartment, the test pressing arrived for my just-finished solo record. We listened to the entire record together. "Nile," he said afterwards, "if you make a record for me half as good as that, I'll be very happy."

I was flattered but a little bewildered. I knew it was a flop right away. I'd been so afraid of being labeled a disco musician that I was too tentative about the album's direction. And the songs weren't hooky enough. Over all, I wasn't clear philosophically or sure what I was trying to say. But during the recording, the cocaine reassured me the record was cool. The problem was, I'd started to believe the coke.

In a Bill Cosby skit, he asks a cocaine user at a party, "Hey, man, why do you do that stuff?" And the user answers, "Because it intensifies my personality." Cosby retorts, "Yeah, but what if you're an asshole?"

Now that I had the record in hand, I had begun to suspect that I was becoming an asshole. I was *trying* to make an innovative and commercial solo record, but I knew I hadn't gotten it right. It would be my sixth consecutive flop in a row. Black radio was the only available outlet to me as a solo artist—I was definitely not getting spins on rock or pop-oriented stations—and the format was not supportive of my experimentation. To make matters worse, the new trend at black radio was rap, which was youthful and street oriented, the exact opposite of old-school, couture-designer culture. I knew my record was over before it started. My only consolation was that *David dug it*. We continually riffed on the state of the music industry and the world in general. At the end of all this musing, we believed that if we did a record together that was artistic, primal, and made us feel good, that'd be a job well done.

Then David really threw me a curveball.

"Nile, darling," he said, using a typical British expression, "I'd like you to do what you do best." His voice had a lyrical power that could mobilize me like Churchill. After his initial praise of my solo record, I thought he was talking about the two of us expanding my new experimental approach to composition. I was beaming with expectant pride—until he finished the sentence: "I want you to make *hits*."

"You want me to make *hits*?" I was a little taken aback.

"Yes, hits. I want you to make *hits*. That's what you do best. You make hits."

"How do you know that's what I do best?" I said, slightly irritated.

"Because you do. It's a fact. I can even hear it in this record, and that's what I'd like you to do."

"Really?" I hid my disappointment. "Okay. Cool. If that's what you want, that's what we'll do."

I WAS A PROFESSIONAL who hadn't had a hit in six attempts, and who dearly wanted a shot at producing Bowie. Still, I felt a little hurt, like after all of our conversations about music and freedom I was being ordered back to the hit-making plantation. David was the last person on earth I thought I'd be making hits with. To be honest, I assumed David's cachet would change the industry's concept of me from disco artist and producer to just *artist* and producer, a big difference. I was sure this conversion would give me the freedom to write what I wanted without worrying about getting radio play on the handful of urban stations.

Plus, what was it that he liked about the solo record, which was anything but a hit? Maybe he could hear something I couldn't? Maybe he was ignoring the fact that it was a black man's record, and to him, trained by the BBC's eclectic format, it was just music, and by that standard, it was actually successful "hit" music? These thoughts rambled through my mind and lingered for a moment, and then reality kicked back in.

I've always believed that a producer's job is a *service* job. I don't get paid to give you what *I* want; I get paid to give you what *you* want. Even if I have to show you what you want, because you don't always know that you want it. David's directive was clear and he was not interested in doing *Scary Monsters 2* (no offense to Tony Visconti). He wanted to make *hits*. The professional producer in me was like the Terminator. I would not stop until my mission was completed.

David's edict forced me to be both Nile and Bernard, complicated and artful enough to satisfy myself (and the former music teachers in my head) but able to throttle back just enough to connect to the masses. This was our tried and tested DHM hit-making formula. All I had to do was exactly what we'd done before. David had chosen the right tool for the right job.

OUR MUSICAL RELATIONSHIP developed rapidly. David asked me to work on some demos in Switzerland, where he lived part of the time. A few weeks later, I touched down in Geneva, landing right in the middle of a picture-postcard winter wonderland. David picked me up at the airport in a slick Volvo model that wasn't available in the States. As we zipped along the icy roads, David confided in me: "I'm legally blind in one eye," he said, or something to that effect. The speedometer seemed to never drop below 100 kilometers per hour. I was scared shitless, but his moves were pretty good.

We arrived in one piece at his beautiful Swiss chalet in the lovely town of Lausanne, on the banks of Lake Geneva, and immediately started the next level of preproduction on the album that would later be called *Let's Dance*.

By now "dance" was a loaded word for me. The Disco Sucks backlash had given me a post-traumatic-stress–like disorder, and I'd vowed not to write any songs with that word in them for a long time. I was shamed out of using a word—"dance"—that represented one of the most primal sources of joy all over the world and throughout human history, not to mention being the key word in several million-selling records that I'd written myself! It gets even more outrageous: In my early twenties I'd studied dance with famed choreographer Syvilla Fort, who taught the Dunham technique, which was modern with a ballet-training regimen. (Katherine Dunham has been called "the Matriarch and Queen Mother of Black Dance";

she and Ms. Fort are among the most legendary names in American black dance history.) Later in life I even had the Nicholas Brothers tap on a Chic record, out of sheer admiration for them. I had a spiritual and a physical connection to the word "dance." How could I be afraid of it? It's not impossible to explain.

In almost every sphere of life, I'd seen the same pattern: The dominant culture manages to direct less powerful people away from their cultural, financial, geographical, and residential base so that the dominant culture can move in and claim it. They rename those assets and, presto chango, you've got gentrification. This dynamic is nothing new: Ask the Native Americans, who had the land they were living on "discovered" right out from under them. So I thought maybe now was a good time to reclaim a word that was already mine as much as anyone else's. Still, I was nervous about the "D" word, because while I didn't want to leave the word around for someone to steal, I didn't want to be seen as a one-trick pony either. It helped that my name wasn't on the album cover: As a well-regarded white rocker, David had the freedom to use the word if he wanted. And when David said, "Let's dance," no one ran into the streets to set records on fire.

NOT LONG AFTER I ARRIVED IN SWITZERLAND, Bowie strolled into my bedroom with a guitar.

"Hey, Nile, listen to this," he said, his skinny frame silhouetted just inside the doorway. "I think it could be a hit."

He started strumming a twelve-string acoustic guitar that had only six strings. What followed was a folksy sketch of a composition with a solid melody: The only problem was it sounded to me like "Donovan meets Anthony Newley." And I don't mean that as a compliment. It wasn't *bad* by artistic standards, but I'd been mandated to make hits, and could only hear what was missing.

The next few minutes felt like hours. We had spent a fair amount of time together in New York, and I thought I knew what he meant when he said "make hits." We'd listened to tons of records—even some rare ones that we'd borrowed from famed music producer Jerry Wexler. We'd listened to Henry Mancini's theme from *Peter Gunn* over and over—and would later lift its horn line for "Let's Dance"—and studied Little Richard. We looked at scores of album covers, press photos, and other artwork and talked about what we considered cool. And then this: a strummy folk guitar part with a moving voice in the chords? It didn't even sound *close* to what I'd call a hit.

I called a mutual friend in New York for some advice. I said, "David walked into my room this morning and played a song for me that he says is a hit. I don't hear it. Is he trying to test me?" Our mutal friend was blunt: "If he says he thinks it's a hit, then he thinks it's a hit. He would never trick you; he's not that kind of person." With that in mind, I went back to David and asked him to teach me the song. I scribbled down the chords and said I'd take a crack at an arrangement.

I headed back to my bedroom with a sheaf of manuscript paper and my guitar and started reworking the song. I soon discovered the diamond in the rough. I emerged with the arrangement while David called Mountain Studios in Montreux, which was owned by Queen. He asked the studio manager, or maybe it was Claude Nobs, creator of the Montreux Jazz Festival, to round up a handful of local musicians to do a session. As it turned out, the musicians were jazz cats and they did a pretty solid version of the charts I'd written. Gone were the strummy chords, gone was the moving voice. I'd replaced them with staccato stabs and a strict harmonic interpretation. I used silence and big open spaces to create the groove and kept rearranging it on the spot, like I always did with Chic. David quickly got down with the reshaping of his song. We had a lot of fun and laughter in that Swiss studio with those terrific musicians (whose names I unfortunately can't remember). Laughter is key to my sessions—the unconditionally loving parent in the room. David dug the session.

"If you *really* like that," I said, "then you'll love it when we get back to New York and you hear *my* guys play it."

We ended our European sojourn with a big celebratory dinner

with the jazz cats at a famous local restaurant in Lausanne. I don't remember cutting anything else in Switzerland. If that was a test, I passed.

BACK IN NEW YORK, David booked my favorite recording studio, the Power Station, along with Bob Clearmountain, my favorite engineer, for a three-week stint. I'm pretty sure the concept was to tentatively see how things would go with my crew, which is why he only booked three weeks. He arrived from London packing plenty of ideas. He had three or four demos at various stages of development, and four tunes that were already released that we would cover. He also had "Let's Dance," the demo we'd made in Switzerland.

The cover songs were the group Metro's "Criminal World," "Cat People," a dirgelike ballad he'd already done for the shared-name film with Giorgio Moroder, and "China Girl," which he and Iggy Pop had written for an earlier project.

The thumbnails would become the songs "Shake It," "Modern Love," "Ricochet," and "Without You."

My first job was to build the morale of the band members, who were playing together for the first time. Though I had my regular Chic keyboardist Rob Sabino, my other go-to players, bassist Bernard Edwards and drummer Tony Thompson, were not on the first session. They'd become less punctual during the last few Chic records. Tony and Nard were so unreliable from drugging, and I was afraid they'd be late for a recording session where David was watching every penny like a hawk. As producer, I was responsible for keeping the project on budget. So I decided they were too risky. They were two of the best players I've ever worked with and I was sad not to have them involved, but I had a job to do. So I hired superstar drummer Omar Hakim, and bassist Carmine Rojas, whose main gig at the time was with Rod Stewart. I figured having a multicultural group made up of experienced rockers was a good way to start, since I didn't know what other material David would be bringing.

The band was acutely aware of the pressure we were under. The level of scrutiny any new Bowie record was sure to face could have given them jitters, so I worked hard to be the same old Nile they all knew. Part of that meant regularly cracking jokes to remind them that they were working for *me,* not Bowie. "After his ass goes home, motherfuckers, I'll still be here," I said to the group. It worked. The joke's purpose was twofold: It made them feel better about being paid single scale (less than what I normally paid session musicians back then), and let them know that I'd make it up to them on our next record together. I had a reputation as a generous contractor, and I had to live with these guys. On every level, I needed them to feel comfortable, and I wanted David to feel comfortable with them, too. So I kicked things off by recording "Let's Dance," which I knew David already liked.

"Let's Dance" was, as David described it, "a postmodern homage to the Isley Brothers' 'Twist and Shout,'" one of the many records we'd listened to during the preproduction phase. The band broke into the groove, which was followed by an eight-bar pocket trumpet solo.

In the words of Billy Idol, *"Fuckin' 'ell!"* The moment we finished off that trumpet solo, I knew we were in new territory and could play by different rules—rules that applied only to white rockers and maybe Miles, Prince, or Michael Jackson. Now I had the freedom to venture beyond pop into jazz territory. I was free to allow cats to *improvise*—on a pop single! It was heaven. I'd played in bands like this before, bands that ranged beyond the usual boundaries of R&B and pop, but we could never get a record deal; the labels always changed their mind when they saw we were black. With Bowie, I finally got to do what so many white rock artists take for granted: just make great music, without worrying about categories. And even if it was only temporary, I was ecstatic.

My instinct to start with "Let's Dance" paid off: We cut the song in one or two takes and it set the tone for the rest of the project. The song was going to be a major hit, and we all knew it. David relaxed into my team's capable, wickedly creative, loving hands.

We knew we wouldn't often get chances like this, so we attacked David's music like an invading army. It was a siege. After years of being denied entry through the front door of rock and roll, we had our battering rams poised to knock down the walls. The rhythm section musicians, who were all black and Latino, were playing like uncaged animals, finally free to push pop to higher levels. After we were solidly into the recording process, I finally brought in Tony Thompson, who struck the drums so hard that the sound pressure levels dimmed the studio lights with each backbeat. It was like, "Yeah, motherfuckers, *take that*!"

Actually, Tony's rage was probably partially directed at me, too. This record would have been a dream come true for the black rocker, but I only called him to play on three songs, even though he was the hardest-hitting rock drummer I've ever known. David was impressed by him, and I knew he was wondering why I hadn't used Tony for the whole record, but David didn't know about the drug use. To be honest, I was in almost as bad shape as my former bandmates. But this was the opportunity of a lifetime and I only had one chance to get it right. I was always committed to Bernard, and wanted him on my "hit" rock-and-roll album, so once I reached the stage where things had passed the point where he could fatally fuck them up, I called on him. He came through with flying colors.

Bernard only played on one song on the album: "Without You." I brought him in to deal with a tricky bass line, one that Carmine Rojas had struggled with.

Nard walked into the control room (precisely on time), said a quick general hello, unpacked his bass, and went out to the studio. He sat in the bass chair and plugged in his gear. He took a look at the short asymmetrical chart on the music stand and said to me, "Is this the song?"

I replied, "Yes, that's it." David could sense there was something uneasy in the air, because unlike the other sessions, there was no laughing and joking on this one. David knew Bernard was my Chic Organization partner, but Nard treated us like strangers.

After taking just a few minutes to get Bernard's technical sound correct (a process that could sometimes take hours, but not with Chic's A-team and in our home base, the Power Station), Nard told the engineer Bob Clearmountain, "Run the motherfucker." One take later he glared through the control-room window.

"Is *that* what you want?"

David and I smiled.

"Yeah, bro, that's what we want."

Prior to that session, I had bet David that Nard would finish the song in fifteen minutes. He did it in thirteen. I was never more proud of him in my life, and it happened on the last day of basic recording. David shrugged his shoulders in approval and disbelief, and I thought to myself: "Chic Organization. That's how we do it! One take, fifteen minutes. These rhythm tracks are *done*."

Bernard quietly packed up his bass and walked out. He was pissed off that I hadn't called him for the rest of the album, but he knew that I was proud to show off his genius. David was so impressed with my guys that he took almost everyone, including the background singers, the Simms Brothers, on the "Serious Moonlight" tour that followed.

A COUPLE OF DAYS before the Nard incident, David played another song for me he said he thought was a hit—Iggy Pop's version of "China Girl." I didn't think it was a radio hit. I liked it, but it was clearly an album cut. We had recorded other smashes earlier that day, and I thought we'd reached a pretty clear understanding on the direction I was trying to steer the project toward. His insistence on this song being a smash was a little discomforting. The original "China Girl" was way overproduced to my tight, minimalist ears, but David insisted that the song was a hit. Confused, I again called that same mutual friend and asked, "Are you sure he isn't trying to play a trick on me?" And again the friend told me, just as he'd said in Switzerland after David performed "Let's Dance" solo in my bedroom, "If David said he thinks it's a hit, he really thinks it's a hit."

Oh my God, what do I do now? I wondered.

Fortunately, the end of the day was approaching. We were working in half-day sessions, as did most black and jazz acts, to reduce costs. I dismissed the band a little early to buy time to think the "China Girl" dilemma through. I needed to find the song's DHM.

At home, I played the song's verse chords and soon discovered that if I changed the held power chord triad to a major chord that moved down to a major seventh and then to the sixth, it sounded sweeter and more Asian. I did a little more fiddling until— *checkmate*—I had a catchy Asian-sounding riff I was very pleased with. This was going to work out after all.

So I did what I usually did when the clock struck 1 a.m.: I went out clubbing all night. I arrived home around 6 a.m., slept about two hours, called Salon De Tokyo health spa and got a culturally sympathetic massage before heading to the studio. I worked on the charts until David arrived, trying to give the song a more Asian vibe, to match the new guitar part I'd come up with.

I worked the guitar riff into the band's arrangement. Accustomed to the supercompetitive world of urban dance music, I kept trawling for an edge. My formula always required starting my songs with hooks and using breakdowns or featuring solo instruments— this new guitar riff sounded very hooky and by itself it did all those things. Now the only thing left was to find the song's DHM. I thought the lyrics of this song sounded like a junkie's ode if ever there was one. One of the nicknames for heroin among users is "China White." On the other hand, cocaine is "Girl." I knew Bowie was sober *now,* but because the song was old, it might have been about speedballing, combining coke with heroin.

So I tried to visualize a pop drug song. Aware of Bowie's commitment to sobriety, I wasn't sure if he'd go along with all this, but mainly I just focused on making our little "drug ditty" a hit. I wanted David to be proud of his record, *whatever* he was talking about. At the end of the day it was his record, and my job was to help him realize his vision.

David arrived at the studio in a very upbeat mood. He looked so normal that it made me more nervous, because at least a wild, wacky, art rocker just might accept my ultra-pop arrangement as absurd, ridiculous, and therefore cool. I was never so scared in my life as when I played that Asian hooky lick for him. He could have easily thought it corny, because compared to the original song by Iggy Pop, my version was not as hard rocking. To my surprise (and relief), he liked it and told me so with great enthusiasm. I said, "Well, if you like that, then listen to *this*." I had the arrangement written out for the entire band. We played it and recorded it right on the spot. There was almost no drama in the recording of the *Let's Dance* album. It was fun and full of surprises, the biggest of which was a then-unknown guitarist from Texas named Stevie Ray Vaughan.

David had seen Stevie play at the Montreux Jazz Festival a few months earlier and knew he wanted to work with him. If you want an example of David's artistic genius, this is it. He saw newbie Stevie Ray play live once, and that was enough to convince him to invite him to record with a group of relatively unknown rocking rookies.

Stevie certainly walked into the Power Station as if he belonged there. He was grandiose, gregarious, and generous. At the beginning of every day's recording session, I would have the assistant take everybody's lunch order so the food would be there when we took our short lunch break. Stevie, instead of ordering that day's lunch, got on the phone and ordered tomorrow's lunch: next-day-air delivery barbecue from Texas, for everybody, and he paid for it all. This was the ultimate bonding gesture. Everybody loved this southern stranger from that moment on. He was the real deal, and he fit right into our little lifeboat. If this record turned out to be a hit, we thought it would be all our passports into the larger world of rock-and-roll pop.

David and I were the only two musicians on the project whose names were familiar to Stevie prior to his arrival. Though David had brought him in on the project, Stevie and I were the ones who'd form a lifelong bond of love and respect. I still remember the look of astonishment on his face when he heard the first track we played for him, "Let's Dance." He could sense this group of anonymous musicians were about to make history. We'd do it again a few years later when I produced and cowrote Stevie's historical recording with his brother Jimmie, *Family Style,* but it was *Let's Dance* that first exposed the world to Stevie Ray Vaughan's spectacular virtuosity.

Both Stevie and David ripped through and completed all their parts in just two days. There was gris-gris sprinkled on every aspect of this record. None of us would ever be the same after its release; all our careers skyrocketed. We were bluesmen at heart, so was *Let's Dance* our metaphorical crossroads? Like Robert Johnson at Dockery Plantation, had we unknowingly sold our souls for this massive success?

MAKING A HIT RECORD IS VERY DIFFICULT. The gates are controlled and restricted, and competition is keen, regardless of who or what you are. I've made so many hits, so many times, but I've made plenty of flops, too—I know that for a record to hit, everything has to line up just right. But making David's hit album was the easiest job of my life. A hit record without a hitch. True, we had four cover songs, but if it was that simple, then why not put four cover songs on every record? True, David was a superstar, but he wouldn't have been the first superstar to bomb. There was some unexplainable voodoo on *Let's Dance.* I was working with most of the exact same people as always and recording in the exact same place as always, and was, by the way, at the peak of my addiction, but that record worked like nothing I'd done before, even with my long string of gold and platinum records.

In the end we completed *Let's Dance* in just seventeen days, mixed and delivered. David was happy and I was in job-well-done party mode. In just over two weeks, I'd reconstructed and rearranged every single song and written all the sweetening charts (horns, backing vocals, and other overdubs), save for Bowie's "head charts," where he *sang* the parts instead of having me write them down on music paper, the first time I'd ever seen that done in a studio situation.

And on top of all that, Bob and I even changed the keyboards on one track without telling David (until now, if he reads this)—he'd given me strict orders not to use a certain keyboard on the album, preferring instead a synthetic version of it. I decided the real one worked better with his voice and we switched it without telling him.

Let's Dance WAS THE FASTEST I've ever produced an album, and Bowie's biggest-selling record. Critically acclaimed, it landed him on the covers of *Time* and *Rolling Stone*. I got to glimpse another world. It was the perk- and privileged-filled world of the global rock star. Everything was perfect—except for David's reluctance to give me the same props he'd bestowed upon his previous producers. He seemed almost embarrassed by the mega-success of *Let's Dance,* even though all along he'd insisted on "making hits." It was such a strange turn for me, because we'd been so close during the production. Maybe I made more out of our relationship than I should have, because of my extreme admiration for him as an artist and the fact that he took a chance on me when the industry must have been pressuring him against it ten times harder than Motown and Diana were pressuring Suzanne de Passe on my last hit record. Or maybe it was because in Bernard's absence, I transferred my feelings for him onto Bowie.

I was hurt by how little I was mentioned in his media coverage and how he tended to prefer discussing his earlier work whenever he was interviewed. Remember, I was working off six consecutive flops and needed the praise and recognition to help rebuild my career. He didn't have to love the record now, I guess, but I knew he loved it when we were doing it. And I understand that just because something sold wildly, you don't necessarily have to like it. To date, "Le Freak" is my biggest—though not my favorite—but I have to acknowledge its achievement. I can only speculate that David, being a real artist, sees his entire body of work as the important thing and felt the world was starting to overidentify him with this single album and its hugely popular songs. I could relate: I felt the same about the way the industry pigeonholed me after Chic's hit singles.

I quickly got over my disappointment. My name was on the record, and the industry—including other artists—recognized my contribution to Bowie's commercial triumph.

Once again I was in demand.

A little over a year after the release of *Let's Dance,* I was named *Billboard* magazine's Number One Singles Producer of the Year. *Let's Dance* topped the charts in both the U.S. and the U.K., selling eight million records and netting three Top Ten singles. The "Serious Moonlight" tour was David's biggest ever, grossing over $100 million. It was a huge moment for him, but not his first: He was always the man. But suddenly, at least to those in the know, I was the man, too.

Despite all that, I still needed, for whatever insecure reason, for David to acknowledge me and what we'd done together. Years later, at a charity function for the ARChive of Contemporary Music, he did. We were at a hip little club called S.O.B.'s in New York's Greenwich Village. While giving his speech, he said, "And this goes out to Nile Rodgers, the only man who could make me start a song with a chorus!" Which of course was my reworking of that little ditty he strummed out for me in Switzerland: "Let's dance. Put on your red shoes and dance the blues." That shout-out made my night. I don't think anybody in the audience had a clue what the hell he was talking about, but I knew, and that's all that counted. Case closed. I love and respect you, David. Thanks.

ten

Who's That Opening-Act Girl?

ON THANKSGIVING DAY OF 1983, AROUND THE TIME I WAS STARTING an exciting new phase of my career, my brother Bunchy was starting the next phase of his. "Exciting" might not be the right word to describe Bunchy's career path. And he was about to involve Mom—who'd been trying her hand at buying and flipping houses—in a new family business.

Like his father, Bunchy was a jack of many trades: musician, comedian, carpenter. Since this was the eighties and everybody was into drugs on some level, Bunchy had decided to switch to narcotics as his main vocation and pretty soon had a fairly profitable business going. Drugs were never taboo in my family, of course, and dealers were always around. It was natural and at times very convenient to have my brother slide into the roster of suppliers for my ever-growing habit.

One day Bunchy had to go to L.A. to drop off two kilos of coke to a customer, only to find that the buyer had suddenly reneged. Unwilling to risk flying back to New York with two bulky keys of blow, he decided to leave the drugs with Mom until he could find another West Coast buyer. In the meantime, Bunchy wasn't opposed to encouraging Mom's entrepreneurial streak. "If you can off them," he told her, "I only want thirty Gs for each key."

"Okay, baby," she said. Ever since Bobby had hooked her for good, recreational drugs had never been an issue for Mom. In this way, as in so many others, she was ahead of her time. By the early eighties in America, coke was a status item among the rich and famous, especially when they were of the Caucasian persuasion. Powdered coke was called "the rich man's drug" in the hood—yes, there were rich black folks and some of them were secure or reckless enough to devote their riches to the acquisition of coke, but let's keep it real: There were not enough of them to fuel an entire drug industry.

My mom, as you might imagine, had a knack for getting into the action quickly. She sold both kilos within two days. My brother scored the amount he wanted, sixty thousand dollars, and she kept the rest for her effort, a tidy little sum for a couple of days' work. So they decided to partner again and make it a family business.

My brother delivered the weight and my mother was soon supplying coke to a cream-of-the-crop customer base of top L.A. professionals. She never succumbed to low-level street dealing (and it's hard for me to imagine her holding down a corner in L.A.). Good times, indeed. Soon she moved to an exclusive enclave called Diamond Bar and started rolling in a cherry red Mercedes with CHICBEV vanity plates.

For a long time, I had no idea what they were up to. I never questioned Mom's upscale move, which seemed completely plausible. After all, I was paying the bills—I'd been covering their bills for years now—and she was also involved in different legitimate businesses that I was seeding. Nobody seriously questioned Mom about her lifestyle—even her police detective boyfriend didn't know how she made her bread.

Yes, here's another wonderful detail about Mom's midlife career as a high-end drug dealer: She dealt right under a detective's nose and he *never had a clue.* They'd met about a year earlier. He'd been investigating a murder that she'd witnessed in front of her former apartment.

Mom may have managed to deceive her detective boyfriend, but the unsavory neighbors in her former hood were far more savvy, which is how she wound up getting robbed and brutally pistol-whipped.

One afternoon my mother made the mistake of giving a female friend from the old nabe a nickel tour of her new Diamond Bar house. During the tour there was a knock on the door, and before she knew it, three armed masked men had pushed the friend out of the way, stormed straight upstairs to Mom's bedroom, and pinned her down on the bed. They started pistol-whipping her, screaming, "Where's the money, bitch?" My mom insisted there was no money in the house, but they kept beating her and demanding cash. Pretty soon blood was running from her head like a fountain. "All I kept thinking to myself," she told me later, "was, 'just don't pass out.' "

Mom decided that if she stayed alert, the robbers wouldn't kill her. So she never stopped talking, which practically drove them nuts.

"The more I talked," she said, "the more they screamed and hit me with the butt of the gun! They then tied me up and started to ransack the house. They kept saying they'd blow my fucking brains out if I didn't tell them where the money was. I stuck to my story and repeated there was no money—over and over."

Even under duress, Mom never let on that the coke money, not to mention a mega-wad of cash from a house she'd just sold, was hidden in the closet—in a pair of boots. After wrecking the house and coming up empty, the interlopers dealt a sharp blow to her head and decided to wait for my brother Bobby, who they knew was on his way over. As it turned out, they'd been casing the house and knew all about my family's comings and goings. So they hid behind Mom's bedroom door and waited. When Bobby walked in, they pounced, pointed a gun to his head, and threw a makeshift hood over his face. Then they took him down to the garage and locked him in the trunk of his car, a blue Mercedes, to soften him up for an interrogation.

Before they got to that, someone knocked on the door. It was Jerry, a sometime boyfriend of Mom's who was also a successful record producer and the partner of Joe Jackson (Michael's father). When no one answered his knock on the door, he picked up the house key from under the mat and let himself in. When Jerry walked blithely into the living room, surprising the crooks, they panicked and shot him three times. He fell back outside against his Rolls-Royce and collapsed to the ground. Complete pandemonium ensued. The robbers jumped into my brother Bobby's Mercedes and drove it right through the closed garage door, Grade-B-action-movie-style, abandoning their own Cadillac in front of Mom's new crib. This was not the Mensa break-and-enter team.

Meanwhile, Bobby was still locked in the trunk. They drove his car to a housing complex, opened the trunk, removed his hood. One of the men pointed a gun to his head and fired. Fortunately for Bobby, the chamber was empty. The gunman tried four more times without a discharge. Undoubtedly exasperated, they untied him, put him behind the wheel of his car, and told him to not look back. A few moments later, Bobby spotted a man walking down the sidewalk and related his ordeal to him. He asked the guy to drive him home as Bobby had no idea where he was. The man instead called the police and gave Bobby five bucks for gas. It turns out the tank was empty.

When Bobby finally got home, the police on the scene told him Mom was in the hospital and that she'd be okay. To everyone's surprise, the perpetrator's car was still parked at Mom's house. This looked to be an easy case to crack. Even the address on the abandoned Caddy's registration matched the location of the housing complex where the kidnappers had tried to fire a gun in Bobby's face.

Incredibly, though, the case was never solved. Of course, because of my mom's drug dealing, she'd never press charges, but the police never seriously followed up on the case even though they had a hot trail leading to the probable perps. For some mysterious reason, they just didn't seem interested in solving the crime.

Bobby thinks the cops were bent out of shape by the fact that all the black people involved in the story owned high-end cars. A Rolls-Royce, two Mercedes Benzes—hell, even the robbers drove a Cadillac. Most black people with very high-end cars have experienced some problems with the police at some point—it's one of the things that unite us. My brother Bobby is Big Bobby's son, so technically he's half-white—only an occasional advantage. When Jerry recovered from his gunshot wounds, he decided that owning a Rolls was more trouble than it was worth, even though one might speculate that his real mistake in this situation was entering the home of Beverly Goodman. Anyway, he traded the Rolls to my mom for her Mercedes.

Of course, Mom wasn't entirely disappointed that the police didn't investigate further. As you might expect, she wasn't eager for the law to keep digging and possibly sniff out her well-hidden drug business.

So the crime remained unsolved and that was officially the end of it. Mom wound up with just a really bad beating and bouts of anxiety. Bobby walked away unhurt. Mom managed to keep most of the money. She even got the Rolls, which in her eyes was a fantastic trade-up.

JUST AFTER DUSK on a sweltering, muggy evening in 1983, I was in the Power Station's Studio C. In the early eighties, Studio C was almost exclusively mine. It was new, extremely private, and capable of generating absurd sound-pressure levels, which is how I liked to roll back then.

As my engineer Jason played back a track I'd just overdubbed at excruciating volume, I snorted a couple of hefty lines off the producer's desk. "Boom!" I said, which meant I approved of my performance. I kept things simple back then. I was heading out to do some quick club hopping.

I jumped behind the wheel of my brand-new fire-engine-red Porsche 911 Targa, turned the key, redlined the engine, and fishtailed out of the garage. I sped west down Fifty-third Street with music pulsating, a crimson disco on wheels. My hair was cropped in a flat-top style called a fade-away, which was inspired by the underground icon Grace Jones, an exceptional artist whose greatest

creation may have been herself; appropriately, I was blasting her classic "Pull Up to the Bumper" as the soundtrack to my ride. I screeched to a halt in front of the Roxy, a popular club that doubled as a roller rink. I strolled right in, past all the civilians waiting in the endless line. The club's owners, operators, and bouncers were all close friends, which meant I could leave

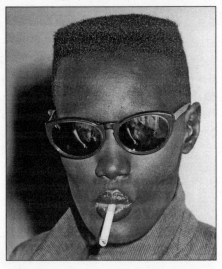

my car out front with the top down.

Thick with cigarette smoke, the Roxy's main room was packed mainly with Club Kids, new wavers, and B-boys and B-girls decked out in foxtails and rope chains. They churned in front of a smoky, holographic backdrop.

I was here tonight to check out a performance by a young artist named Jenny Burton, an attractive chanteuse I was interested in producing but had never actually met. I really didn't need to look for *more* work: 1983 was right smack in the middle of an especially good stretch for me. That year I'd had at least seven projects come out, many with major artists such as Paul Simon, Hall & Oates, Southside Johnny, and INXS. Soon I'd meet Duran Duran and embark on what would be my longest continuous relationship with a band other than Chic.

But Jenny Burton was hot. She was like a club version of Lena Horne, and had the look of the R&B stars who would conquer the world twenty years later (Beyoncé, Rihanna, etc.). She was the lead singer of C-Bank, an electro-R&B band that was important in what was known as the freestyle movement—a Latin-and-hip-hop-flavored dance music that was threatening to migrate from the clubs to the mainstream. She was as trendy and hot as the Roxy, and she was riding a monster club hit at the time, called "One More Shot."

Like a real pro, I'd perfectly timed my arrival to sync with her start time, or at least I thought so, but I soon realized that the opening act hadn't even gone on yet. I walked across the dance floor and openly tooted up next to a cute lesbian Latina B-girl couple. One of the girls had just finished kissing her partner. The kiss was particularly wet and she was licking the excess off the girl's face when I abruptly asked, "So, um . . . who's the opening act?"

"Madonna," she said, half pissed and half startled by my intrusively timed question.

"*Madonna,* really? The chick that sings 'Everybody' Madonna?"

"Yup, her." In a very huffy tone.

"Cool! You guys want a bump?" (This instantly redeemed me.)

"Yeah, *papi.*" They both did a couple of hits, just a little less conspicuously than I did.

Now, this Madonna person wasn't a total stranger to me. Jellybean Benitez, a hot DJ, producer, and businessman, had told me about her already; he'd probably even mentioned this gig. Before Jellybean, I'd first heard about Madonna from a friend named Michael Zilkha, the owner of alternative music label ZE Records, best known for Was (Not Was), Kid Creole, and Lydia Lunch. Michael had told me about this *wonderful artist.* Michael's got a public school, Oxford accent, and when he speaks, every word sounds important, especially adjectives like "wonderful." I remember him telling me, "Nile, you and Madonna simply *must* work together, because Madonna's *fantastic* and you're *fantastic*."

"Lot's of people are fantastic," I countered. "And I'm not sure she qualifies."

(I really didn't know much about her then. I'd assumed she was Puerto Rican, because I knew she was associated with Jellybean and the freestyle scene. I liked her song "Everybody," but I didn't have any reason to believe Madonna was special. She had one okay club hit. Not even Nostradamus himself could have predicted she'd become one of the most successful recording artists of all time.)

"My friend keeps saying Madonna's bananas," I shouted over the club's pounding sound system to my new B-girl friend. "Are you down with her?"

"I'm not down with her yet, but my honey says she's most ill."

"OK." I pointed to the fem girl. I decided to turn her praise into a wager. "You've got to give me double my blow back if she's whack." Then I laughed and asked, "Word?"

"Word up," she answered.

"Bet!" Then I waved and headed over to the DJ booth. I was trying to kill time and was buzzing pretty nicely. I ran into an old pal of mine, Mike, who was one of the few brothers I knew who was deep into this scene, which was good news: It meant I could check out two acts and square my reaction with a hip black man's second opinion. "Yo, Mike, how great is this shit?" I said, serving him up the obligatory double bumps of blow.

He answered, "It's pretty dope."

"Not the toot! I mean getting to check out two acts tonight for the price of one!"

"Jenny's most def, but I ain't clocked Madonna's show yet."

Suddenly someone announced "*Madonna!*" over the PA, the track dropped, and I recognized the song. I'd heard it the night before at a club, Paradise Garage. A good sign.

What I saw next startled me: a toothsome white girl *stepping* (doing dance routines while performing). Stepping is what R&B

bands like the Jackson 5 and most others used to do until the likes of Prince, Parliament-Funkadelic, the Isleys, and Rick James moved the scene to more rocklike performances—rock-star poses and spontaneous, improvised movement instead of choreographed moves. By the mideighties many black bands of real significance weren't stepping at all, but now here was a *white girl* doing intricate choreography, all while crooning:

> *"Holiday-ee, Celebra-eete.*
> *Holiday-ee, Celebra-eete."*

Mike, myself, and some of the other patrons of color in the club were momentarily shocked. I wasn't ready for this. Not only was Madonna *stepping,* she had a stageful of fly-looking dancers stepping right along with her. She was akin to a young, sexually suggestive, white Gladys Knight—and they were her Pips.

Black acts rarely used extra dancers, because the musicians themselves danced, making any additions unnecessary. Somehow, Madonna and her crew made it work, sort of. But something was off. The whole thing reminded me of my days at the Apollo and the Chitlin' Circuit, where singers and dancers had every last detail choreographed. Ah, the missing thing was a live band.

AFTER HER SHORT SET, which to my surprise included the song "Burning Up," which I'd heard around town but hadn't connected to her, I went backstage to meet Madonna. The moment I walked into her makeshift dressing room, I noticed that the cigarette smoke from the club (a no-no for singers) had completely overpowered the room's ventilation. She was curvaceous and cute, but raw, and her toughness was impressive, even to a homegrown New Yorker like myself. She looked like she was living a hard life, but seemed pleased to meet me—maybe because she knew I had charting records coming out every few weeks. Or maybe she was just being polite.

"Hey, Madonna," I said.

"Yo, what's up?"

"Coolin'," I said. "Your show was pretty tight. By the way, I'm a friend of Michael Zilkha's and he thinks you're the shit."

She accepted the compliment with a little nod of acknowledgment and a fairly big grin.

We chatted for a minute and then I headed back out to the floor. I'm sure Jenny's show was great, but I was too high to remember it at all. And I didn't know what to make of Madonna. Her short opening act had left me slightly puzzled. I didn't know of any other white artists that were doing Latin hip-hop–sounding music. It was weird. I was intrigued, but not convinced it worked. I also had another artist I wanted to see that night, so I split.

From the Roxy, I tore up Tenth Avenue to a new spot called F-Sharp, where the band Bow Wow Wow was giving a press conference. I wanted to meet their stunning Mohawked Burmese singer, Annabella Lwin. F-Sharp was on the West Side Highway in a Hell's Kitchen enclave dubbed the Trucks, because the city's garbage trucks parked there, providing cover for the bustling male prostitution trade.

Bow Wow Wow's thing was open to fans, and during the course of the press event, the band said something that offended a club employee. All hell broke loose, in a fashionably hip underground New York sort of way. It was a *stylish* fight. When I walked in, I couldn't believe what I was seeing. I went out almost every night and witnessed only a surprisingly small amount of altercations. We were lovers, not fighters.

When I arrived, the melee was at its apex, and like so many events in my life, a chance encounter occurred: It turned out that the fight was between the band and the club's DJ, Robert Drake, who was my closest friend in the world next to Nard. Robert had recorded and premiered Chic's first song, "Everybody Dance," at the downtown buppie club the Night Owl back in '76.

I waded through an ocean of people until I reached Bow Wow Wow and somehow chilled them out. After they calmed down, I told them, "This dude is my friend," and introduced them to Robert, the guy they were trying to kill moments before. And with that the fight was over. Bow Wow Wow was from the U.K., and like most English bands, they relished a good scrap. But they also respected my work, and talking music and getting high trumped busting heads any day. So I and the band member who'd been fighting moments ago talked tunes and got wasted. I'd become an international peacekeeping force! And much to my delight, I learned that the current crop of new wave bands, especially U.K. bands, were inspired by Chic's sound.

After partying with Bow Wow Wow, I left F-Sharp for the downtown hot spots. I skipped the Pyramid and Brownies and wound up at Save the Robots, an after-hours club I loved. It was completely illegal and for that reason alone pushed the party envelope harder than any club I can remember. In those days many clubs were in Alphabet City, an irony that wasn't lost on me. My old neighborhood still *looked* the same, but was now called the Lower East Side, and the rents were as high as I was.

I FEEL ALIVE WHEN I WORK HARD, especially when I have no choice in the matter. Bowie and Chic were both unsigned when we succeeded with *Let's Dance,* and the slight air of desperation was great fuel for my work—it was a nice simulation of the struggling atmosphere of most of my life up to that point. So now, even though I had my pick of superstars to work with, I continued to pursue and produce opening acts. I knew that an opening act could end up being the headliner with the right nurturing. I loved turning the Eliza Dolittles into My Fair Ladies, probably because I've always felt like the ultimate ugly duckling.

Chic always considered itself an opening act, regardless of how we were billed—even at our peak in the late seventies we never saw ourselves as *stars*. And even though we sold millions of records, neither did anyone else. When we performed "Le Freak" on *American*

Bandstand, Dick Clark said something like "This is the biggest act that nobody knows, doing the biggest song about a dance that nobody knows how to do. Ladies and gentlemen, Chic with Le Freak!"

Madonna was the opening act for Jenny Burton. A couple of months before, at a Culture Club gig at the Palladium, I met the opening act Spoons, from Canada, whom I later worked with. On that same trip north, I caught a funky new-wave rock band opening for Hall & Oates called INXS. I'd never heard of them. Blown away by their set, I went backstage to meet them and we hit it off immediately.

Like so many Anglo-Australian bands breaking in the early eighties, INXS was crazy about Chic, which was hard enough for me to get my head around. But when they said they loved my solo album, I thought they were bullshitting me. To prove me wrong, the band launched into "Yum-Yum," a song from *Adventures in the Land of Good Groove*—in four-part harmony no less:

"Poontang poontang, where you want it?
Slept all night with my hands on it
Give me some of that Yum-Yum
Before I sleep tonight"

"This is how we warm up our voices at sound check," they confided.

"Yum Yum" had flopped commercially, but they dug it so much that they'd even crafted an original arrangement. That sealed the deal. On the spot we decided we *had* to work together. Later that year I produced a track we cut in one take, called "Original Sin," the band's first international hit, and with that, INXS soon moved from opening act to headliner status.

Michael Hutchence, the lead singer, who died at the tragic age of thirty-seven, was a dazzlingly charismatic front man and a really good bloke. Unfortunately, after we cut "Original Sin," we rarely spoke, which is what typically happens: I become so engrossed in the next artist that I don't have time to keep up with the last one.

"Original Sin" was not only a monster smash for INXS, but it was an extremely significant project for me because the song brought Duran Duran into my life.

The band's lead singer, Simon Le Bon, had heard "Sin" at a party in Australia, and decided he had to work with the producer. At the time, Duran Duran was an opening act, too. I met them on the group's first U.S. tour—they were opening for Blondie, whose co-leaders Debbie Harry and Chris Stein were two of my best friends—and soon Duran Duran and I were thick as thieves. Though they were openers for Blondie, they already had a series of huge hit singles—"Planet Earth," "Girls on Film," "Save a Prayer," "Rio," "Is There Something I Should Know?" and "Hungry Like the Wolf"—and were international stars and MTV darlings. They were on their way to headlining status on their own speed.

After Duran's masterful show, I introduced myself backstage. We were all flying high, on a number of levels. John Taylor and I were so giddy and stoned that we ran around the theater playing games like tag and hide-and-go-seek. Our sense of mutual respect was so tangible that we immediately began planning our first project together. A few weeks later, I did a remix of a song of theirs called "The Reflex."

Unfortunately, as much as Duran Duran liked the remix, their record company wasn't happy, and I was soon in an oddly similar situation to the conflict Nard and I had had with Diana Ross's people.

Nick Rhodes called me moments after the band had excitedly previewed my retooling of "The Reflex" to the suits at Capitol Records. "Nile," he began, his monotonic stiff-upper-lip English accent barely hiding his despair, "we have a problem."

My stomach tightened. "What's up, Nick?"

He struggled to find the words. "Capitol *hates* the record," he finally said.

I was stunned. "The Reflex" was a *smash*. I was sure of it. This was déjà vu all over again.

"How do *you* guys feel about it?" I asked a little defensively.

"Nile, we love it, but Capitol hates it so much they don't want to release it. They say it's too *black* sounding."

Too black sounding? I tried not to hit the roof, but in a way it was nice to hear it put so plain. Finally someone had just come out and said it. As far as I was concerned, this was straight-up racist. And dumb. The record was fantastic. And I was in a very different place than when I'd faced this nonsense before. I was no longer so invested in what these people thought.

"Fuck them," I told Nick. "If you guys like it, tell them to kiss your ass and put the fucking record out anyway." Even though I believed what I was saying, I felt bad because I could hear the distress in Nick's voice. Then he said something that even my too-black ass had never heard before (or ever since, thank God).

"The label said that if we forced them to put the record out, they'll want to take points back on our deal because it's going to cost a lot to promote it, and it's not fair for them to bear the extra cost of a record that won't sell."

"Tell them OK," I said with a mix of extreme confidence and total outrage. I was that sure we had a hit on our hands. "Yeah, give them the fucking points back if it doesn't sell. Fuck 'em, Nick! I've never heard of anything so ridiculous."

"THE REFLEX" WENT ON TO BECOME the biggest-selling single of Duran Duran's career. And thus was sealed a long and productive partnership. I had a great run with the the Fab Five, as they were dubbed by the U.K. press, producing "The Reflex," "Wild Boys," and "Notorious," collectively selling tens of millions of units.

Not only were we involved musically, we were partying and shopping buddies. Bassist John Taylor was my main partying buddy; we hit clubs all over New York and London. Keyboardist Nick Rhodes and his then wife, Julie Anne, came next. Together we embarked on gargantuan shopping sprees at the most fashionable shops in eighties London. Nick was tight with the top designers: He hooked me up with Manolo Blahnik, who was turning out a men's collection, and the queen's hatmaker Phillip Treacy. Guitarist Andy Taylor and I would also hit the occasional pub and have a few pints together. He's a solid musician and a highly opinionated dude with a fiery personality. Roger Taylor, the band's drummer, was the most laid-back in the band, and we mainly had a studio relationship.

Simon Le Bon and his wife, Yasmin, a successful fashion model, led very different lives than the rest of the band. Simon was a risk-seeking sportsman. He embraced competition as if his life depended upon winning, even through a major motorcycle accident and nearly drowning in the Whitbread Round the World Race when his yacht's keel broke and the boat capsized. What he had wasn't a death wish, but a life wish. And he wasn't alone; we all lived to the limit. It was the first time in my life that I was so completely absorbed in the privileged lives of superstars.

But it didn't feel quite right. As exciting as superstardom was, there is something comforting about being an opening act, because you're very aware that the world doesn't revolve around you, which at least means that you can take a day off without the planet coming to an end. Perhaps that's why I embraced Chic's status as an eternal opening act. As an opening act, you share the same gravity as the rest of the world. Whereas superstars are monitored as closely as the stock market—their value is quantifiable and constantly fluctuating.

On a hot day, at least hot for London, John Taylor and I stopped for afternoon drinks at the St. James's Club. At the peak of his popularity, John was constantly mobbed by fans. Once we got past the fans and were inside the club, I noticed Paul McCartney sitting at a table by himself. Not a soul bothered him when he left. John, on the other hand, was swarmed by screaming fans. He needed a bodyguard to protect him. The tumult was just one notch down from sixties Beatlemania. This newly found superstardom had come at a price.

I still vividly recall a surreal evening in which the band and I were marched off to London police headquarters for our own protection after Scotland Yard issued a high-alert watch. A riot had

nearly erupted. Evidently a group of soccer hooligans—not exactly
Duran Duran fans—had heard that the band's studio was next to the
Chelsea football stadium, which they didn't like. We were escorted
from the studio by police before a hostile crowd. It was a chilling
spectacle of the kind that only English soccer hooligans can conjure,
and stays with me all these year later. The crush of love at the St.
James's Club in the same city was only two days away, a vivid dem-
onstration of the whiplash of stardom.

Over the next few months, Duran Duran ascended globally
with a little help from me. We'd all made it to the top. But just
when I thought I'd already won the World Series, my biggest opening act ever stepped up to the plate.

eleven

Anything Worth Doing
Is Worth Overdoing!

THE SUN WAS ALMOST DIRECTLY OVERHEAD AS I ROLLED UP TO MOM'S condo in Redondo Beach, California. Mom's place was set near a beautiful spot called the Horseshoe Pier, aptly named for its unusual shape. You could start your stroll over the ocean at one end of the beach and finish it at the other end. The family spent the day in the usual way, laughing and joking—not to mention drinking, smoking, and coking—until I had to head back to L.A. for some music business. I'd just finished a new Duran Duran record and needed to quality-check it before it hit the street. (Unfortunately, no one had thought to quality-check my family before allowing us to hit the street.)

A few days later, I sent myself off on vacation to Tecate, Mexico, to a health spa called Rancho La Puerta. I was following an equation I thought would make sense of my wacky life: Party like crazy, then go to a spa, lay off booze and drugs, eat health food, and work out like an Olympian. I'd even do those incredibly hard Jane Fonda workout classes, which were made more bearable by the fact that I always seemed to wind up directly behind shapely actress Amy Irving. A recurring coincidence, I'm sure.

I also spent a lot of time hiking through the surrounding hills, where I could find enough quiet to hear my own interior voice. One day, while hiking along a mountain trail, I was struck by the conviction that all the events in my life were connected: They were bound to happen because they were, in fact, bound—fixed in place and inevitable. Everything that had happened to me was always going to happen.

I sat yogi-style at the summit and considered this idea and other paradoxes. I saw the mountain I'd just trekked up as a metaphor: It had taken strenuous work to get myself to the top, and the reward was getting to coast all the way down, submitting to the pull of gravity rather than fighting it, just to end up where you started. But in my profession, staying on top was the only option. You never wanted to come down in show business. No one wanted to go back to where they started. If everything in life is connected, like the steps along the trail I'd just hiked, and just as fixed, where was that trail leading next? Would I stay up—or begin the long journey down?

What I didn't know as I sat atop that stunning mountain was that the next part of my life was already falling into place in a suburb of Los Angeles.

WE'VE ALL HEARD THE EXPRESSION "Success has many fathers." You'd be hard-pressed to find a better example than the making of Madonna's *Like a Virgin*. Everyone who had anything to do with it has taken credit for its success. The album had as many fathers as Genghis Khan had descendants, and he probably fathered nearly half of China.

On a typically smoggy day in "Beautiful Downtown Burbank"

(as they used to say on *Laugh-In*), two local songsmiths, Billy Steinberg and Tom Kelly, strolled into Warner Brothers Records for a pitch meeting. They were trying to score a deal for i-Ten, the group they'd recently formed. They were successful songwriters, and Tom was a killer L.A. session singer with a great track record of collaborations. But for whatever reason, the i-Ten presentation didn't wow Warner A&R executive Michael Ostin. Fortunately, Michael not only has good ears, as we say in the business, he's a nice guy. So before they split, he gave them the chance to play one more song.

Billy and Tom had a tune they weren't sure what to do with, or who to give to for recording. It was called "Like a Virgin," and truth be told, playing it for Warner was a last-ditch afterthought. Just one listen later, Michael said he had the perfect artist for the song.

MADONNA HAPPENED TO BE IN THE BUILDING to brainstorm with Michael and Lenny Waronker, another Warner heavyweight, about her next album. So far her career was rolling along but hadn't exploded. Her self-titled debut album had sold a grand total of 700,000 units. OK, but not an earthshaking number back in the days when people actually bought records. At the time, the industry was debating whether Cyndi Lauper or Madonna would ultimately break out and take the heavyweight title. Cyndi was the front-runner. I even heard that one major-label CEO straight out said about Madge: "The bitch can't sing!"

But numbers and industry buzz weren't everything. The suits at Warner knew they had something special in Madonna. She was the classic diamond in the rough—she just needed a few great tunes and the right producer to cut and polish her up.

Before she got to his office, Michael played the "Like a Virgin" demo for Lenny and Steven Baker, another top Warner exec. They didn't get the song at all. This was a common response. A lot of people didn't get "Like a Virgin" at first listen.

At some point during Madonna's meeting, Michael played her the song. After one verse and chorus, Madonna made up her mind:

"She got it quicker than anybody," according to Michael, "including me." She was so buzzed that she decided "Like a Virgin" should be the first single—and title—of her next album. She made this decision in less than two minutes. Classic Madonna. Decisive—and right.

Inspired, Madonna, Michael, and Lenny wrote a wish list of producers: The top two were Narada Michael Walden and me. Michael and Lenny didn't know that Madonna and I had already met at her Roxy show or that we had friends in common. So why did Madonna ultimately choose to work with me? Good question. After our first meeting, our mutual acquaintances certainly continued to talk to each other. Knowing how Madonna makes up her mind, I suspect she'd already decided that I was her guy.

Some rock historians claim that Madonna decided to work with me because David Bowie referred her, but that's pure and complete nonsense. It's true that Madonna and I had lots of common friends. But the night we met at the Roxy, David Bowie wasn't one of them. That said, I wasn't the least likely choice to produce a record for an opening act with one minor hit. In 1983 not many producers were hotter or more productive than me. Though I didn't win Producer of the Year honors for *Let's Dance,* which became David Bowie's biggest, I had seven major records out and the U.K. music magazine *New Music Express* said, "Nile Rodgers should win some sort of award for sheer volume alone."

So my confidence was pretty high: I would boast during our negotiations, "She's going platinum-plus," because I believed in myself. And by then—after a few meetings where I was fully exposed to her now-legendary blond ambition—I *really* believed in her. I knew I could take her to the next level.

The record company and Madonna clearly thought so too, or they never would have agreed to the terms of my contract. The agreement we reached—again, a testament to what Madonna had yet to accomplish in her career—was absurdly in my favor. They ultimately signed off on a deal that paid me as much as any *artist* would expect to end up with today.

I'm pretty positive she hasn't paid a producer that much since.

Still, I guess you could say that history proved they made a good deal: As I write, *Like a Virgin* has sold more than twenty million units. And the record continues to sell, every day, almost thirty later.

OUR DEAL FIRMLY IN PLACE, we got right down to the business of making a record. Madonna was ready to go from day one. The first step was to have her lay out her artistic vision for me, so I could help her realize it.

One afternoon the doorman rang my intercom. "Mr. Rodgers," he said, "there's a young lady here to see you."

I overheard him ask her name.

"Madonna. Tell him Madonna is here," she said.

"It's *Madonna,* Mr. Rodgers," said my bemused doorman. He'd obviously never met a Madonna before.

I opened the door to one of the sexiest, friendliest, and happiest women I'd ever seen—and that's really saying something. Any number of happy, friendly, and sexy women crossed that threshold in the eighties. She was dressed in her soon-to-be iconic street style with her hair tied in a bow and black rubber bracelets dangling up and down her wrists. She looked very young.

"Yo, this is a nice place," she said. My apartment was a combination bachelor pad and nightclub, with Art Deco and Japanese antiques, an old-fashioned jukebox, and a multicolored neon stork, inspired by the famous club of the same name. I offered her a drink. She chose something nonalcoholic. I was already nursing my top-of-the-morning bottle of Heineken.

She knew a thing or two about art and commented on my posters and gouaches by Paul Colin and Van Caulaert that the now famous jewelry designer Loree Rodkin had sold me. We sat facing each other at the Ms. Pac-man two-player console table in my living room.

We ran through a few of her demos, never listening to anything twice—I didn't need to. My time at the Apollo and doing countless recording sessions had taught me to memorize entire songs in one listen, so one listen was enough for me. I didn't show much emotion; I was only thinking about how the songs connected. In short, what was the album's DHM? Everything she played was pretty catchy, but songs are just songs, and she had hired me to make an *album*.

After I downed a few more Heinies, we listened to the rest of her songs. By the time we were through, the tone of the meeting abruptly changed. Madonna's metamorphosis from a happy-go-lucky post-teenybopper to a hard-core career woman blindsided me.

"If you don't love all of these songs," she said to me in a very matter-of-fact tone, "we can't work together."

I was shocked. I hadn't received an ultimatum since that crew of enforcers flashed their guns at me when Chic threatened to sue the makers of "A Rapper's Delight" for sampling "Good Times." I liked Madonna a lot, and I knew we'd work well together, but I had no choice but to speak the truth.

"Well, to be honest with you, I don't love *all* these songs," I said, "but I can promise you this: By the time we're finished with them I will."

I don't remember if she laughed, but she didn't break the deal.

THE FIRST TIME I STOPPED BY Madonna's apartment in SoHo, I was a little surprised by its modesty. Of course it's funny today, because she's a hell of a lot richer now than I am, but at the time I actually felt sorry for her. She was closing in on a platinum album but didn't have much to show for it. Madonna clearly didn't roll like my artist friends Peter Beard or Joseph Kosuth, who had spacious designer lofts a stone's throw away. She didn't even have a decent sofa for guests to sit on. The only furniture I can remember was a mattress on the floor, which reminded me of Woody's Avenue C crash pad, where I bunked when I was a teenage runaway. I was raised in this area when my family was doing well and when we weren't. Even by Beverly and Bobby's heroin-chic standards this wasn't making it.

A couple days after my first visit, I told my handyman to bring her a leather couch from my Connecticut office. After he helped carried it upstairs, he told me he couldn't believe that Madonna lived in a place that wasn't half as decked out as his own suburban home.

OVER THE NEXT FEW MONTHS, I grew as close to Madonna as I've ever been to a woman without being romantically involved. We spent every spare moment we could together until her record hit the streets. When we weren't working, I picked her up in a vintage forties limo for nights on the town.

It was usually just the two of us, even though we both had significant others and plenty of friends. We were like Gable and Lombard thrust into the eighties, and our dapper chauffeur completed the retro elegance. When we pulled up to a club, any club, we were treated like stars at a Hollywood premiere.

I got a big kick out of this role-playing game. I obviously can't speak for her, but you'd be hard-pressed to convince me that this wasn't one of the most exciting periods of Madonna's life. It certainly was for me.

We'd always hit our favorite spots. My preference was a new club called Area, which featured rotating art installations called themes that would change every few weeks. They ran the gamut of visual fantasies and included work from art stars like Jean-Michel Basquiat and Kenny Scharf. Indie-punk filmmaker Amos Poe used the club's installations as eye candy for his film *Alphabet City,* which I scored. Area fit me like a jumpsuit and I loved it there. During the Area days, I felt as close to being a star as I would ever become. I can't begin to document the endless coke raps and brief encounters I'd have there—and probably shouldn't. Area was maybe the most perfect club in the world, second only to Studio 54 when it reigned supreme—but I'm talking a very close second.

Then there was Madge's favorite spot, the multileveled Danceteria. As much as I dug it, it didn't feel as sexy to me as it did to her.

It did have a diverse roster of live acts, from the hippest of avant-garde jazz (Sun Ra and others) to the newest of new wave (Devo and others), but it never gave me that "I have to be here and nowhere else" feeling. A great nightclub feels like the center of an otherwise cold and lifeless universe. It makes a seemingly frivolous night out feel *necessary,* life-giving—it's a communal space where the people, the art on the walls, the art walking around, the dancing, the conversation, the music, the theater of it all, hit the same vibration—and there you are, your whole being humming at the same frequency. Danceteria didn't quite do all that for me.

Madge, on the other hand, shook like a tuning fork when she walked into the space—and she tried to convince me of how hip it really was. But I was born in New York, and I'd seen every possible club concept by then. For me, Danceteria—which has gone down in

downtown history as one of the essential clubs of the era—was just one of the great club options the vast city had to offer, which I took for granted given the sheer abundance of nightlife on our menu. It's like  the way we New Yorkers feel about visiting the Statue of Liberty or the Empire State Building: We leave it for the tourists and head for the side streets, where the real action is. I'd go to Danceteria a few times with Madonna, but I'd rarely go on my own.

We sometimes took in restaurants like Marylou's in the West Village, whose regular patrons, like Jack Nicholson and various CEOs, hardly constituted Madonna's normal crowd—at least back then.

I was never the kind of star who'd have a whole street of strangers rubbernecking when I walked by, but in my hometown I've always known a lot of people, especially in my old downtown stomping grounds. Though Madonna was still a relative newcomer from Michigan, her presence dominated any room the moment she walked in. I've been around celebrities all my life, but she already had that certain something only a handful of people have. Wherever we showed up, I always heard the same refrain:

"Who's that girl with Nile?"

Madonna didn't do my kind of drinking or drugging, so I kept my cool around her. I always waited to get truly fucked up at the early-morning clubs like Brownies in Alphabet City and the Toilet (a nickname—I don't remember the club's real name) on the Upper West Side, long after I left her somewhere or dropped her back home.

MADONNA WAS VERY SERIOUS about making her record.

She was much more intense about the process than I was. Maybe I was more relaxed because I was more experienced or had less at stake—or maybe it was because I knew that I was making a record with an emerging star with a crop of great material, which was the easiest job in the world.

One of my first responsibilities was to convince Madonna that a digitally programmed record would make her sound too pop and not soulful (i.e., black) enough. Her demos were very pop sounding and could've lived and died as fly-by-night hits if we didn't properly capture the soul at Madonna's core. The tunes were hooky, but on the radio they might be indistinguishable from every other pop song of the moment. We had to be unique. Since computer sequencing now essentially allowed anybody to be funky and groove, I wanted her record to have the classic R&B-based sound that only live players give you. A true artist approached a breathing groove differently from a computer track. The solution was to use my band Chic as the bedrock.

She let me have that one.

Ironically, I was now the one with race-based theories about music. As with Bowie, I figured making hits with Madonna was going to be a piece of cake compared to doing the same with Sister Sledge, Chic, or, the hardest of all, Diana Ross. As with *Let's Dance, Like a Virgin* was a walk in the park because I had a stacked deck: Madonna was mainstream pop with just enough urban influence to crowd-please across the board. Whether it's early Elvis, the Beatles, Tom Jones, Roy Orbison, or even Al Jolson, white people doing black music has always been a tried-and-true formula. Especially when white listeners have no idea they're really listening to black music.

It had worked with Bowie and Duran Duran. And now, with this astonishingly charismatic girl who turned on every room of strangers we entered, I was sure that I could deliver the goods.

THINGS WENT SIDEWAYS ALMOST IMMEDIATELY. The demo for one of the first songs we were set to record, "Material Girl," which was written by Peter Brown (author of some of the greatest dance-floor records of all time, like "Do You Wanna Get Funky with Me" and "Dance with Me"), was fantastic. Still, we had problems.

To begin with, the song's key wasn't right for Madonna's natural singing voice. She's comfortable and very warm sounding between alto and mezzo-soprano (think of her voice on her song "Live to Tell" and the verses of "Holiday"), but this version forced her to sing as a mezzo-soprano going up to a B-flat, which was less than flattering, to my ears. She was singing it all with a slight nasal quality. Unfortunately, she'd learned the song that way and she *loved* what she was hearing. I tried to convince her to let me change the key, but strongheaded Madonna? She was not having it.

I knew that it was the artist's name ultimately on the cover of the record—not mine. I also knew that we were on a budget, and was committed, as always, to working fast and coming in on, or under, budget. In Madonna's words at the time: "Time is money and the money is mine." So I had no choice but to help her nail the vocal in the demo's key.

We worked long and hard to get "Material Girl" right. It wasn't easy, but Madonna's legendary work ethic immediately shone through—she didn't mind putting in the time to get the song in shape. And we didn't have auto-tune devices, the now commonly used studio tool that can make a hyena sing on key, to help us. The thing is, Madonna's voice is actually very in tune. And even when it's not, she still has enough control of it to make it sound like music. Pitch is important but expression and emotion make a performance. Remember, the artist is telling a story, one that we must believe—the ability to convey powerful, resonant feelings is the key to pop, not perfect technique. After toiling over the vocals for hours, we finally nailed the performance. "Material Girl," as you surely know, went on to become a massive hit. But, as usual, it took some convincing before we could get it out to the world.

At the label's request, I turned over a rough mix. I also gave one to Madonna's then manager, Freddy DeMann. Freddy was Michael Jackson's former rep, and he'd just come off the biggest record of all time, *Thriller.* Freddy was a terrific manager and an even-keeled thinker, so he dealt me a major blow when he called to ask in a dismayed tone, "What did you *do* to her voice?"

"I recorded the shit in the key she insisted doing it in. And I worked my ass off to get her to sound good. Don't blame *me* for getting it right."

He didn't exactly *thank* me, but he chilled out. Once I made it clear that I'd fulfilled his artist's wishes, he must have taken another listen, because he never complained too much about anything again (which is good, because the vocal for "Like a Virgin" was even further out of the pleasant part of her natural range, in the key of F-sharp, and getting it on tape required the exact same arduous process).

Our next battle was over song order. When I make a record, I always know the sequence of singles from the moment I start recording. I was positive the first single *had* to be "Material Girl," which I knew was a smash. After all, I was hired to give her a smash.

Madonna had an entirely different point of view. She wanted "Like a Virgin." It's funny: I'd worked with so many international superstars, but I'd never come across such an iron will before. On this subject, however, neither of us would budge without a fight. Of course, as I said before, I knew the song order was ultimately Madonna's choice. It was her career and her record. The problem was, I couldn't get over the powerful sense that she was making a *huge* mistake.

In my quest to prove my point, I played both songs ("Material Girl" and "Like a Virgin") for everybody I knew, trying to gin up enough evidence to back up my gut instinct. I remember one colleague's reaction as clear as day—that of my friend Gail Boggs. Gail was a real pro; she'd sung with Bette Midler and costarred as one of Whoopi Goldberg's spiritual assistants in the film *Ghost*. I can still recall the day she sat in my car to take my musical version of the Pepsi challenge.

Unfortunately, it didn't last very long. Once I blasted "Like a Virgin," I never got a chance to follow up with "Material Girl." After one listen she uttered these prophetic words:

"Nile, this record is going to be No. 1 for *at least* six weeks."

It was. Gail was right! And I, well, I had to admit I was wrong. Gail's enthusiasm was so compelling that I could no longer deny that the song was something special. Madonna had captured its essence and put it right in my face. Already things were changing with Madonna: People were starting to follow her scandals, the guys she was sleeping with, and her outrageous fashion moves, but they were willing to pay for her music because it spoke to them. All true artists have this gift, and her delivery of what could've been a cute pop song with a provocative hook really *touched* people—especially young women.

My young charge clearly had serious instincts.

★ ★ ★

IN THE RECORDING STUDIO, Madonna's superintense let's-get-down-to-business attitude sometimes rubbed people the wrong way. I tried to protect the musicians on the album—after all, they were my secret weapon—from her tougher side. Their loyalty to me drove her crazy, and she tossed off some fairly insulting stuff. When they were directed at me, I could laugh her insults off because we really did love each other. Much like with Nard, we'd developed a relationship that allowed for the constant hurling of insults. It was how we entertained ourselves during the lengthy methodical process—but it was supposed to stay between us.

Unfortunately, other people weren't so comfortable with her verbal abuse. One day Madonna's insult slinging went too far. Our assistant had the temerity to go to the bathroom, and she freaked out on him.

"*Where the fuck is he going?*" she said, loudly enough that he could clearly hear. Unsatisfied that she'd made her point, she then let off a fusillade from her usual arsenal of one-liners: "Time is money, and the money is mine," etc. But today her tone was laced with a cruelty that I hadn't heard before. She was being mean. So I confronted her.

"Madonna," I said, "you can't treat people like that. He's just a guy trying to help you make the best record he can. And he needs to go to the bathroom."

"Fuck that," she said, "he didn't ask *me* if he could go."

And with that she and I got into it. This was not the Madonna I knew, and I didn't appreciate it. Our exchange got so heated that I actually quit the record. I got up and said, "If you are going to treat people who are working for you that way, I can't do this anymore." I promptly collected my belongings and stormed out of the studio door.

I was seething with anger, waiting for an elevator that couldn't arrive quickly enough, when she ran out.

"*Nile!*" she yelled. Once she realized that she had me cornered, she pivoted and said in her best girlish voice, "Does that mean you don't love me anymore?"

I looked at her and smiled. The smile then turned into a full-out laugh—her transparency was comical, but she was also right: I couldn't fight the affection I had for her. With that I went back to work, ending what has to be the shortest producer strike in history. That would hardly be the last of the blowouts we'd have before the record was finished. Some of the scuffles were my fault: Sleep deprivation and too much partying probably made me act a little crazy. Meanwhile, my crew was doing lots of drugs, too. They'd show up late or even miss a session, and I had to lie to protect them from Madonna's wrath. I once made a call to the police in front of Madonna to convince her that Nard had gotten into a traffic accident, even though I knew *exactly* where he was. Deceptions were necessary to keep the project, my people, and myself on track.

SPEAKING OF CRAZY:

One day, as I was leaving the studio at the end of the workday, Madonna asked me out of the clear blue sky, "Hey, Nile, do you think I'm sexy?"

"Madonna, is that a serious question?"

"Yes."

"You have to be one of the sexiest people I've ever known."

"Then why don't you want to fuck me?"

"What? Well, er, um, because I'm your producer."

"Well, that never stopped any of the other ones." She turned her back and stormed into the studio. I was left standing there with a silly look on my face.

She never made clear what the point was. What made her question even weirder was that I knew Madonna was never sexually attracted to me. She only went for great-looking guys, the kind that girls obsess over and then end up getting treated like shit by. If Madonna went out with a guy like me, it would've been as confusing to the public as when Julia Roberts married Lyle Lovett. And even if she *had* found me attractive, as a few other girls I've considered out of my league have over the years, I wouldn't have taken the bait. No, I'd learned a massive lesson much earlier in my career: Don't shit where you eat. The last thing I wanted was to ruin what I thought would be a long and fruitful relationship with an artist I believed was going to become an Eternal Pop Superstar.

RIGHT BEFORE WE WERE about to wrap up the record, I got a phone call from Michael Ostin, Madonna's A&R exec. Michael was my sole contact at Warner on the Madonna project, and by now we'd become very close. We had an honest relationship and could discuss anything about her and the record with complete candor.

I could tell from his tone we had a problem. Michael was in a pickle.

"Nile," he said haltingly, "I know you guys have finished the single and Madonna is chomping at the bit to put it out, but 'Borderline' is taking off like a rocket ship. No one expected it. It's killing the charts and burning up at MTV. What would you do if you were us?"

Without dropping a beat, I said, "When 'Borderline' starts to fall off the charts, follow it up with 'Lucky Star.' It's one of the best songs on the album."

"But that could put you back *months*—and Madonna is itching to put this new record out."

"Michael," I said, "you already have the product in the stores. And you've got another single on the album that's smoking. You'd be a fool not to try and take it all the way." Michael is a smart exec. He was probably going to do this all along but was just being courteous. It was smart, respectful, and correct.

IT MAY HAVE SEEMED like I was on the label's side, advocating holding the record I'd just completed in favor of milking Madonna's previous album. But by now I knew every song on that first record, which meant I knew those tunes had a lot more shelf life. If her first album had a chance at a second life, why wouldn't they jump at it? And it would only increase the anticipation for the new album.

"Like a Virgin" would now have to wait for the earlier singles to fade. Such an embarrassment of riches is almost inconceivable now, when whole careers come and go in a few weeks, but Madonna suddenly had a backlog of hits because she also had a few hot songs from films she'd recorded. We knew that, as a general rule, the marketplace only affords an artist one single at a time.

So we waited. And we waited. And sure enough, both songs were hits, which meant that Madonna's first album started to move some major units. So we waited, and we waited some more.

The wait lasted many months, during which time I made a ton of records and Madonna promoted her first album like crazy. We worked very hard. And we played even harder. I wound up spending more time socializing with Madonna than recording with her.

She joined me at La Samana, a luxury resort in St. Martin where the clique I was hanging with spent every Christmas. Despite the growing success of her first record, Madonna still hadn't become the fully realized *Madonna,* but she was in good company with my extended crew. Back then, my top pals were Daryl Hannah, her family, and her boyfriend, Jackson Browne; NBC bigwig Dick Ebersol and his actress wife, Susan Saint James, and family; Oprah Winfrey and her boyfriend Stedman Graham; politician Vernon Jordan and his wife-to-be, Ann Dibble Cook, and family; music mogul Marty Bandier and his family, including wife Dorothy, an ex-model who was connected to my best friend from the Black Panther days, Jamal Joseph, and his wife, Joyce, another model/actress; and my main man and closest friend, publishing mogul Jann Wenner and his then wife, Jane.

Our crowd also included Bob Johnson, who was just starting BET (Black Entertainment Television), and with whom I regularly played tennis; and Harry Belafonte and his daughter Gina, whom I loved debating with (we were on the same side—it was just stimulating to have another ex-street-level lefty to shoot the shit with in this super bourgeois hedonistic resort). There was also my then girl-friend Nancy Stoddart, who single-handedly introduced me to this lifestyle. Though I'd become financially well off, I had never had a true vacation until I met Nancy. In fact, the very first time I did, I went kicking and screaming, but to my surprise I actually wound up having a good time.

By now I had to have coke everywhere I went. Every day. Most of my friends and colleagues never knew the extent of my addic-tion. (At least I don't think they knew.) I remember the day we ar-rived in St. Martin, Madonna, Jellybean, Nancy, and I lunched on the resort's terrace. Though coke accompanied most of my meals, I hadn't flown down with any. But I wasn't worried. It was the eight-ies and I knew I could find drugs anywhere. Or more correctly, the drugs would find me.

The rest of my party never suspected a thing. But in the drug world, word travels fast. A high roller had landed. The moment we passed through customs, I was on a local drug dealer's radar. Every-where I went on the island, I had someone laying in the cut to keep my nostrils filled. I gave the word that I'd happily pay extra if they didn't step on it too much. The baby laxative and sugar they cut it with ruined the intensity of the high. I'd become accustomed to close-to-pure stuff back in New York. But none of my friends seemed to notice how deep I was into the drugs. I was still at the top of my game professionally, and my work ethic powered me through the days. They have a saying in recovery programs, "God protects drug addicts and fools." I was both, so I was especially well pro-tected.

Really, everything had worked according to our Chic master plan. My music was well known, but for the most part, my face wasn't. This unique blend of anonymity and affluence was all very convenient: I could go anywhere and do anything I pleased. As Oprah said when I appeared on her Season Two "Rags to Riches" show, "You are one of the richest people I know," which is sort of funny to think about, given that Oprah is now probably the richest person I—or anyone—knows. Money wasn't my goal, just a yardstick to measure success.

On New Year's Day 1985, my situation was near perfect. Life was fantastic, almost blissful. We'd finished *Like a Virgin* in just six weeks. We knew the record was great, and we now had time to relax in the sunshine. Meanwhile, my relationship with Madonna continued to grow. When her promotion schedule opened up, she joined me on Martha's Vineyard.

A PLAYBOY BUNNY FLIGHT ATTENDANT I once dated used to tell me how great "the Vineyard" was. Her name was Renée, and for many years she'd worked on Heff's corporate jet. The famed Playboy jet was black, sleek, beautiful, and classy—and so was the drop-dead fine Renée. Not only was she gorgeous, but genuinely nice, well mannered, and very popular. One day she and I went shopping in an upscale Chicago department store, and baseball superstar Reggie Jackson walked up and greeted her by her first and last name. I was proud that she was with me. Renée was superconnected and worldly; she could have easily been a politician, diplomat, or royalty.

"Martha's Vineyard is where the rich black folks hang," she'd repeatedly told me. I think her whole family had been summering there most of their lives. Cool. I'd become a certified rich black folk, and I certainly knew how to hang. And so in the summer of 1984, I rented Seven Gates Farm, a massive house with its own private beach, in the town of West Tisbury.

I'd envisioned the Vineyard as La Rive Gauche for black people. I pictured everybody from Muhammad Ali and Pam Grier to Jean-Michel Basquiat and Angela Davis would be lounging beachside, locked in heady conversations about art, high fashion, sports, and politics. Based on Renée's description, the Vineyard sounded similar to the best aspects of my childhood. I suspected the fascinating personality types of my youth would be there tenfold: armchair philosophers, artists, chess and Scrabble players, and envoys from every possible affinity group, and I'd be freer to be me. I couldn't wait to be welcomed into the fold of my fellow overachieving brothers and sisters.

And then from the moment I touched down on the island, I felt much more racially alienated than I'd ever felt anywhere else.

When I rolled around the Vineyard with the likes of Madonna, Carly Simon, or any of my many white friends, things were always cool, but if I flew solo or with black friends, things were not. I was used to that, but as I said, I expected life would be different in an idyllic enclave of American black affluence. I've always struggled just to fit in, and I'll be the first to admit it. I know I'm somewhat, well, *different,* maybe extremely so, but on top of that, I have that extra difference, which is the American black thing.

Since I was six years old, I've traveled all over this country and more than half the world, and for the most part we black Americans have a style that's uniquely ours. Even if I'm in a crowded foreign city, I can spot a black American in a crowd easier than a Parisian can spot an American in a bistro. Now here I was on the Vineyard, ready to enjoy the relaxed joyfulness and racial harmony. Unfortunately, it turned out that race still mattered. And here's what made things so wacky on the Vineyard: It wasn't the white people who made me feel unwelcome.

It turns out I'd come back around to the same color caste system that I'd first experienced in my own family growing up. This phenomenon isn't folklore or fantasy. Like many darker kids who were the butt of juvenile jokes such as "Your mama's so black she can stand next to a Cadillac and charge the battery," I was left without a suitable comeback. I'm dark-skinned. And like most people, I get even darker in the summer. It quickly became apparent that many Vineyard visitors of color had been given the same instructions as my mother's ancestors: "Marry light!" Now, I hadn't come here to the Vineyard to marry anyone, but the message carried over to other forms of socializing as well.

My brother Bunchy—who at the time was a sometime musician, carpenter, and drug wheeler-dealer—has light skin like our mom. Though he wasn't wealthy—and he wasn't even particularly employed, legally at least—he was accepted almost everywhere on the Vineyard, especially in Oak Bluffs, a village about ten miles from my summer place that was a haven for some of the richest black folks in America. But I was given subtle grief from the moment I set foot in town. People were never overly hostile, but I got just enough negative attitude to let me know where I stood.

On my very first trip to Oak Bluffs after sundown, I was refused entry to an upscale house party—a party I'd been invited to—by the bouncer guarding the front door. I was totally perplexed.

As Renée had said, the Vineyard was where *rich* black folks hung. I was probably richer and absolutely blacker than ninety-nine percent of the people there. I quickly realized that the standoffish posturing I'd been experiencing was simply based on my hue. Of course I can't swear to what was in his head because I'm not a mind reader, but I've encountered this before. My skin color was the only information the doorman at the exclusive Oak Bluffs party had to judge me. And for him color, which masquerades as a key to one's status, was what mattered. Fortunately, the situation was resolved when an ex-girlfriend, who had spotted me being turned away, told the doorman, "Hey, that's Nile Rodgers, the leader of Chic and Diana Ross's producer," at which point he let me in—along with my entourage.

The funny thing is, he probably shouldn't have let me in—for an entirely different reason:

My friends and I all stank powerfully of skunk.

A few days previously, my girlfriend Nancy's dogs had trapped a skunk under our house. As any self-respecting cornered rodent would do, the little fellow sprayed the dogs, drenching them nearly to the point of drowning. We tended to their burning noses and eyes, bathed them in cool water, and washed the pooches in tomato juice, as Fin the groundsman had instructed. We then dried them with about ten bath towels.

That would have been the end of that, but my housekeeper, in a particularly forgetful moment, washed *all our clothes* with those skunk-infused towels. The scent stayed in everything for weeks.

After a few hours, we more or less got used to the smell. But that was just us. Once we were inside the party and past the point of no return, we unknowingly offended everyone's olfactory systems. You should have seen the facial expressions. After a few minutes of appalled wincing, one of the bourgie black revelers yelled out, "*Damn, I smell skunk!*"

During the skunk phase on the Vineyard, Madonna's A&R chief, Michael Ostin, and his wife were among my houseguests. They went straight from the beach to Paris. When they checked into the exclusive George V Hotel later that week, and the bellman brought their pristinely matched Chanel suitcases into the elegant lobby, they emitted a distinct fragrance, Eau de Skunk, by the house of Monsieur Pepé Le Pew.

Our Martha's Vineyard rodent perfumer would continue to make his presence felt for some time. In fact, his work traveled all the way back to the Ostins' California home, about a month after the original incident.

Like a Virgin hit the street on November 6, 1984, after a seemingly endless wait. It went quickly to No. 1 on the *Billboard* pop chart and hit No. 6 on the R&B chart. The white-artist-singing-black-music formula worked better than with any previous artist of mine. The single stayed on the pop Top 40 chart for three months. The album became the biggest-selling record of both of our careers.

I knew Madonna was a superstar-in-waiting, but even I was surprised by *Like a Virgin*'s unprecedented success. A few months earlier, I'd taken her to Madison Square Garden to see Duran Duran, and she sat relatively unnoticed in the audience. Only a couple of girls in the upper level screamed and waved at her. Seven months later she'd return as a headliner, and didn't dare step into the audience. Her near-riotous fans were completely uncontrollable.

I saw Madonna at a party after she played the Garden, in a club we both loved called the Palladium, and I'll never forget the statement she made to me: "Nile, I can't believe this shit," she said. "Every time I go outside, there's always fucking reporters and photographers, and it really pisses me off."

I'd never met anyone—ever—who worked so hard to become famous, which is why I did a double take. So I said the first thing that popped into my mind: "Madonna, get the fuck out of here. The day you're going to be *really* pissed off is the day you come outside and they're not there."

ON A MONDAY MORNING IN JULY OF 1985, I awakened in my New York apartment from my typical two- to three-hour slumber. I contemplated skipping work, thinking I'd better stay in bed because the room was spinning. I didn't even remember going to sleep. And regardless of how hard I tried, I couldn't recognize the names and numbers on the paper scraps that littered my night table, except one.

The only name that registered was Madonna's. But the number was written in a very different hand, so I knew I hadn't written it. I could only assume she must have. How long had I had the number? Since the Palladium party? Who knew? At some point during the day, I called her and we spoke about our upcoming gig—Live Aid. Despite my increasingly foggy mind, I was still in good enough shape to work all the time. My latest project was with the Thompson Twins.

I was surprised by how pumped up Madonna was about the gig—she was close to obsessed. Live Aid, as most people know, was the second phase of the charity project that recorded the song "We Are the World." Six months earlier the newly dubbed Material Girl had been snubbed from the original project, even though the "We Are the World" organizers chose participants from American Music Awards attendees, which included Madonna. On the night of the recording session, a group of us stopped at Morton's Restaurant in L.A. for dinner to celebrate Madonna's performance on the AMAs.

Afterwards Michael Ostin and I headed over to A&M Studio for the session. Madonna didn't join us. She was keenly aware of the slight. As I said earlier, I could always tell when she was hurt—that night she was hurt and furious.

We were all perplexed. By then Madonna was a household name. The only explanation was a breaking controversy about some racy photos that were supposedly about to come out. The chatter about it dominated industry gossip. And maybe the "We Are the World" organizers were just worried about bad press.

Like many struggling artists, Madonna had indeed posed nude a few years earlier. No big deal. Now that she was a star, the pictures were coming out in *Playboy*. Sort of a big deal. And they were full-frontal shots. Okay, that was kind of a huge deal. Though I never saw the pics, I remember the frenzy they caused. Who cares? In my opinion, she should have sung on that record. But then, she was my artist, so what else would I say?

Of course, instead of derailing her career, the scandal propelled her into the stratosphere.

MADONNA TOOK THE LIVE AID STAGE overdressed for the scorching summer heat in a classic eighties pantsuit complete with shoulder pads and a Nehru collar. Her opportunity to address the swirling controversy was immediate: A voice broke through the cacophonous crowd noise, yelling "*Take it off!*"

Without missing a beat, she replied, "*I ain't takin' shit off today!*"

The rest of her set was almost irrelevant. Nothing could top that zinger. With one line she told us she was human. She'd been poor and had to do a job for money to make ends meet, and who can't relate to that? But she wasn't anybody's boy toy, no matter what her belt buckle said. After her set was through, she graciously played tambourine and sang backing vocals with the Thompson Twins. Most of the day's musical press was about Bob Geldof, David Bowie and Mick Jagger's "Dancing in the Streets" (which I also produced as a single), the band Queen's historic London performance, and

Phil Collins's transatlantic London-and-Philly adventure (he performed his own set in both venues, and in Philly also played with
Led Zeppelin alongside Chic's drummer Tony Thompson). But
Madonna's perfect one-liner captured a moment in its own right. It
was never just the music with Madonna.

It's too bad that she's become so good at being a star that I
doubt she'll ever tell anyone what she really thinks about anything
now. Certainly not in public, on a stage, in front of the world. She
has too much to lose. That's the downside to all those paparazzi and
press stalking her, who still haven't gone away: Maybe by now she
really wants to be free to walk out of her house without a supernova
of flashbulbs exploding around her. But I doubt it. She'll likely be a
perfect promotion machine to the very end.

Madonna used to call me about the silliest shit in the world, and
no matter how inconsequential, it always felt substantive.

"Hey, Nile," she said one time, calling me from Morocco or
somewhere in the Middle East, if I remember correctly.

"What's up, Madonna?"

"Freddie [her manager] put me in a fucked-up seat on the plane,"
she began, and the story went from there, never quite working its
way to a larger point. I was in a recording session half a world away,
but I took a break to hear her long-distance melodrama. I have no
idea what she thought I could do to help and I don't know why I
stopped the session to try, but Madonna had a way of making her
interests feel vital, especially during the period before *Like a Virgin*
came out. During that phase I watched her transform from what she
was into what she'd become. I've worked for many famous people,
but Madonna was very different—and still I can't quite put my finger
on why. In a low-res world, she was high-definition hyperrealism, as
if her body had greater atomic density, every strand of her hair and
thread of her clothing brighter and more colorful, more real.

MADONNA'S FIRST VIDEO MUSIC AWARDS appearance was pure pop
history, the equal of Michael Jackson's moonwalk on *Motown 25,* or

the Beatles on *Ed Sullivan*. Though her vocal performance wasn't pristine—remember, the song is out of her natural range and difficult to sing—she gave a do-or-die effort that shocked the world at a moment when the whole world was watching.

I watched the performance with Mick Jagger and another friend in a recording studio lounge—at the time I was producing Mick's solo record *She's the Boss*. After Madonna performed "Like a Virgin," my friend said, "Madonna is just style and no substance." I said, "You just don't get it, do you? This is show business—style is substance!" Mick nodded in agreement. I was a little ticked off and wanted to make my friend understand me—and get a laugh out of Mick.

"I wish I could bottle what she's got and give you a drink of that shit," I said. "Then I could produce your ass and we'd both have a lot more money."

I DIDN'T GO TO THE VMAs with Madonna that night because Jagger's project was close to missing our deadline. Mick had taped a speech for the event so we could keep working. But my then girlfriend Nancy was at the VMAs to support her. Madonna had really connected with Nancy while waiting for *Virgin* to come out. For a while they were extremely close. Madonna realized she needed a cram course in the folkways of the upper classes. Nancy was the perfect tutor.

Nancy was born in Chestnut Hill, Philadelphia. Her Social Register parents were sticklers for manners and proper behavior. Nancy's thank-you notes were written promptly, her handshake was firm and came with solid eye contact, and she knew which fork to use. She'd attended a snotty all-girls private school and graduated from Sarah Lawrence College, then lived in Rome and Paris, where she became famed socialite Baroness Marie-Hélène de Rothschild's pet protégée and observed firsthand how the truly rich and titled lived.

Madonna's nose for advancement picked up the scent of Nancy's blue blood. The two women were fascinated with each other.

Madonna, I believe, reminded Nancy of Dickens's Artful Dodger when she first met her. Madge dressed like a hip ragamuffin and lived in an empty loft; Nancy's digs at Eightieth and Fifth were lavishly decorated and full of antiques. The midwestern college dropout was about to get schooled. She seemed to prefer Nancy's fancy uptown Victorian digs to her downtown boho loft, and often stayed there with Sean Penn. Nancy hardly minded. An interior designer, she had hooked up my new pad and often crashed at my place.

Madonna soon developed a taste for Denning & Fourcade sofas and especially loved the richly embroidered sheets that adorned Nancy's ornate bed. When she got engaged to Sean Penn, Nancy told her, "We need to register at Tiffany's. And Frette."

Madonna chose very tasteful china and silver and fancy Frette linens. She even got engraved Rizzoli stationery for the notes that Nancy taught her how to write. She was an apt pupil all right, but she must have missed a couple of Nancy's classes on life at the top. At her '85 bridal shower, she received all sorts of presents, from her downtown friends as well as Nancy's uptown friends. A pair of berry spoons from James Robinson's antique shop awoke the Detroit girl in her.

"Berry spoons! What the fuck are berry spoons?" shouted Madonna.

I bet she knows now. At Sting's birthday party a few years ago, she greeted me with an English accent, and certain guests were talking about her love of shooting pheasant. I've heard she had one thousand unlucky birds delivered to her estate for that sole purpose. I believe I've seen photos of her gleefully partying on "the Glorious Twelfth" (August 12), the first day of the shooting season for grouse and ptarmigan. On that day many poor unsuspecting birds lose their lives, and culinary delicacies are served up at grand parties throughout the British Isles with beautifully engraved antique sterling-silver berry spoons.

"Music makes the bourgeoisie and the rebel."
—MADONNA LOUISE CICCONE

twelve

Vive la Révolution!

BACK IN 1970, GIL SCOTT-HERON SAID, "THE REVOLUTION WILL NOT be televised." With all due respect to the great poet and musician, he was wrong. In the searing summer heat of 1985, a televised event called Live Aid, a music-superstar-driven, dual-stage concert to help save Africa, became the largest pop event of all time—and I was part of the core band.

Live Aid certainly felt like revolution, kind of, sort of, or at least what passed for a revolution in 1985. It was definitely a huge moment in my life—proof that everything I'd devoted my career to truly had the power to change the world. The good news for me was that Live Aid wasn't exactly a call to arms or a demand for any personal sacrifice. Since I was now over thirty, developing a little paunch, and getting high daily on toot and common store-bought grog, it's probably all the revolution I could handle.

In retrospect, I see that '85 was certainly a revolutionary year for me. I was at war with myself, in the middle of an epic personal identity crisis of sorts. Who was I? Was I an over-the-counter countercultural zealot who'd achieved some higher state of cool? Or was I just a humdrum alcoholic with enough money to buy tons of coke and enough talent to still hang on to a good job? It was a tough call.

Eventually I'd have many occasions to question my path toward garden-variety alcoholism, but July 13 wasn't one of them. Live Aid was the payoff for a lifetime of hard work. I was practically tripping over music legends—Led Zeppelin, Eric Clapton, Mick Jagger, Phil Collins, Lionel Richie, Joan Baez, Bob Dylan, Ashford & Simpson, Tom Petty, Hall & Oates, Teddy Pendergrass, Duran Duran, and Madonna—all gathered together like a walking collection of *Rolling Stone* covers.

I'd admired almost every artist here since I was a teen. Now I was a peer, which was hard for me to believe.

LIVE AID SHOULD HAVE REPRESENTED the highest peak in my professional life, but for some reason I kept pressing on, in search of a higher mountaintop.

Like a Virgin, the biggest record of my career, guaranteed a certain amount of financial security and freedom. After that my life started changing very quickly. I was now working exclusively as an independent producer. Chic was officially dead. Since I no longer had Chic for my artistic expression, I started pouring even more of myself into my own career. I left the Power Station for Skyline Studios, in Koreatown at 36 West Thirty-seventh Street (which later became the Wu-Tang Clan's famed "36 Chambers").

At Skyline, life was very different. My cars were repeatedly broken into, my assistants were mugged, and Koreatown was dangerous after dark. Still, I loved it there. I was completely fearless. Instead of lamenting the loss of security, my former partner Nard, and the band, I reveled in my newfound freedom. I was morphing into an odd and fairly dangerous hybrid addict: the junkie workaholic.

As the eighties pressed on, I started to become more and more cavalier about my health and safety. I was like a ravenous vampire at dawn. I consumed everything as if it was my last night on earth. I piloted my various speedboats as wildly as a Roaring Twenties dare-devil, maneuvered my exotic sports cars like I was in the Indy 500, ingested more drugs than I ever had before, had tons of sex in a convenient room that overlooked the studio, and began to believe in my own immortality.

I took on more projects than one human being could manage, forcing myself to work ungodly hours, aided by coke and liquid courage. Though Bernard wasn't around to edit me, I'd started to overcome my natural instinct to overcomplicate my music. I became very confident in my abilities, and backed that hubris up by churn-ing out a Herculean number of TV commercials and film scores, not to mention dozens of records and the occasional live gig. Sur-prisingly, they were all good—well, almost all.

My career was smoking hot, but the truth is, no matter how successful I was, I knew I was never the first choice for the easy gigs, or "layups," as we call them. I was usually a label's last resort. I don't know why this has always been the case, but I believe most labels categorized my sound as too black or offbeat. Maybe I don't play the political game well; or perhaps the absence of a manager pro-moting me behind the scenes while I toiled in the studio kept me from the choicest projects. For the most part, I got called in from the bullpen to save a losing game, like when music business legend Clive Davis called me in to rescue the Thompson Twins record *Here's to Future Days* (which went on to be a hit).

I pretended this was the way I liked it. I would have definitely welcomed a Céline or Whitney record thrown my way. But, hey, c'est la vie. My hard-partying, fast-living style probably wouldn't have suited them anyway. Well, maybe.

By then I'd basically met every big rock star I'd ever admired as a teenager. It's funny what happens when you meet the people you've idolized as a kid. For one thing, I quickly discovered that I wasn't the only one with hearty appetites. I was often amazed by the drinking-and-drugging blackout stories I'd hear from stars I was working with. I would be deep into a story about how their work had profoundly influenced me, how touched I'd been, only to learn that he or she *didn't even remember making the work!*

"No way this amnesia could be real," I thought to myself. "Bullshit, you don't remember recording the song that changed my life. It's just feigned humility." But the truth is, shockingly long-term blackouts are not uncommon among the creative set. Dozens of iconic superstars I'd meet lacked any genuine memories of their own groundbreaking achievements. They had zero recall of events that had gone on to become rock-and-roll history. As I moved in more rarified circles, the Lost Weekender list continued to grow.

Don't believe me?

1. When I first met David Bowie, I mentioned that I'd loved many of his infamous glam-rock records. When I asked him about *Pin Ups* specifically, he said: "Nile, I don't remember doing that album. I know it's my work. I know it's my picture on the cover. But I have no independent recollection of doing it." At the time, I believed his memory loss was a by-product of the traumatic childhood incident that altered the color of his eyes.

2. My fear from the *Let's Dance* sessions finally came true during the recording of *Like a Virgin,* when my ex-partner and bassist extraordinaire Bernard Edwards got so high one day that he completely missed a session. When he showed up the next day, Nard had no idea that a full day and a session had gone by. In fact, he was almost confrontational, as if I'd made the whole thing up. I sincerely believe he didn't know that he'd gotten so high that he lost a day of his life.

3. Speaking of Nard: In an attempt to keep our increasingly diminishing friendship intact, I once invited him to see Paul McCartney at Madison Square Garden. Nard had recently had his own big hit, producing the Power Station and Robert Palmer's "Addicted to Love," and I'd wanted to introduce him to new prospective relationships in the rock world. We were seated in the VIP section next to Chris Squire, bassist of the group Yes. I'd seen Chris at the Gar-

den at least twice in the early seventies, and more recently, performing Yes's recent smash "Owner of a Lonely Heart." After we'd
discussed how great Sir Paul's sound was, the legendary musician
said to me, "Do you think we [meaning Yes] should play this place,
too?"

I thought he was joking, so I comically replied, "Oh, for sure.
You'll sound a lot better when you play here now."

"What d'you mean, mate?" he asked seriously. *Was he joking?*

"Yeah, I'll bet the sound system's new and improved since
then," I cautiously replied. Blank stare from Chris. So I just came
out and asked, "I think I've seen you here at least twice before tonight, right?"

He gave me a confused look. Oh shit, I thought, he actually
doesn't remember playing one of the most famous venues on earth.
I was also positive he'd played there the year before as part of a big
Atlantic Records celebration that my band Chic, the act with label's
largest-selling single, "Le Freak," was not invited to participate in,
but that was beside the point.★

Other people's mind-boggling memory loss due to drug use
should have been a warning. But I honestly believed I was different.
At that point in my life, even after multiple binges, I still had almost
total recall. I could remember minute details of even trivial events.

Boy, was I in for a surprise.

AND SO I KEPT ON GOING, faster and faster, running from something,
the way I used to run from bullies as a skinny little kid. It was the
perfect time for someone in flight from reality: It was the eighties,

★Right before this went to press, I called Chris Squire. We had a delightful conversation and his mind was crystal clear. He had all the dates for his upcoming Yes tour
memorized. We laughed our asses off about the Garden incident and in the end he said
to print it. I said, "But if you don't remember seeing McCartney, maybe I got the rock
star wrong." He laughed and said, "It really could have been me, so just say it was." I
was confident in my memory because I noted at the time I was in mega-bass player
heaven: Chris and Bernard on my left and right and Paul McCartney onstage.

after all, an era of truly historic excess. Here's the dizzying account of artists I worked with during that wild ride, in no particular order: the Thompson Twins, Steve Winwood, the B-52's, Sheena Easton, Cyndi Lauper, Hall & Oats, Grace Jones, Mick Jagger, the Honey-drippers (with Robert Plant), David Lee Roth, Depeche Mode, Jeff Beck, Ric Ocasek, the Vaughan Brothers, Jimmie Vaughan, Bryan Ferry, Southside Johnny, the Dan Reed Network, Sister Sledge, Paul Simon, Al Jarreau, Michael Jackson, Michael Gregory Jackson, Laurie Anderson, Peter Gabriel, Philip Bailey, Diana Ross, Stray Cats, Bob Dylan, Eric Clapton, David Bowie, Paul Young, Wet Wet Wet, Toshi Kubota, Seal, Marta Sanchez, Slash, Taja Sevelle, Spoons, Lorelie McBroom, Mariah Carey, David Sanborn, Samantha Cole, Will Powers, Christopher Max, Kim Carnes, Jenny Burton, the System, Carole Davis, Terry Gonzalez, Outloud, Paula Abdul, SMAP, the Southern All-Stars, Claude Nougaro, and my own solo projects. This list is not complete; it's just to give you a sense of scale.

On each of these records, all of which I still vividly remember, my role was basically always the same. I was the guy managing and working around problems and variables, from the songs to the equipment to the personnel. If you take what you now know about the often highly knotty process of making a record and multiply it by the preceding list of artists, it's not hard to imagine the mental, spiritual, and physical damage I was doing to myself. My only defense is that my over-the-top lifestyle brought a certain order to my life. Think about the way turbulent weather patterns look from outer space.

THE SPRING OF 1988 marked the end of three especially intense years of back-to-back projects following Live Aid. In addition to producing many of the artists I just mentioned, I'd also been hired to score my first major film and was really excited to write a full orchestral score. Though I was a novice film composer with only a few scores under my belt, somebody had told the film's director, John Landis,

"Nile Rodgers, oh, he's a genius," and on the strength of this rec-
ommendation, he pursued me. I didn't even know what the film
was because it didn't have a name, only the working title "The Za-
munda Project."

The film turned out to be the Eddie Murphy vehicle *Coming to
America,* and it would provide me with yet another level of pop-
cultural cred. I'd thought my rock-and-roll life was excessive and
over the top. The truth is, I was still living minor league compared
to the lifestyle I could enjoy subsidized by a major league film budget.

It all began when Paramount temporarily gave me my own studio, built *over the weekend* on the lot to meet an absurd production
deadline. Apparently, Eddie Murphy had been moved by an Orson
Welles docu-style movie in which Nostradamus predicts the exact
date of the Big California Earthquake. Unfortunately, that date happened to be a few months after we started shooting. Eddie insisted
that he wrap all his scenes before the Golden State plunged into the
Pacific.

In order for Eddie to escape before the big disaster, Landis
wanted music in place in order for him to sign off on a scene. But
he didn't want just any temporary placeholder music, he wanted the
right music, or a reasonable facsimile thereof. This meant I had to
score dailies. Let me explain the process: After they filmed a scene,
the film was developed, rough-edited, and scored to determine if
they had it in the can. Landis, a veteran director, knew a decent
Hollywood composer would never agree to such a thing. He was
betting my lack of experience would result in my agreeing to inden-
tured servitude.

He was right. After I signed on, I had my new assistant, Rich,
and my Porsche 911 Slantnose Targa 3.0 shipped to California.
They even granted me my own handpicked top-shelf engineer. We
worked day and night and basically lived on the Paramount lot.

I still remember the first day I arrived for work. The welcoming
committee was John Landis himself, waiting for me at my official
parking area, and a slightly disheveled elderly white man. I thought

the man was John's dad, so I was very respectful, speaking very slowly because he seemed hard of hearing.

After a few minutes of inconsequential chitchat, the old man suddenly spoke to me in a markedly different voice.

"It's Eddie," he said.

I didn't quite understand. So he repeated, "It's Eddie," this time in a slightly more assertive voice. I still didn't get it.

"Yo, it's *Eddie*."

"What?"

"Nile, man, it's Eddie," he said, louder now, and in his familiar East Coast–urban timbre.

"*Oh shit!*" I screamed. And with that the old white man and John Landis got their guffaw on. This was their way of welcoming me to the big leagues and making me comfortable. Genius!

Eddie's old-Jewish-man-from-the-barbershop makeup job was completely convincing, and I knew it would look great on camera. The joke was not only funny as hell, but had the additional benefit of jump-starting my gray matter. I started writing music in my head right there on the lot. I was instantly into the project, and oh, what a project it was.

I got any and everything I wanted, like a spoiled child. Money was not an issue. I had all the comforts of New York and then some. My girlfriend visited me whenever she could. Many of my L.A. friends stopped by regularly. My purpose-built Paramount studio soon became the place to be—and drugs, of course, were the reason. But I was hiding them from select people.

As I fell further into addiction, I was still lucid enough to know who was—and who wasn't—cool with getting high. Oprah and I had become very close and I knew she didn't do blow. She was in town working on a movie of her own, *The Women of Brewster Place,* and decided to drop by. I hid the toot. I don't believe she ever witnessed me getting or being wasted, although she's obviously very sharp and intuitive, so she probably suspected something funny was going on.

Either way, she never judged me. Later, when my life started falling apart, she tried to help me by suggesting respected therapist Harville Hendrix. Unfortunately, the referral marked the beginning of the end of our relationship—but that was a ways off. She used to refer to me as "her little brother." Even though I'm older, she was infinitely more mature. I'm usually drawn to brightness and maturity, but I was starting to feel more and more comfortable around chaos and bedlam. *Coming to America* provided the perfect backdrop: Life had served up the perfect frenzied situation, exactly when I needed it.

But like the conclusion of any good movie, the curtain was getting ready to come down. I'd soon be heading for the blackout highway like my rock-and-roll brethren.

HERE'S SOMETHING I'VE ALWAYS WONDERED about my life back in the day: Was the cocaine trade completely out of control? Or was it just me?

Sometime during the summer of '85, I began to assimilate dealers into my social life—I realized that an in-house supplier was far more convenient and safer than sending my studio staff to cop. And just as I was bringing dealers into my personal circle, my personal circle started dealing themselves. Everybody close to me was getting in on the lucrative action. And a lot of these people seemed to be part of my family.

During those heady days, my best supplier was probably my younger brother Bunchy, who by now was making frequent trips to South America. Bunchy wasn't working for me, exactly—I was just his best customer. He made more money during that period than any other time in his life. Had he saved and invested what he made off of me, he could've just laid back forever. (I don't even want to think about the amount of money I burned up my nose.) Meanwhile, my mom, a dabbler in the drug business since I was a kid, had delved back in with a vengeance.

I didn't know the extent of my family's involvement in the drug trade until they started spilling the beans years later during one of

our family Thanksgiving bashes. During that same feast, my brother
Bobby confessed that he'd been selling pot since he was six, unbe-
knownst to my whole family. (We thought the reason he always
seemed to have cash as a kid was his formidable gambling skills.)
Then there's my youngest brother, Dax, who had the toughest luck
due to drugs: He was sentenced to eight years in the can for the least
lucrative role in one of the biggest drug cases in the history of North
Carolina.

For years I'd been caring for them all, but they couldn't resist
selling drugs for quick cash.

They also couldn't resist getting high. Everyone in my immediate family maintained some kind of habit, even my brother Tony,
whom my mother let her aunt adopt.

So much for nature versus nurture.

And let's not forget my stepfather, Bobby, the patriarch—or
what passed for one in my unique clan.

For as long as I could remember, Bobby was either high or
drunk. Once, while doing a stint in the VA hospital residential program, they'd tried to get him to admit to his alcoholism. He beamed
with pride and said: "Man, dig it. Alcohol is nothing to me. I drink
when I want and what I want. I'm a dope fiend, baby."

It was harder for Bobby to admit to being an alcoholic than for
Pete Rose to admit to betting on baseball. Every Thanksgiving at
the family gathering in Vegas, he'd proudly say, "Pud, I'm the
world's oldest living junkie." But never an alcoholic, at least in his
own mind.

IT'S EASY FOR ME to point out my family's shortcomings, but my
problems were worse than all of theirs combined.

I should have known better. After all, I knew as well as anyone
how common accidental overdoses and intentional suicides were in
the music business, but the funny thing was, I continued to live my
wild life without fear. I've never thought drugs would whisk me out
of this world. When I popped my drug cherry sniffing glue, I es-

sentially overdosed. Given my poor respiratory health and low body weight, passing out could have easily killed me. Obviously it didn't. Instead, I came to and said, "Let's go again!"

Since the tender age of eleven, I'd been dabbling in mind-altering substances, living on the edge and behaving as if I was invincible— and I'd had no reason to think there was anything wrong.

I was about to discover what it feels like to fall off the mountain-top.

madonna

like a virgin

part 3

I Made It Through the Wilderness

thirteen

The Dance, Dance, Dance of Death

I SOMETIMES REFER TO SEPTEMBER 13, 1982, AS THE OFFICIAL BEGIN-
ning of the Grim Reaper's Sex, Drugs, and Rock & Roll-Call.
That's the day almost all my friends and pop culture associates started
to die.

The first to go was Chic's trumpeter, Ray Maldonado, who
passed away while I was across the street from his apartment ordering barbecued ribs. Ray was soon followed by Robert Mapple-
thorpe, Keith Haring, Stevie Ray Vaughan, Miles Davis, Vitas
Gerulaitis, Andy Warhol, Michael Hutchence, Robert Palmer, Tony
Thompson, Luther Vandross, and at least ninety-five other Nile-
world regulars.

What I didn't know was that the Reaper was coming for me,
too. The signs were all around me, I just wasn't paying attention.

One of the most unexpected and tragic passings during this funereal stretch had to be Stevie Ray Vaughan, who went on August 27, 1990, at 12:40 a.m.

When I first met Stevie during the *Let's Dance* sessions, he was a relatively unknown opening act with a huge personality and a penchant for getting high like there was no tomorrow. Since that first meeting, he'd become a superstar. Of late, he was also clean, sober, and happier and friendlier than ever. I was in the midst of producing the next chapter of his exciting musical life: His record with his brother Jimmie, called *Family Style,* which was going very well. Between recordings, Stevie toured with his band Double Trouble, and on one such occasion he and Jimmie headed to the Midwest for weekend gigs with Eric Clapton. After a performance at the Alpine Valley Music Theater in East Troy, Wisconsin, Stevie wanted to turn in early, so Clapton offered Stevie his seat on a chartered helicopter out of town. They lifted off in a souplike fog. The pilot failed to climb high enough to clear a hill that wasn't visible through the low ceiling. The crash killed everyone on board.

All his years of death-defying boozing and drugging hadn't killed him, but, tragically, Stevie didn't live long enough to enjoy his sobriety to the fullest. Meanwhile, I flirted with the void daily. I knew the moment I started chasing highs, I was chasing death. But I was fairly comfortable with the arrangement.

ABOUT SIX MONTHS AFTER STEVIE'S PASSING, I came home from another night of debauchery—I parked my newest Porsche at about 6:30 a.m., said hello to the doorman like I always did, and headed toward the elevator. I stumbled into the elevator and pushed the button marked "14," which made no sense because I lived on the twenty-eighth-floor. Somewhere between the lobby and the fourteenth floor, my heart stopped beating. I literally dropped dead.

Luckily, I collapsed into the hallway on fourteen, aspirating on my own vomit, Hendrix-style. A porter miraculously happened to be on fourteen picking up the trash. He called the EMTs.

I can't explain why I pushed "14," but had I not pressed it, I would have remained dead. The twenty-eighth floor was deserted at 6:30 a.m. The trash had already been collected for the day.

When the EMTs arrived, I had no pulse. They rushed me to the emergency room, barely clinging to life. The ER docs tried various resuscitation techniques, but I continued to flatline. After they'd done all they could, they gave up and decided to "call it."

As they were recording the time of death, an orderly in the room said, "Hey, Doc, we've got a live one here."

"What?" the ER's attending physician replied.

"Yup. His heart just started beating again, all by itself."

How do I know this story almost word for word? The attending physician decided to stick around to tell me how hard they'd worked to save my life. He hoped I'd appreciate what the ER team had done to save me. He was right. I felt beyond appreciative. I was humbled and ashamed.

But not ashamed enough to learn my lesson! And to make matters worse, this wasn't even my first near-fatal incident due to intoxicants. I'd already done a tour in the Intensive Care Coronary Unit at New York Hospital a few months earlier. (I roomed next to the shah of Iran; coincidentally, one of his relatives had hired a band I once played in called the Master Plan, which had gigged in Iran a few months before Chic blew up.)

I'd also wound up in the hospital after a flight from Hawaii to L.A., during which, on a dare, I downed every whiskey sour they had on board in less than six hours. "That's some kind of record," the flight attendant informed me while serving me the last round. After we landed, I passed out and was whisked off to the ER with my second bout of acute alcohol poisoning and pancreatitis, which could have easily resulted in the pushing up of daisies.

Death had visited me on countless occasions, but never long enough to exercise the option. The Ferryman threw me back like an undersized fish. I can't explain why I feared sleep more than death. I seemed to pursue death like Indiana Jones searching for the Lost Ark, but not from some kind of death wish: I was just an addict, like everybody else in my family. I can say this now with dignified relief. For years I'd awaken with the room spinning and soon find myself kneeling at the toilet, swearing, "Oh, God, if you help me through this, I'll never do that again." But by nightfall . . .

ONE HUMID SWELTERING NIGHT about two weeks into August of '94, I bumped into Madonna at a club in Miami's South Beach district called Liquid. We were surprised and happy to see each other after so many years, and we exchanged pleasantries for a few minutes. As I prepared to take my hang to the next level, she said, "Yo, Nile. I'm having a party over at my place this weekend. Wanna come?"

"Cool," I said, while Ingrid Casares, her close friend at the time (she'd long since split with Sean Penn), jotted down the address.

I was in Miami working on preproduction with Cuban musical genius Nil Lara, one of the most meticulous artists I'd ever met. His home studio was practically an archive on a scale that rivaled the library at any institution of higher learning. On the night I arrived, he happened to be performing at a local club in South Beach. He asked me to sit in, which I happily did.

When I hit the stage, *I kicked ass.* I unleashed every guitar trick I knew; I played behind my back and lay on the floor as if overcome by the voodoo of funk while jamming. I may have even stooped to the lamest low: playing with my teeth.

The next day, I strolled over to the artist's place feeling light and confident. "Hey, do you want to hear what you played last night?" he said.

"Wow, you recorded it?"

He nodded impassively.

I was eager to listen, because all I could remember was the cheering crowd and how great I felt. How cool that he had thought to record the show!

When the music started, I was shocked at how bad I'd played. *What a fucking joke.* I sucked. Years of mentoring by great musicians were erased in an instant. My father, our ancestral blood, and every person who'd helped me become a professional musician? *Betrayed*. I wasn't being overly dramatic—every musician can have a bad night once in a while—but when you suck like I sucked, it's disturbing. I don't remember what excuse I gave to the artist, but I do remember him saying something to the effect of "You thought you were good, didn't you?"

Forget *good*. I actually remembered being great. I couldn't reconcile the feeling with the shit I was hearing. The evidence was clear—I'd gone insane. I'd been shamed by my behavior before, and I'd always resolved to restrain myself from further embarrassment. But this was different. For the first time, I believed that my ability to create music had been compromised by my lifestyle. I couldn't face the artist again and I politely extricated myself from producing his record.

Back at the Marlin Hotel, where I was staying, things started to get worse. I began to hallucinate. I hadn't slept since I'd stepped off the plane, about thirty-six hours ago, not counting the sleepless night before I left New York. I was terrified because I no longer trusted myself to judge reality.

"Physical reality is consistent with universal laws. Where the laws do not operate, there is no reality—we judge reality by the responses of our senses. Once we are convinced of the reality of a given situation, we abide by its rules," said Mr. Spock on an episode of *Star Trek*. I one hundred percent agreed with the wise Vulcan.

Though I stopped working in Miami, I didn't stop playing there. Partying had become more important than playing music. Despite bowing out of the production gig and my horrible performance at the show, I stayed in great spirits from my now-increased diet of cocaine and booze. I quickly accepted this shake-up in my priorities: Partying trumped working!

I was a new Nile, a different person altogether. Don't get me wrong; I loved to hang, but never more than I loved to work. I've always felt very fortunate, because I'm paid to do what I was born to do. Now I was at the mercy of my addiction. Shame or no shame, my world was completely topsy-turvy.

* * *

PART OF MY PROBLEM may have been the company I was keeping. The after-hours scene, once the height of glamour, was no longer exciting to me. And though the drugs flowed like a river, I could never get enough. Consequently I'd started hanging out with more people in the drug trade. Forget the club crowd. These were the real party people. I increasingly hung out at their apartments instead of after-hours clubs. Hard-core killers were part of the mix, but they were, for the most part, very likable and a lot of fun. And I knew this breed. Mom's old contract killer friend, Bang-Bang, had always been nothing but kind to me and my first girlfriend, Deborah. Of course, at the time I didn't know that he'd violently raped Mom and dangled my newborn baby brother out the window.

My oldest friends and colleagues were worried about me, but I simply couldn't be reasoned with. My girlfriend in New York, Jane, knew that I was doing huge amounts of blow and running without sleep; she also considered my new crew highly undesirable. But I didn't care what she thought. They were my friends.

Jane and everyone else were powerless to intervene. Since I was still capable of remarkable clarity during our conversations, she thought that I was lucid enough to take care of myself. I assured her that everything was all right, that I was just having too much fun to sleep. "I might miss something good!" I'd shifted into high gear and was now pursuing death, *con brio*!

TWO NIGHTS BEFORE MADONNA'S PARTY, I bumped into a girl I knew from New York, the girlfriend of a very scary dude I'd been hanging with, and her friend. I had more coke than Scarface. The three of us were certifiable. I have no idea what actually went down, but I'm willing to bet the sex and drugs we did are in the "legendary, even in hell!" category.

Meanwhile, my increasingly lethal lifestyle was exacting huge economic repercussions on my bank account: I was burning through money like crazy, though I was far too gone to believe my accountant, who'd called an emergency meeting a few months before I left for Miami. He didn't exactly beat around the bush.

He looked me square in the eye and asked if I had a drug problem.

"No," I said. "I just go to a lot of parties."

"Then why do you buy so much coke?"

"I want people to like me, so I share it with everybody."

"Do me a favor."

"What?"

"The next time you go to a party, buy a bag of gold ingots and give 'em away. Gold only costs three hundred bucks an ounce and cocaine is three thousand an ounce," he said. "I guarantee that if you give people gold instead of blow, they'll *really* like you. And you'll save a hell of a lot of money."

I fired him. But of course, he was right.

ON THE NIGHT OF MADONNA's thirty-sixth birthday party, I hadn't slept for four days.

My date for the evening was a stunning brown-skinned movie star named Theresa Randle, who was in Miami filming *Bad Boys* with Will Smith and Martin Lawrence. I don't remember how we met. Sometime that evening, I picked her up at the Biltmore Hotel. Her manager had confided in me that she thought I was "one of the nicest people she'd ever met." By the next day, she probably had the opposite opinion: Her client wound up finding her own ride home, and I never heard from Theresa again. I am so sorry. From what little I remember of Ms. Randle, she was wonderful.

The only snippet of conversation I remember was Theresa's remark, right after I downed my sixth or seventh bottle of sake at the Japanese restaurant where we dined before the party: "Wow, I'm scared of you," she said. In the black community back in the day, that was a compliment. In retrospect, I don't think that's what she meant. After dinner this beautiful brave soul actually rode in the car with me behind the wheel, even though I wasn't in a position to operate a doorknob.

I vaguely remember arriving with my gorgeous date, and that's about it. The rest of the night is almost a complete blackout. I pissed off plenty of people, I'm told, but I can't recall what I did to deserve their ire. One of the few memories I can still conjure involves Mickey Rourke and me commandeering one of Madonna's bathrooms to engage in a typical coke rap, complete with the obligatory tears and the inevitable "I love you, man" endearments.

We were going to save the world before sunrise. Or at least we would have, but I passed out before we could get started. I had to be hand-delivered to my hotel by a team of concerned friends. Madonna has forgiven me, but I'm not sure I can ever forgive myself.

I wish that was the end of the story.

WHEN I AWOKE from my comatose state a few hours later, things went rapidly downhill.

First I called my answering machine in New York. A message started playing with a voice that sounded like Chazz Palminteri doing his worst mafioso accent. "I heard you waz wit my girl dee utta night. I hope yas had a good fuckin' time because it's gonna be your last, ya piece a shit."

Click. I froze. It was the guy whose girlfriend I'd been, uh, hanging out with the other night.

I freaked out. I ransacked the minibar, but I'd already downed all the vodka, gin, champagne, white wine, and beer. The only remaining booze was brown in color. Believe it or not, I was still holding to my "Only real alcoholics drink brown liquor" theory, even four days into an epic bender. So since I was *not* an alcoholic, I wouldn't touch the stuff. Still, I was in some deep shit and needed a drink to relax and think things through.

Desperate, I swigged down a bottle of straight Scotch. Then I noticed the shutters on my window weren't closed. I heard people outside my door planning to break in. I still had two half-ounce

Baggies of coke on my night table, so I took a couple of hits and finished off a second bottle of the brown stuff. To my surprise, it tasted great. Then I called a martial arts supply store and had them deliver a sword. Yes, a sword. I called one of my new Miami coke friends and asked him to let me borrow his .45 automatic, which sounded reasonable to him. He said he'd drop it by. I started calling every connected guy I knew.

I whispered to a friend, who shall remain nameless in the interest of not incriminating him, "There's a contract out on my life."

"How did you hear such a thing?"

I told him about the answering machine and the bad dude's girlfriend.

He called me an asshole for crossing the line. "What the fuck were you thinking?" he said.

Still, he promised me he'd look into it. After what seemed like an eternity, but which was probably only about twenty or thirty minutes, he called back. His next words were slow and deliberate: "Nile, are you doing coke?"

I screamed back, *"What the fuck does that have to do with anything? Come on, man, is somebody after me or not?"*

He then said something that even I, given my long drug history, had never heard before.

"Nile, that's the coke talking to you." He kept repeating it over and over, which made me angry, scared, and confused.

Finally it dawned on me: Oh shit, I thought to myself. *He's in on it.* I've read all those books and seen all those movies. They get to someone who you trust to set you up for the hit. *I can't believe it's him.*

Actually, of course, I was in the hallucinogenic depths of full-blown cocaine psychosis. At the time, though, my situation felt intensely real, and I didn't know where to turn. I rang up an even older and closer friend. After I related my story, he said an unexpected thing: "Nile, listen to me, that's the coke talking to you," which surprised and annoyed me. *Et tu, Brute?*

Then my connected friend called me back to scream at me.

"Throw that fucking coke away or I'll come down and kill you myself!"
Thinking I could buy my life by flushing an ounce of coke down
the toilet, I did as I was told. But this small act of contrition proved
futile. I still heard people whispering—their voices were clear and
succinct. I was moving in and out of reality, but I wasn't aware
which state was which.

In what may have been my final act of lucidity, I called a retired
New York City detective I knew named Bo Dietl, who was familiar
with my Real Deal crowd. "We have to take it to them," he ad-
vised. "Get it out in the open."

So I frantically packed my bag and rushed off to the airport,
hopping on a plane back to New York. Hours later in my apartment, with a crushing hangover and cokeless due to the company of
real cops, I tried to play the threatening message on my answering
machine for Bo and the other ex-cops he'd brought with him. I was
appalled to discover that the tape was blank.

"Oh shit, he somehow managed to erase the message," I told
my protectors.

As THE COKE-FUELED PSYCHOSIS receded, and my rational mind returned, I slowly realized that the voices I'd heard so clearly in Miami
were all inside my head. That didn't make it much better. What
really scared me was the thought that less than twenty-four hours
earlier I'd been in a closet, clutching a gun and a samurai sword. I
thought to myself, *Shit, what if the housekeeper hadn't honored the Do
Not Disturb sign?* Would I have shot her or cut her head off?

Then, to make matters worse, I picked up a newspaper article
that said Keith Richards, of all people, had just kicked drugs. I knew
Keith pretty well because of my work on Mick's solo album. I'd had
tea with him in London in what may have been the weirdest meeting ever—to sober himself up he'd taken an ice-cold bath fully
clothed—to discuss the possibility of me producing the Stones.

Are you kidding me? Keith Richards got sober? If he could do it, I
could do it. The gauntlet had been thrown down.

* * *

WHEN I ARRIVED at Silver Hill Hospital in New Canaan, Connecticut, I was a mess. I felt naked and fragile and hadn't touched my guitar since the embarrassing public performance a few weeks earlier. I'd convinced the admissions staff to allow me to keep an instrument in my room. They reluctantly agreed.

I now understand why they didn't want me to have access to my guitar. Suicide attempts are regular events in rehab, and guitar strings are perfect for hanging yourself. The staff at the hospital was sure that I, patient Nile Rodgers, was not ready to succeed in rehab, at least not this time around. They thought I was just too self-centered and too entrenched in my lifestyle to stop.

What the staff didn't know was that thanks to my bender on Madonna's thirty-sixth birthday, three days before I arrived at Silver Hill, I'd already stopped. I had had enough. The thing is, *stopping* wasn't hard at all. Every addict I know stops all the time—over and over and over again. And I, like every good addict, had stopping down cold. Stopping was easy; staying stopped was the hard part.

So I refocused on *staying* stopped, which, paradoxically, meant doing something instead of doing nothing. Hmm . . . this made sense to me. Anything of value (even drugs) that I had ever achieved required action and discipline. Double hmm . . . I remembered one of my teacher's words at the end of a lesson: "The only thing to remember is this simple definition of the word 'discipline': *the ability to delay gratification*. It's an easy way to visualize the training required to adopt a behavioral pattern."

Suddenly so much was clear to me. The embarrassing guitar performance, the contract on my life, the message on my answering machine, the voices—they were all mental mirages, and all egotistical ones at that. I was just like my dad, lying in the gutter, or naked on the Hotel Greenwich fire escape, babbling about how his uniquely gifted life had been short-circuited because of my mother's betrayal. In recovery programs they have a saying: *An addict is an egomaniac with an inferiority complex.*

And that described my family and me perfectly.

Over the next few weeks at Silver Hill, I was introduced to several simple slogans that answered complicated problems:

The door to hell swings both ways and it's never locked; you can leave anytime you want.

What other people think of me is none of my business.

I'm one bad decision away from complete devastation.

An addict's uniform is a crown, a scepter, and a diaper.

Keep It Simple, Stupid!—or KISS. I particularly liked that one because of KISS's role in the birth of Chic. Maybe KISS could save me again.

For eight months I practiced these principles daily with the same diligence I'd brought to learning how to play the guitar. Everything in my life got better.

My first day out of rehab, I walked into a Westport, Connecticut, restaurant to pick up some takeout. While I waited for my order, the maître d' said I had a phone call.

"Who is it?" I asked, surprised.

"Don't worry, you know him."

I took the call. "Who is this?"

"Hey, Nile, mate, it's Keith. You got a bump?"

After eight months in recovery, the first person I heard from was the man who'd unwittingly inspired me to get clean and sober, Keith Richards, looking to score.

"No, man, I don't," I responded. "But I'll give you back to the owner. I'm sure he can hook you up."

DON'T THINK THAT RECOVERY was a piece of cake, but, eventually, I got it. I love logic, and rehab's tenets were the essence of logic to me. Accepting the fact that I was just an addict lifted the psychic burdens that had plagued me all my life. It's a good thing I got there in time. If I hadn't stopped partying, I'm sure I would have lost my ability to make music.

When you're an addict, even if you don't use, you're still an addict. The urge is always "right outside the door doing push-ups," goes the classic refrain. In the sixteen years since I left rehab, I've never relapsed. The death of loved ones is one of the main triggers for relapse, which continually tested me. For most of my adult life, hardly a week has passed without someone close to me dying.

Though most of the suddenly dead or dying around me were famous people, the riskiest to my sobriety involved a talented friend, Reginald Brisbon (Briz), who's unfortunately relatively unknown. He was working with Paul Simon as a vocalist when he died in Le Bar Bat, a club on West Fifty-seventh Street in New York. On the night of July 15, 1995, while dancing with a friend, he suffered a fatal aneurysm and died on the dance floor. Like Stevie Ray Vaughan (whom he also worked with), he was clean and sober.

The news of his death caught me by surprise, and planning a musical memorial for Briz was a serious test for my sobriety. Briz died just a few months after I left rehab, and my addiction wanted me back in a big way.

At the memorial, Paul Simon paid tribute along with the recently re-formed Chic's newest lineup, which included Jill Jones of Prince's *Purple Rain* fame and the Uptown Horns. My greatest fear was performing in front of people without the aid of my usual high, and my emotions were all over the map. I'd suffered from stage fright my entire life.

Many people had turned out for the memorial and to offer words of support to Briz's distraught mother. I was happy to let them all speak. But finally the moment of truth was upon me.

The last time I was in Le Bar Bat, I was the life of the party. Coke, a gorgeous female posse, and all sorts of hanger-ons made up my entourage. But now, I was the loneliest person in the world; I'd returned to being the sickly little boy in the plastic bubble. Sure, I was grieving the loss of my dear friend Briz. In retrospect, I was grieving too for the loss of my old lifestyle.

Dozens if not hundreds of people spoke to me that night, but all I heard was the voice in my head. "You can't play worth shit," it said. "You're a joke. Remember that night at the club in Miami? It was the last time you played in front of a live audience, and what happened when you finally heard what you really played like?"

The only other voice that got through to me was Nard saying, "Yo, man, let's do this." I don't remember what we played for our first song. I don't know who spoke or how we were introduced, or if the tone was somber or New Orleans–style celebratory. But I do remember what happened when we played. My mind raced a million miles an hour through the set, with the Voice in my head asking for the last time: "Do you think you deserve to be out here with Bernard and this crew of top-flight musicians?" But it was amazing to be there, sober and rediscovering a Nile I thought I'd lost.

After we finished the first song, I screamed, "*I belong up here!*" The audience was stunned by my outburst. They had no idea what I meant. We were at a memorial, which made my comment even more strange and inappropriate. But I had just defeated a demon. My addiction was doing push-ups all right, but my recovery was doing Pilates, aerobics, and training for an Ironman Triathlon.

We played the rest of the set flawlessly. Even though Bernard thought my outburst was whack, he was grinning from ear to ear because he could sense that we were back on the beam.

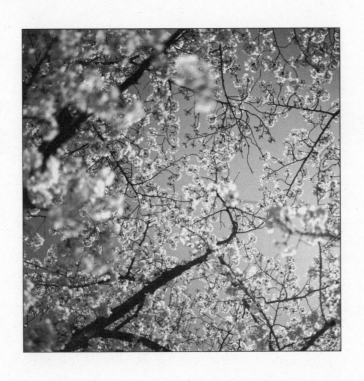

fourteen

We're Gonna Party Like It's 1996

I AWOKE ON DAY ONE OF 1996 WITH A SMILE. IT WAS MY SECOND consecutive New Year's Day without a hangover. That day, as a completely stone-cold sober civilian, I could have a blast just walking my dog. Who knew frosty marine air could make a man feel so alive?

That same day, the evening news was brimming with reports on Michael Jackson's "HIStory" tour. He was apparently performing in Brunei, promoting his current album of the same name, which I'd had the good fortune to play on.

The news was all good, but I was concerned about Michael. During the making of "HIStory," he'd revealed things to me in the studio that made me think he was searching for something that he couldn't define. His longing wasn't about music—he always knew exactly what he wanted me to play. His musical decisions happened in minutes. His concerns were more philosophical. We'd spent hours just talking.

Before we started recording, I reminded Michael that my old band New York City had opened for the Jackson 5 during the American leg of their first world tour. To my utter surprise, he remembered almost every minute of our time together on the tour bus more than twenty years ago, including my obsession with the *Fabulous Furry Freak Brothers* comic books, which I read to him when he was sixteen years old. Michael loved the *Freak Brothers* and we both laughed at the thought of his strict, straitlaced dad discovering the comic's actual contents. I was awed by the detail of Michael's recall; he'd memorized the names of all the main characters.

Michael remembered how drastically different I was from my bosses in New York City, "the guys who wore suits and regular clothes," he said in his trademark high-pitched giggle. "You always wore ripped-up skintight jeans, and I remember you had your own thing going on in those really high snakeskin platform shoes." Michael Jackson remembered *me* (Sally Field moment!), the skinny black nonconformist in one of his *opening acts*? He also remembered how I marveled as they performed "Dancing Machine" at sound check. I'd had a number of encounters with Michael over the years, and we'd always reminisce about the old days, but we'd never taken it to this level of microscopic detail before.

It was strange bonding like this with the King of Pop. I was flattered and surprised at the depth and texture of his memories of that moment in our lives. And to think this was a session that almost didn't happen.

A FEW WEEKS BEFORE the Jackson recording session, I'd officially decided to leave the music business to become a gentleman of leisure, which was pretty precocious, considering that I was just forty-three years old. But I was in the early days of sobriety, and anything associated with show biz felt dangerous.

One of the first steps in my exit strategy was relocating my recording operation to my Connecticut home, where things felt safe, and sticking strictly to small projects until I could figure out the big picture.

Then I got a call from Michael Jackson's camp.

At the time, the King of Pop was getting beaten up in the tabloids daily. He decided to fight back with his most potent weapon—his music. When I was asked to play on the record, I politely and quickly said, "No, I'm not available," without so much as asking about the details of the session. When they reported back to Michael, I honestly think he was shocked, which is probably why he promptly called back himself.

You'd think a direct call from Michael Jackson might have been enough to change my mind, but I just couldn't do it. My reluctance to play on his record had nothing to do with Michael himself. I loved the guy. I'd do anything for him—except risk my sobriety. But Michael had a bee in his bonnet and wouldn't take no for an answer. We kept playing tug-of-war until I finally blurted out my reason. "I can't play on the record," I said, "because I've just come out of rehab and I'm still in the day program." That seemed to catch him off guard.

"What's a day program?" he asked.

"I do what I used to do when I was inpatient at rehab, but I sleep at home."

"Really?" he said.

"Yeah. The studio feels unsafe to me. Too many memories of the good old days, and once I'm back in that environment, I'm not sure if I'll be able to stay humble."

He didn't quite get the concept of surrendering to addiction, of being afraid and staying humble. To be frank, neither did I. I was just repeating what rehab told me to do. But it was working. My careful approach had kept me drug and alcohol free for a great many months.

We finally landed on a compromise: Michael would send a car

for me. I would sit in the limo until he needed me. Then someone would send an assistant out and I'd come in and play my part. "After you approve it," I said, "I'll leave and head back up to Westport right away." He agreed.

When I arrived at the studio on the first day, after our little "remember the good old days" routine, I recorded my part and Michael approved the recording. I was starting to pack up to leave as per our agreement, when Michael asked:

"Hey, Nile, can I talk to you a little more?"

"Of course. Absolutely," I said, thinking this was about more playing.

"Let's go over to the lounge."

"Cool. Should I finish packing up?"

"Yeah, we're finished with the part. It sounds really good."

I packed up my gear, said goodbye to the engineers, and popped over to the studio's lounge.

We chatted for a while, and to my great surprise and relief, I didn't have a pressing urge to drink or drug in the studio lounge. I actually felt comfortable. From that point on, Michael carried most of the conversation. He continued reminiscing about the early days on the road. I could tell he missed the music, as well as the love and camaraderie, not specifically mine, or his brothers' or his crews' or his family's—it was more general: He missed the adulation that he had always elicited up to that point in his life. Unsurprisingly, I sensed that he was happiest when the world really loved him and everything he did, before his personal proclivities sparked constant tabloid fodder.

The tone of the conversation changed. His mood shifted and something happened that I would have never thought possible in a million years: He opened up to me about his dark feelings. Until that point our rap was all upbeat—typical musician laughing and joking around.

He said gossip in the news upset him and ultimately saddened him. I was very fragile and so was he, and we connected over our mutual state of mind. It was as if we were on the bus in the early seventies, only this time the secrets we shared were far less innocent. I'd made it clear I wanted to play guitar and go home. But I was also so grateful for the fact that Michael Jackson felt comfortable enough with me to share such intimate revelations. He confided that he was having marital problems and would probably be getting divorced. This was a full year before the slightest mention of his split with Lisa Marie Presley hit the press.

Why share this with me? I thought to myself as Michael continued to unload. Maybe because I outwardly seemed very happy and well adjusted, and he could sense that I was trustworthy. And I *was* feeling peaceful, both physically and mentally happy. It was almost like being high, but better. Some people call this "being on a pink cloud." I wanted Michael to experience some of my newfound peace.

Eventually, Michael asked me about Silver Hill's day program. I was curious about his interest in rehab. I assumed it was just idle chitchat or a response to my portrait of the place as a chill destination for famous people. I didn't think he was drinking or drugging at all—not with that memory recall.

He quickly brought the conversation back to the press's hounding him, which I'd grown tired of rehashing. I made a sincere suggestion: "Michael, if you want to come to a place where you can get away from that madness, come stay up at my house in Connecticut for a while."

"Diana has a house up there," he observed, talking about Miss Ross.

"Yes, she does, but at my house the press won't bother you. Madonna stayed at my crib and she never had any problems at all. In fact, it was almost as if nobody cared she was there."

After I said those fateful words, I watched his face drop as he seemed to contemplate a vacation into insignificance. Of course I didn't literally mean that nobody would care about him. All I meant was that my place was laid-back. But that's not what seemed to register. I quickly realized my misstep. Not wanting the opportunity to pass, I attempted to play missionary and added, "Paul Newman,

Joanne Woodward, Donna Summer, Martha Stewart, Phil Dona-
hue, Marlo Thomas, and Ashford and Simpson live quietly in Westport, too."

But it was too late. Whatever momentary Xanadu vision he'd
had of Silver Hill's day program had evaporated. He'd made up his
mind.

As a record producer who's used to dealing with mercurial talent, I knew we were done. If we'd been making a record, I'd have
suggested a movie, meal, or trip to the video game arcade to shake
off the coming blues. But now I could feel it was simply time to go.
Besides, I was still a little nervous about spending any more time at
the studio than I'd intended. I didn't feel the urge to drink, but who
knew how long that would last?

Instead of hugging it out, we shook hands as we said goodbye.
His hands were unusually rough for such a gentle person.

I never saw Michael again.

AND SO I RETURNED by limo to Westport, alone as planned, and continued with my new life. I had my own issues. I was starting to believe that my sobriety was entirely dependent on the institution. In
fact, I was so afraid to leave the day program voluntarily that they
finally *asked* me to.

"Nile, this is a short-term program," said Gerrard, my Men's
Group counselor.

"I know," I said, "but the routine has kept me grounded and I
need that."

"Bro, you've been going to the day program for more than eight
months," he said. "There are other tools to help you live life over
the long haul. Try going to meetings and know that we're always
here for you in case you need to come back."

And with that I finally left Silver Hill to see if what I'd learned
would stick.

Over the next few months, many of my friends would die, even
ones that were clean and sober. They were all young and this was

shocking to me. The most shocking were my rehab friends who bit the dust, because most had been pretending to be sober. It puzzled me, because the *big* lesson I'd learned was that people are not supposed to judge you. You could even show up drunk at the recovery programs. You didn't need to pretend to be sober. The idea is, you get it when you get it—or you never get it. People understand that's just the way it is.

I still love all my friends who choose to use drugs. One post-recovery birthday, while I was gigging in a foreign country, I reconnected with a friend whom I hadn't seen in about two decades.

"I have the greatest birthday present you can imagine," she said, laying out a massive line of blow.

In the most nonjudgmental way, I kindly refused the drugs.

"Wow!" she said. "Somebody told me you didn't get high anymore. But I didn't believe it, because I remember how much fun we used to have."

I laughed and said, "I still have fun."

She apologized, then said, "Do you mind if I do some?"

"Of course not," I said. "I only mind if *I* do some!"

I continued to work on a number of projects that were basically a series of one-offs, but what I was most excited about was rekindling my relationship with Bernard and rebooting Chic. I knew Chic would never be the same again. It couldn't be. Times had changed and I had changed.

APRIL 1996. I was in Japan in prime cherry blossom season. The warm spring air was filled with their perfumed scent, and I was delighted whenever I caught sight of their delicate beauty. Cherry blossoms are called Sakura, and they bloom for a very short period. It is the most sacred time of the year in the Land of the Rising Sun.

I was here being honored as JT's (Japan Tobacco's) Super Producer of the Year, an award that culminates in a two-hour television special that is rehearsed over a three-day series of live concerts, the last of which is shot for broadcast. I was flying high, overwhelmed by the honor of being recognized for my body of work with my very own TV show.

I'd gathered a handful of people near and dear to me to perform at this event, which was basically *This Is Your Life* in song form. I had Steve Winwood, Sister Sledge, Duran Duran's Simon Le Bon, Slash, the Crowell Sisters (a new group I'd been developing), a host of qualified sidemen whom I'd considered to be stars in their own right, and, of course, the newly re-formed Chic—with my old partner Bernard on bass.

Although this was an homage to my past work, I believed Chic's future was incredibly bright. This was just the beginning. Much like the Vaughan brothers, who'd come together in search of a new musical direction, our task was to figure out what Chic should be. We weren't worried. Chic was eternally optimistic.

During the trip certain rock-and-roll bonds were sealed for life—with Slash, Steve Winwood, and of course all of our Chic Organization alumni. "We Are Family" could have been our battle cry as we performed our nightly three-hour show with military precision. Everything just clicked, at least until the third and final show, a sold-out performance at the Budokan, which was shot to be televised.

We'd played the night before and were better than we'd ever been, but just twenty-four hours later, things started to quickly go wrong—very wrong. Nard arrived at the dressing room feeling a little sick. "I need to lay down for a minute," he said. "I wonder if I can get a vitamin shot to give me a boost of energy." I told our promoter/agent and she called a doctor. He arrived almost instantly.

After examining Bernard, he informed me in no uncertain terms, "The show must be canceled and Mr. Edwards has to go to the hospital immediately." I didn't hesitate. I told the promoter that we had to postpone the show and reschedule the shoot and concert. Nard was lying on the dressing room couch, but when he overheard the plan, he said, "Let me talk to the doctor."

Nard convinced the doctor that the show had to go on. So he got his vitamin shot, and they agreed he'd head to the hospital directly after we wrapped the show. Even the promoter, who spoke perfect English, said postponing the show wasn't a problem. The doctor seemed alarmed. But Nard wasn't having it. "Do you think I'd come all the way over here," he said to him, "to let my boy down?"

"Bernard, it's OK if we do this another day," the promoter said. But Nard wouldn't budge. He said the show must go on.

After a quick, astronaut-style nap, Nard seemed to recover. By the time the show was about to start, he was damn near the same old Nard, laughing, joking, and quoting Parliament-Funkadelic's "Let's Take It to the Stage."

This show was extra elaborate for us. We had dancers, a huge stage with opposing ramps; it was even tiered for a multiple-camera shoot, like a major sporting event. Before they announced our names, Nard and I peeked out at the audience. "We did it," he said in an emotional tone. "They didn't come to *see* us—they came to *hear* our music. It's bigger than we are." He was almost crying, which was so completely out of character for him. I, however, was completely in character: "Who the hell are you, Socrates? We've got a damn show to do. Why is your ass getting all philosophical on me now? Let's hit this shit."

A few minutes later, in a combination of Japanese and English, the announcer roared "JT Super Producer '96—NILE RODGERS!" Nard responded with "Three, four" to the band. We came in on the downbeat and blasted off.

Everything proceeded along brilliantly until we got to the next-to-last song of the first half, Bowie's "Let's Dance," which was being performed by Simon Le Bon. During the verse the bass unexpectedly dropped out. I recall saying to myself, "Wow, that's genius. Why didn't I do that on the record?"

I quickly looked back to give Nard a wink of approval, but I didn't see him. We continued playing the song and the bass returned in exactly the right place. I wasn't quite sure why he wasn't on stage, so I counted off the next song, Duran Duran's "Wild Boys." And lo and behold, there was Nard back on stage, playing along. At the end of the set, we left the stage triumphantly for the intermission.

Nard and I met in the dressing room for a quick clothing change. While stripping off his sweaty clothes, he said, "Damn, did you see that?"

"See what?" I replied, still trying to catch my breath.

"I passed out."

"What?"

"I passed out," he repeated.

"What do you mean you passed out?"

"Remember when the bass dropped?"

"Yeah."

"Well, that's what happened."

I was stunned. After all, the drop-out was so *musical*. It couldn't have been more perfect. "I was playing one minute," Nard continued, "and the next thing I know I'm on the floor and they're shaking me and saying my name. When I came to, I heard where you guys were, so I joined back in."

At the time, this was all too much for me to fully digest. I was frantically dressing, hydrating, and going over our second-half set list.

Nard didn't complain about feeling overly sick. He simply said, "Yo, I'm going to play the second half sitting down, if that's cool?"

"Of course that's cool," I said. Then he remembered we were doing some Chic numbers that were choreographed, so he said, "I'll get up when we get to the parts that I have to stand for." And with that, we hit the stage for the second half of the three-hour show. We played well, but I could sense a difference. Nard was playing on adrenaline, guts, willpower, and, of course, his uncanny musicality, which had bailed us out of countless close calls in the past. But he was running on empty. Somehow, though, we got through the rest of the show.

We returned to our hotel and Nard said he was going to bed. I reminded him of the doctor's orders, but he shrugged me off. He said he was fine—just tired. We were all tired—the show was a three-hour marathon—but I was hungry, so I had dinner with a Japanese friend named Masako. Before she and I left the hotel, I called Nard to check in on him:

"Hello," he answered in a gravelly voice.

"Hey, man, I'm going out to eat, do you want me to bring you something back?"

"No, it's cool."

"You sure you don't need anything?"

"Everything's all right. I just have to rest."

DURING THE NIGHT I was awakened suddenly from a nightmare and found myself on the floor. At the time, I thought an earthquake had thrown me out of the bed, but my friend was soundly sleeping. I woke her up. She hadn't felt anything, she said. We checked CNN. Nothing. A few months earlier, I'd experienced the Northridge, California, earthquake and was terrified that I was about to have the earth snatched from under me again.

It was 1:33 a.m. I was too afraid to sleep, so I convinced myself that I was rested enough to stay up until my early morning editing session. Nervously I rewound the nightmare:

I was one of the last two people on earth. We were holding hands. Suddenly the other person started to rise from the ground as if filled with helium. I tried to hold on to him, but I couldn't. I was afraid of being carried up into the clouds, afraid of heights even in my dreams, so I finally let go. He floated off, and all I could do was helplessly watch him fly away. I was completely alone.

In the dream, I dropped back to earth. In real life, I fell out of the bed.

I ended up falling back asleep, but was awakened by the telephone between 6 and 7 a.m.. "Mr. Edwards will not answer his wake-up call and the whole band is waiting for him in the lobby. They have to leave for the airport soon," the hotel manager said. "What should we do, sir?"

"Let the band leave," I told him. "I'll get him up. He's directly across from me." I knocked until my knuckles grew raw. No matter how hard, loud, or long I knocked, he refused to answer. I finally asked housekeeping to open his door.

The housekeeper opened the door to Nard's room and my eyes adjusted to darkness; the only light in the room was the flickering of his television. Nard's feet hung off the end of the couch. He was lying on his side, with his hand behind his head, like he'd been watching television. His blood had pooled to the bottom of his feet, which were grotesquely swollen.

I shook him vigorously. He was completely rigid, so when I shook his arm, his feet moved in the same motion. I screamed his name, thinking that this would really piss him off, and that he'd scream back, *Muthafucka, I can hear you*! Then we'd laugh and he'd hurry to the airport. But that didn't happen. My mind refused to accept what was right in front of my eyes. He was dead. When I could no longer deny what I knew to be true, I touched his cheek with my fingertips. His body was the same temperature as the coffee table.

I lost it. I cried hysterically. The housekeeper didn't know what to do. The hotel staff called the police.

As I mentioned, unexpected situations can often be a relapse trigger: The classic examples are divorce, job loss, sickness, and, of course, death. This was as unexpected as anything that had ever happened to me. Bernard had been my protector since we'd become friends some twenty-five years earlier. Now he was dead.

The only thought that broke through my hysteria was, *Now it's your time to look out for him.*

A RUSH OF ACTIVITY ensued immediately after I discovered Bernard's body. It was, to say the least, a complicated situation: An American had died in a hotel room while the president of the United States, Bill Clinton, and his entourage were staying next door; we were in Japan; the police and coroner had to do a complete investigation; the deceased was a musician in a country with a zero-tolerance drug policy; the Japanese don't embalm their dead; the flight to New York is fifteen hours; you can ship dead bodies only with special permits and in containers that take time to acquire.

There was an endless list of things requiring action that only I could attend to. And on top of all of that, I had to edit, mix, and deliver a TV show with a confirmed airdate.

Nard and I had *always* subscribed to "the show must go on." Ironically, had Bernard not been so committed to our age-old motto, he might be with us today.

Once the medical examiner filled out the death certificate, he needed my account of events. In perfect English he told me, "From the state of rigor mortis, I estimate time of death to be between 1 and 2 a.m."

"Around the time of the earthquake?" I asked.

"What earthquake?"

I told him about my nightmare and falling out of bed. After carefully listening to my story, he changed *estimated time of death from between 1 and 2 a.m.* to *time of death 1:33 a.m.* Then he looked at me and said, "We did not have an earthquake. We have many earthquakes in Japan, and they are recorded very accurately. That was your friend leaving you. The time of death is 1:33 a.m., just like you said. Thank you for this information."

I did everything the police asked of me at the station to expedite returning Bernard's body to his family. After I finished, they still wouldn't take me back to my hotel. I figured that we couldn't travel because Clinton was in town and they had the zone secured. Then the head detective took me to the garage. As I was about to get into my car, he said, "Please come over here and be with your friend." I wasn't sure what he meant, so I said, "Pardon me?"

"Please come here and be with your friend," the officer repeated while gesturing with his hand, "and stay as long as you want." Instead of getting into the car, I went over toward where he was now standing.

I walked into a small room that they'd converted into a make-shift temple.

Bernard was in a coffin with a glass front, and he was dressed in a white kimono. The saddest day of my life was also one of the most beautiful.

We Are Family

MORE THAN FOURTEEN YEARS HAVE PASSED SINCE NARD'S DEATH. DEspite our ups and downs, I always knew my old partner had my back. When he died, I had no choice but to step up. I'd been warned that such a catastrophic event could be a trigger to drink again, but it turned out to be a trigger *not* to drink, to get it and *keep it* together. I've found great solace in finally taking care of myself and others.

It's been a busy decade, to say the least. Life has paid off pretty well, considering how poorly it started. Though my royalties have allowed me to maintain a comfortable lifestyle, I never really became a true "gentleman of leisure." For me to be truly alive, I have to stay in the world of music.

Over the past few years, I've been busier than ever. I've worked on more than a hundred projects, with such diverse artists as Bob

Dylan, Britney Spears, Elton John, Dweezil Zappa, Joss Stone, Angélique Kidjo, and Steve Vai, among many others. Earlier this year I worked on an album called *Olympia* with Bryan Ferry, thus bringing me full circle to one of Chic's original influences. I also expanded my range by composing my first musical, and founding a distribution company and record label called Sumthing, which specializes in blockbuster video game soundtracks (primarily composed of classical music).

You may find it ironic that a guy who was once tainted with the Disco Sucks scarlet letter is now furthering the reach of new traditional composers in the world of theater, film, and video games, but for me, it's all part of the same artistic truth: A great hook is a great hook, whether it's for "Le Freak" or *Halo*.

ON SEPTEMBER 10, 2001, I took a United Airlines red-eye flight home from one of many *Halo* meetings at the Microsoft campus near Seattle. Hurricane Erin was just off the Atlantic coast, causing extreme turbulence as we entered New York's airspace just before dawn the next morning. As we touched down, the captain said, "That's some storm we got out there, folks. It looks like we just made it."

About an hour after I got home, my girlfriend Nancy was in the kitchen watching CNN. "You've got to see this," she said. As I tried to wrap my mind around the smoldering hole in the World Trade Center's North Tower, the second plane struck the South Tower.

I stayed awake all day watching news updates. As the names of the dead were announced, I recognized that of an old friend: Berry Berenson. A model and actress turned photographer, she'd snapped my image many times. When I was named *Billboard*'s Number One Singles Producer of the Year, she shot the magazine's full-length photo.

By nightfall my phone was ringing off the hook with calls from concerned artists and friends from around the world. One friend suggested I use "We Are Family" to jump-start America's healing process, in the tradition of "We Are the World." It didn't make sense to me, because Nard and I had written that song specifically for the group Sister Sledge as our take on their specific family dynamic. But the idea began to grow and everyone who heard it seemed to concur. After giving it a bit more thought, I called Tom Silverman, the head of Tommy Boy Records, and he agreed to finance it.

We decided to record in L.A. and New York. In a matter of days, I had organized a diverse roster of over two hundred celebs, from Diana Ross, Patti LaBelle, Bernadette Peters, Luther Vandross, Joel Grey, and Eartha Kitt to Queen Latifah, Pink, the B-52's, Jackson Browne, Mila Jovovich, Afrika Bambaataa, Rev Run of DMC, Mario, Matthew Modine, David Hasselhoff, the Pointer Sisters, Macaulay Culkin, and even Sister Sledge. We had legendary sports figures John McEnroe, Rebecca Lobo, Rod Gilbert, and at least three of Muhammad Ali's daughters. But we also had emergency workers, too. We wanted to repay them in the best way we could, with music and a few hours of peace, love, and tranquility.

When we gathered together in New York, at the same studio where the original Sister Sledge production had been recorded, it felt like the safest place on earth.

After the New York session, the television host Montel Williams and I hopped on a flight bound for L.A. to record yet another group of bighearted people. When we boarded the flight, every crew member's face was familiar to me, and mine to them. They were the same crew that I'd flown in with during Hurricane Erin, and this was their first flight since. We all hugged, laughed, and greeted each other as if we were long-lost family members just come home.

During the recording, there were many memorable performances. Sophie B. Hawkins put a spin on the groove and started us off on hand drum. Queen Latifah followed with a pep-talk rap to the ensemble. Patti LaBelle hit a note so high it made all our heads spin, then Luther Vandross's voice cracked when he went for a tricky riff—the first time I'd heard him hit a bad note in thirty years. Steve Van Zandt fired off a guitar solo in the breakdown section, and Diana Ross drove all the way cross-country during the no-fly period just to sing in the chorus.

Filmmakers Danny Schechter and Spike Lee made a film called *The Making and Meaning of "We Are Family,"* capturing the beginning of the project, and how we eventually realized that we could build it beyond what had started out as a one-off. I called an old friend from *Sesame Street,* the television producer Christopher Cerf (whose father Bennett cofounded Random House). When I told him what we were doing, he said, "I've always wanted to do a charity music project." So we wound up coproducing a children's version of the song, starring more than 150 children's TV characters.

We showed the film at a special screening at the Sundance Film Festival, where we received a standing ovation for the music-video doc, and the children's version was roadblocked (meaning it was broadcast in sync on all three top children's TV networks) on March 11, 2002, six months after 9/11.

AND SO WAS BORN the We Are Family Foundation. My team started small but performed big. Since then we've funded the building of seventeen schools in Africa, Central America, and Nepal, distributed over eighty thousand children's DVDs, and brought first-run films and poetry slams to kids in hospitals. We've adopted thirteen-year-old *New York Times* bestselling author Mattie J. T. Stepanek's "Peace is possible" message and developed an innovative year-round mentoring program called Three Dot Dash (• • • —), the Morse code symbol for the letter V, or what's become known as the peace sign.

Three Dot Dash, our chief program, now searches the world over for Global Teen Leaders who share Mattie's vision of achievable peace, and whose successful programs are dedicated to the furtherance of basic human needs: water, food, health, safety, shelter, education, and the environment. Our original thirty Global Teen

Leaders have already positively affected more than four million people with their programs.

WHEN "WE ARE FAMILY" was originally composed for Sister Sledge, I never thought it would become a phrase that would have such great meaning in my own life. Last week the foundation had a huge celebration with friends, family, and supporters who flew in from all corners of the globe. It was one of the most life-affirming parties of my entire life. I was ecstatic.

The next day, as I was leaving for a concert in Rome, I got a call from my doctor. He asked me to sit down. I told him, "I'm running late to the airport, so hold that thought until I get back." He said, "We must talk now. You have an aggressive form of cancer and I need to see you right away to discuss your possible options." I was stunned, but I had a job to do.

When it comes to my life, I'm never at a loss for irony. This information had come less than ten hours after one of the most optimistic days of my life.

Since getting sober back in '94, I've reflected on all of my close encounters with the Grim Reaper and have learned to be truly grateful for the gift of life:

Yesterday's history,
tomorrow's a mystery,
today's a gift,
that's why they call it the present.

That's a slogan they used to recite at my old day program. Another was, "Live every day as if you think it's your last, because one day you'll be right!" I like to look at it like this: I'm going to die living—instead of live dying. So I went to Rome and, trust me, the show smoked!

* * *

TODAY I GOT HOME after the routine (smoking) Roman gig. It's a brisk early November morning and there isn't a cloud in the sky. A few days ago, we had our first frost of the year. The cold chills my bones but it's just what I need to keep me moving. I'm running late again and I need to hurry if I'm going to catch my plane. I'm heading out to Las Vegas to see Mom and the family. I know even without Big Bobby it's still going to be a blast and, like always, completely dysfunctional and out of control.

For years my family's kept secrets from me, and in the end they were never really a big deal. This year I'm going to keep one from them—my cancer. I feel like I can't share it with Mom because she'd worry too much. Maybe in the end it just might turn out not to be a big deal. And I plan to celebrate. Tomorrow is Thanksgiving Day.

Acknowledgments

David Kuhn, for inviting me to lunch, asking me to tell my story, convincing me to write it myself, and introducing me to Andrew.

Andrew Essex, for everything. Your musical background enabled you to speak to me in a language that I really understood: form, structure, verses, choruses, and repeatedly asking me, "Do the words sing to you?" Finally they did. You'll eternally have my utmost respect, admiration, and friendship.

Debbie Ford, for letting me read to you on the beach during vacation.

Nancy Hunt, for simply being you and hanging in there with me. I love you.

Joseph Harris, M.D., for looking up the emergency room records of my father, Nile Rodgers Sr., which led me to the cemetery of the unclaimed dead.

Chris Jackson, who was a pleasure to work with because he always went that extra mile. I'm happy you were not offended at our first meeting when I said, "Damn, you must be the Colin Powell of editing."

Cindy Spiegel and Julie Grau, for taking a page out of my book and working with an opening act.

The great staff at Spiegel & Grau: publicist Maria Braeckel, who tirelessly took my crazy emails that started with, "Ooo, maybe we can . . ."; the marketing team led by Avideh Bashirrad and Erika Greber; the art director Greg Mollica and designer Evan Gaffney; Julie and Chris's assistant editor Laura Van der Veer; and assistant editor Mya Spalter, who offered useful notes early in the process.

Illustration Credits

All images courtesy of the author except for the following:

Index